SPOILS AND SPOILERS

THE AUSTRALIAN EXPERIENCE: NO 2

mike Shelton

THE AUSTRALIAN EXPERIENCE
Series Editor: Heather Radi

ALSO IN THE SERIES
Geoffrey Sherington   *Australia's Immigrants*
Richard White   *Inventing Australia*
Richard Broome   *Aboriginal Australians*

GEOFFREY BOLTON

SPOILS AND SPOILERS

Australians make their environment 1788–1980

GEORGE ALLEN & UNWIN
SYDNEY LONDON BOSTON

First published in 1981 by
George Allen & Unwin Australia Pty Ltd
8 Napier Street
North Sydney NSW 2060

National Library of Australia
Cataloguing-in-Publication entry:

Bolton, Geoffrey.
Spoils and Spoilers.

Bibliography.
Includes Index.
ISBN 0 86861 218 9
ISBN 0 86861 226 x Paperback

1. Man—Influence on nature—Australia. 2.
Europeans in Australia. 3. Australia—History. I.
Title. (Series: The Australian experience; 2).

304.2' 8' 0994

Library of Congress Catalog Card Number: 80-71054

Set in 10 on 11.5 Times by Filmset Ltd, Hong Kong

Printed in Hong Kong by South China Printing Co.

Contents

Acknowledgements   *vi*

1   A Timeless Land   *1*

2   The British Impact   *11*

3   The Weather   *25*

4   They Hated Trees   *37*

5   The First Generation   *49*

6   Urban Beginnings   *59*

7   After Gold   *69*

8   The Pastoral Impact   *81*

9   Towards Conservation   *97*

10   Suburban Spread   *109*

11   Planners and Improvers   *121*

12   Rural Australia, 1900–1945   *135*

13   Affluent Society   *147*

14   Rescue Operations   *159*

15   Backlash and Forecast   *169*

Notes   *175*

Bibliography   *185*

Index   *187*

Acknowledgements

No work of historical writing is a one-person effort, and I have many people to thank for support and encouragement during the planning and writing of this book. I am especially indebted to:

The Department of History, Institute of Advanced Studies, Australian National University, and the Master and Fellows, St John's College, Cambridge for generous hospitality to me as a visiting Fellow.

To Alan Atkinson, Ged Martin, Joe Powell, Lorna Robertson, Mike Bosworth, and Tom Stannage for helpful advice and suggestions.

To Carol Bolton for the cottage among the orchards at Balingup where much of this book was written, and for all that goes with it.

To Melanie Harris and Lianne Blackwell for typing various drafts of the manuscript—and to Melanie as well for her help in making the space in my working routine which enabled it to be completed.

To Stephen Murray-Smith for his generous help with material, to Max Kelly for photographs, and to the Public Transport Commission of New South Wales and the Mitchell Library for assistance with illustrations.

To Heather Radi who created the opportunity for the book to be written.

To Howard Smith for compiling the index.

To Judith Wright and Les Murray for permission to quote from their poems published by Angus & Robertion; and to Thomas Shapcott for his poem published in the *Australian*.

And to the students and colleagues at Murdoch University who were present at the creation of the course on which this book is based, and to whom I dedicate it.

"THESE SUBVERSIVES, THESE FRIENDS OF THE DIRT"

Joh Bjelke-Petersen

The Enemies Of The Dirt might dabble
in real estate with a nod to the local council
but they'd swallow a rainforest before breakfast
and are planning to skillet the Barrier Reef
that is, after the hard work of quarrying
has been dealt with in the telex room.
The Enemies Of the Dirt pride themselves
on their cracked hard-work nails. Their vivid necks
bulge above regulation white collars. They know
all the hardships of was it really almost forty years back?
They do know what bludgers are. The Enemies of the Dirt
know too well the dirt they grew from (before the subdivision):
From high windows there is a million-dollar view
of the nearly new freeway that blots out the riverbank
(all those mangroves). Necks creep at the thought of mozzies.
The big floods might still rise to tackle this denuded topsoil
and good luck then to the friends of the dirt, who are under
each arch looking for chinks with soiled khaki shoulderbags
crammed with seeds. Seeds, growth—in this climate?
"Green shoots can split the rock," someone said. No,
someone wrote that: language, another subversive.
"If it moves, shoot: if it doesn't, chop." Up so high,
The Enemies Of The Dirt have an affinity for axes, they sense
the vulnerability of towers, they have a sudden instinct
for Protected Species.

THOMAS SHAPCOTT

1   A Timeless Land

The timeless land, we call Australia. The phrase implies that before 1788 the ancient, bony, scoured-down Australian continent had no history. Many writers have seen it as a static environment impervious to any change less powerful than the impact of modern Western technology. 'Civilization did not begin in Australia until the last quarter of the eighteenth century' is the opening sentence of Manning Clark's *History of Australia*, first published in 1962. Thirty years earlier an able naturalist, H.H. Finlayson, complained of the difficulty of finding a corner of Australia where the balance of nature was undisturbed—by which he meant in the same condition as it was before the Europeans came. Half a century before him G.W. Rusden wrote of 'the mysterious slumber which reigned over so vast and neglected a portion of the globe' as Australia before the navigators: again this suggestion of total inertia.[1] There is an inkling of this concept of a timeless, changeless Australia in Sturt's reaction to the western Riverina in 1829:

> Neither beast nor bird inhabited these lonely and inhospitable regions, over which the silence of the grave seemed to reign.[2]

But this reaction of being an intruder upon an ancient and untouched environment could be a source of hope and energy. Major Mitchell, happening upon that fertile tract of western Victoria which he named 'Australia Felix,' exclaimed:

> Of this Eden I was the only Adam; and it was indeed a sort of paradise to me, permitted thus to be the first to explore its mountains and streams—to behold its scenery—to investigate its geological character—and finally, by my survey, to develop those natural advantages, all still unknown to the civilized world, but yet certain to become, at no distant date, of vast importance to a new people.[3]

Whether attracted like Mitchell or repelled like Sturt, the first European comers shared the view that history, the measurement of the passing of time as a significant factor in the shaping of an ecology, began only with the coming of Western society.

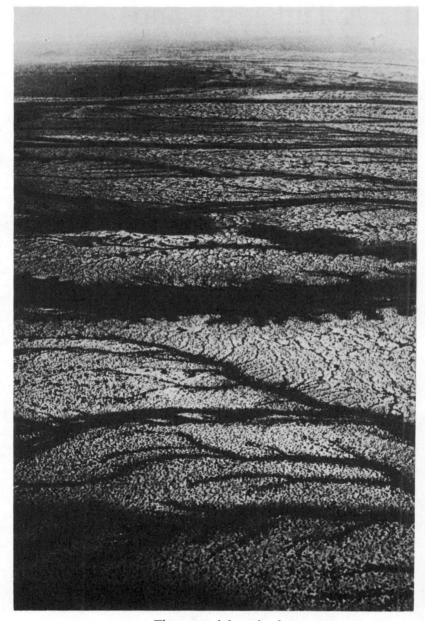

The scoured down land
From C.J. Lloyd, *The National Estate: Australia's Heritage*, (Cassell, 1977)

Before the first half of the nineteenth century most Europeans had a foreshortened sense of time span. The science of geology was in its infancy, and many even among the educated possessed bibles which fixed the moment of Earth's creation at 10 a.m. on Friday, 28 October 4004 B.C. When the poetic judge Barron Field wrote in 1819 of Australia as an 'afterbirth' he was probably thinking of the theory that it was the last continent to be formed, surfacing only after Noah's flood. This was refuted by the discovery of fossils in the Wellington valley in 1830. It was with visible satisfaction that a Sydney official informed the Colonial Office: 'we now have many other proofs that this country was once inhabited by beasts of prey and that it is coeval with the rest of the world.'[4] For some, such as Sturt, this still pushed the origins of Australia no further back than the Great Flood. Commenting on the discovery of a fossilised shoreline in inland New South Wales, he wrote: 'the marks of that awful catastrophe which so nearly extinguished the human race, are every day becoming more and more visible as geological research proceeds.'[5]

Some intellectuals already argued that such stories as the Creation and the Flood were 'judiciously accommodated to vulgar minds'[6] rather than providing a sure guide to the Earth's age. But there were few intellectuals among Australia's pioneer settlers. To most of them the Australian environment would have seemed dishearteningly changeless. They would have thought, as until recently almost every white Australian thought, that the Aborigines made very little contribution to the shaping of the Australian landscape. Sparse in number, scant in needs, the Aborigines were apparently quite untroubled by that drive to mobilise the earth's resources and transform its environment which to the Western mind marked the beginnings of civil society.

Even before the acceptance of Darwin's evolutionary theories Europeans tended to place the Aborigines very low in the hierarchy of human beings. Dampier in 1688 thought them 'the miserablest people on earth'. Two centuries later in Queensland the pastoralist Walter Scott described them as 'Like beasts with lower pleasures; like beasts, with lower pains'.[7] Most white Australians accepted a scale of human perfection placing the Anglo-Saxon at its peak and the Aborigines, together with the Bushmen of South Africa and the Veddas of South Asia, at the bottom. It was almost as if the Aborigines were seen as a fossil remnant of bygone eras, much as the marsupials were among mammals; a kind of dead-end anabranch of the mainstream of human progress. Unaware of commerce and agriculture, invincibly ignorant it seemed of any sense of economic motivation, the Aborigines in all their centuries of occupation contented themselves with the lives of nomadic hunters, merely scratching the surface of the continent.

By contrast the nineteenth century Europeans prided themselves on transforming the wilderness into a great pastoral empire, a tempting source of gold, and a working man's paradise sustaining the thriving cities of Melbourne and Sydney. If the Europeans found Australia hard to tame it could at times be conceded that the Aborigines, though lacking in the gifts of civilisation, possessed compensatory skills of a no doubt lower order which accounted for their survival. The practised keenness of their eyesight enabled them to live off the land. They seemed to possess qualities of endurance fit to accept levels of discomfort and pain unsuited to the European physique. They communicated across distance with a speed suggesting telepathy. All this was well known, but it was hard for most white Australians to appreciate the extent of the Aborigines' achievement. During the nineteenth century the two races were in mortal combat for the possession of the land, and during the first forty years of the twentieth century the Aborigines were seen by most as a dying race, fit only for the protection of the reserves. Most white Australians by then were city-dwellers, unequipped to guess at the subtlety and complexity of traditional Aboriginal adaptations to their environment. Hardly anyone realised that the presence of the Aborigines had a profound effect on the face of Australia. Only a handful of anthropologists were concerned to study them systematically. As a result before 1930 many opportunities were lost of finding out about Aboriginal influences on the ecology.

Much information perished with the disintegration of Aboriginal society under European contact. Within a little more than seventy years after white settlement the entire Aboriginal population of Tasmania came to 'extinction', though this term ignores the survival of many with some Aboriginal ancestry. A very similar story could be told of the Bowen district in North Queensland, the Monaro in southern New South Wales, and the Swan River coastal plain.[8] In such circumstances there could be little hope of gaining a full and accurate picture of traditional Aboriginal society. Sympathetic and patient observers conducted interviews, compiled vocabularies, and wrote down what they could discover about Aboriginal myths and legends, but the recorders were not trained to ask the right questions or to understand the implications of what they were told. Too often Aboriginal folklore was seen as merely picturesque and fanciful, and not as an account of practical responses to environmental problems.

This tendency to underrate the value of Aboriginal testimony about their own culture may have been fostered by another belief common until recent years among white Australians. This was the idea that after their first landfall in Australia the Aborigines were cut off from contact with other races and cultures. Isolated, they could be seen as simple primitives incapable of developing techniques for the more effective exploitation of the natural resources around them. Given regular patterns of outside contact—and it is known that the Makasar Indonesians and the Papuans were visiting northern Australia for centuries, and that there may have been at least indirect and second-hand exposure to Islamic and Chinese culture—it is hard to see Aboriginal culture as static and unchanging. At least it is possible to formulate questions about Aboriginal influences on the environment.

It look a long time for serious attention to be paid to Aboriginal archaeology. To many otherwise intelligent and liberal-minded people in the first half of the twentieth century the only interesting archaeology was the archaeology of 'high' culture: Sir Arthur Evans at Knossos, Howard Carter at the tomb of Tutankhamun, the scholar excavating the ruins of the great buildings to reveal works of artistic merit. Even among prehistorians working on preliterate cultures there was a tendency to attach greatest importance to those societies which graduated from the use of stone tools, and thus to underrate the achievement of 'primitive' groups in south-east Asia and Australia.[9] It was only after the Second World War that the balance was tilted. In 1952 the technique of carbon dating was perfected, enabling greater precision in the dating of artifacts, and stronger certainty in piecing together the story of the development of preliterate cultures. Two years later the University of Melbourne began teaching and research in the field of Australian Aboriginal prehistory. Nearly all that we know about the impact of the Aborigines on the Australian environment dates from those two events.

Thanks to the researchers of the last quarter century we now know that the Aborigines have been in Australia for at least 40 000 years. Only China, Java and East Africa have so far revealed human remains of greater age. Australia may yet be found to match them. So far the most ancient traces of human life have all been discovered in the southern part of the continent, whereas the evidence suggests that the first Australians arrived from the north, so that we would expect to find the remains of the Aborigines' most remote ancestors in the Kimberleys or Cape York Peninsula.

There is still doubt about whether the Aborigines derived from one common stock, or whether they represent the outcome of two, three, or even five distinct waves of immigrants from the north. Most of the genetic evidence suggests a common origin for all modern Aborigines, with minor differences developing since they arrived in Australia. The trouble with such speculation is that we have nothing better than informed guesswork about the number of Aborigines living in Australia before white settlement. The highest guess is about 1.4 million, but most scholars accept an estimate of around 300 000 in 1788, one to every 25 square kilometres.

This Aboriginal society was organised very efficiently on a basis of small kinship groups. Each small group—a dozen, twenty, rarely more than thirty—operated over clearly defined territories. Within these bounds they led a nomadic life which guarded against the overexploitation of any particular area of land, and allowed scope for game and grass to recuperate. At times these groups would come together in considerably larger bands for religious or ceremonial purposes, or in order to exploit a seasonal bounty or an unexpected prize such as a whale beached on the seashore. There was a flexibility about Aboriginal society which helped them through extremes of drought and plenty. In hard times they could live on very little; in times of plenty they gorged themselves. A people capable of devising social disciplines of this nature were also able to exercise some measure of control over their numbers. Some have seen the Aborigines as among the first and most deliberate practitioners of zero population growth, maintaining numbers which matched the availability of resources. Marriage laws, tribal taboos, a certain amount of abortion and infanticide, the abandonment of the aged in seasons of scarcity, all limited the human demands on the Australian environment.

These measures were knitted into the central fabric of Aboriginal culture over a thousand generations. Over that long period the resources of Australia were gradually becoming scarcer. At the most obvious level there was simply rather less of Australia. About 15 per cent of the continent's land surface has sunk below sea level since the first Aborigines settled on it. Nor was the interior of Australia as arid as it has since become, although historians of climate are still not quite certain of the stages by which the great dryness descended. The Australia of the first Aborigines was sufficiently hospitable to support a bigger range of fauna than the Australia of the first Europeans. Thirty thousand years ago there were emus and kangaroos twice as large as their modern counterparts. Marsupial lions and thylacines were found as readily in Arnhem Land as in Tasmania. And there were the diprotodons, kin to the wombat but of hippopotamus bulk. None of these beasts was formidable enough to deter human settlement. In fact it was to be the humans who exterminated a number of the beasts. It used to be thought that the diprotodons were driven to extinction by drought, for they were extensive grazers requiring a good deal of herbage. Now that their remains have been found in regions of almost every climatic type in Australia, it seems that the diprotodons, like their cousins the wombats, were capable of adapting to considerable ranges of drought and plenty. The most likely agent of their destruction, as for so many of the world's fauna, was humans, in this case Aborigines.

How could a race of skilled hunters resist the promise of plentiful meat offered by these large slow creatures? It is probably also because of the Aborigines that the thylacine, the Tasmanian tiger, disappeared on the Australian mainland, although in this case some of the responsibility must be shared by the dingo. Possibly as recently as four thousand years ago the dingo was introduced to Aboriginal Australia, though nine thousand years is a more usual estimate. It was time enough for the dingo to prove a more efficient hunter of bandicoots, lizards and various other members of the humbler creation, and thus to doom its competitor to extinction. The survival of the Tasmanian tiger was due to the fact that Bass Strait separated island and mainland well before the dingo appeared on the scene. When dogs arrived with European settlement in 1803 the Tasmanian Aborigines were quick to adopt them as their hunting companions; but their own destruction followed so soon afterwards that the dogs cannot have done significant harm to the Tasmanian fauna. That task, together with the extermination of the Tasmanian Aborigines themselves, was to be reserved for the white settlers' technology.

Aboriginal hunters commanded a resource more powerful than their weapons in changing the Australian ecosystem. This was fire. Early European navigators often mentioned the great clouds of smoke which were to be seen in summer rising from the coastline. Sometimes in admiration, sometimes exasperated by the destructive consequences, many of the first generation of inland pioneers noted the Aboriginal use of fire-stick farming. Fire was used to drive game out of hiding in scrub or bracken, and also to burn off old feed and promote new growth to attract game. Once started a fire was never put out, and this uncontrolled burning sometimes caused bushfires of devastating proportions.

These conditions favoured the growth of plant species which reproduce after exposure to fire. This has given rise to an argument among botanists, some claiming that it was Aboriginal firing which fostered the development of this odd characteristic, others contending that even before the Aborigines arrived the Australian terrain was frequently scoured by fires caused by lightning strike. Against this, it seems that lightning is not more prevalent in Australia than in many other regions of the world; and (except in Greek legends about Zeus) it is not usually necessary to be struck by lightning before reproduction can occur.[10]

Beyond any doubt this repeated burning off in regions of good rainfall regenerated growth and produced the open, park-like country which satisfied European canons of landscape. Otherwise, wrote Major Mitchell in 1848, 'the Australian woods had probably contained as thick a jungle as those of New Zealand or America instead of open forests.'[11] This facilitated European exploration and produced grasslands which were a lure for pastoralists: 'What was good pasture for kangaroos was good pasture for European stock. It has been made so by the *work* the Aborigines had put into the systematic management of their runs.'[12]

Fire was not wholly beneficial. In the sparser woodland of the interior Aboriginal fires probably robbed the soil of nitrogen, and contributed to erosion, salt creep, and the eventual spread of the central Australian desert. Probably there was a major shift to aridity in the Australian climate between four and six thousand years ago. This left tracts of semidesert with long straggling salt lakes as the only reminder of the running waters of the past. Climatic shift was no doubt the main cause of the change, but Aboriginal fires may well have hastened the process. Certainly the Inland was once more supportive of animal life than it is now, and Aboriginal archaeological sites suggest that the hunters of ten or fifteen thousand years ago enjoyed a more varied diet than their modern descendants, because of their access to species now driven to extinction. Those who would see the Aboriginal as a noble savage, better attuned than white Australians to the needs and moods of the environment, must reckon with the possibility that the Aborigines left an impoverished ecosystem behind them.[13]

Yet the Aboriginal achievement was considerable. They were fine botanists, who learned to maximise the available resources, in an environment without cereal crops and with a poorer diversity of plant life than was accessible to most other cultures. The whole of Australia was their farm, and it was a farm which they exploited with care for the needs of later generations. It may be that the increasing aridity of the land taught them forcibly that resources could not be regarded as infinite, but that they must practise disciplined nomadic habits, restriction of numbers, and conservation of sources of water and food. In addition their pattern of life was imbued with a deeply felt sense of religious tradition which identified the people with the land and its natural features. The individual was subordinated to the good of the community, and the community was subordinated to the environment. There was no scope for motives of individual profit which might tempt the venturesome to either improvement or exploitation. The concept of land as private property which might be cultivated, possessed, inherited, and transformed was unknown in Aboriginal Australia.

At the other end of the world, first in the Mediterranean and later throughout Europe, ideas of individualism were to change society until Europeans had hardly a point of similarity to Australian Aborigines except their common humanity. When after 1788 the two cultures came into close contact there was no real prospect that they could achieve mutual understanding, still less that the technically superior Europeans would dream that they had anything to learn from the Aborigines about the care and control of the Australian environment.

2   The British Impact

In the years following 1788 the first white settlers brought with them
a number of intellectual and aesthetic attitudes, some so deeply
ingrained that they were unacknowledged. Some have seen the
Christian inheritance as important in shaping attitudes towards the
environment. The Bible taught in its first chapter that God, having
created Adam, gave him dominion over every living thing.[1] In an era
when anyone who could read at all read the Bible, this produced a
frame of mind which allowed man to consider himself as separate
from and superior to the rest of creation. Man would exploit nature
to his own benefit. The British who came to Australia from 1788 were
nearly all nominally Christians, but they were probably more influenced by growing up in a society which on rational principles
believed that men had a right and duty to transform the environment
into greater productivity. One of the most eloquent writers of the
eighteenth century, Jonathan Swift, stated that 'whoever could make
two ears of corn or two blades of grass to grow upon a spot of ground
where only one grew before, would deserve better of mankind, and do
more essential service to his country, than the whole race of politicians
put together'.[2] Politicians have been quoting the first part of this saying
ever since.

If there was one political notion of which all eighteenth century
Englishmen were convinced, it was the idea that the protection of
liberty and property were the main purposes of government. These
beliefs were vindicated by more than a century of economic and social
change which placed the British Isles well ahead of other European
countries. Unlike their forefathers the Englishmen of 1788 did not
believe that man's rights as a citizen arose from his standing as a
child of God, of equal value with his fellow Christians. Unlike their
modern descendants they did not believe in democracy. They thought
the essential mark of a citizen was the ownership of property. Property
was what belonged to a specific individual, and distinguished that
individual from others. Land was the most highly regarded form of

property, but merchandise, hereditary legal rights, even the tenancy of an official position could all be regarded as forms of property. Without property, without that sense of self-regard which came of having a stake in the country, the individual would be powerless to protect his rights or to utter independent opinions. It was the government's responsibility to provide, through its defence and foreign policy and its administration of the laws, security for the rights of property; but governments should not interfere with the rights of the individual, and should tax no more than was required for the upkeep of essential services. Coercion by government was to be resisted even when it claimed to be acting in the interests of society. These attitudes ruled out much likelihood of effective government action towards environmental conservation, but in eighteenth-century Britain they were offset by a number of factors, some of which had their bearing on the colonisation of Australia.

The British of 1788 believed themselves to be one of the world's most advanced civilisations: not perhaps as ancient as China or as polished as France, but superior to all in liberty, initiative, and prospects for economic enterprise and growth. Britain stood at the threshold of industrialisation. Probably no part of the world had previously undergone such rapid economic development as England and Scotland during the eighteenth century. This growth was partly a reflection of a rapid rise in population, itself the result of improving diet, and the disappearance of such epidemic diseases as bubonic plague. In the England of 1788 it was 150 years since a serious famine in any part of the country. Even in Ireland as in most of Western Europe only the elderly could remember a time when deaths from starvation had been many.

The eighteenth century in Britain was thus a time of rapid population growth. Between 1700 and 1800 numbers rose in England from 5.5 to 10 million, in Scotland from 1.5 to 3 million, in Ireland from 3.5 to 6 million. In Ireland a colonial system of land tenure discouraged peasant initiative, so that this increase in population brought with it a resource problem. Although the reclamation of bogland and the development of primary exports averted disaster for some decades, many of the peasantry lived on a subsistence diet mainly comprising potatoes and skim milk. But in England, Wales and Scotland increasing demand stimulated the transformation of agriculture from local subsistence farming to the growth of cash crops. Market opportunities were sought with increasing activity as road and canal transport improved. Different localities came to concentrate on specialised lines of produce. Scotland and Ireland, for example, became major producers of beef; it was in walking cattle on the hoof to distant markets that the drovers of Galway and the Scottish Highlands perfected many of the techniques and terms which would later be used by Australian overlanders.

The shift towards a market economy brought hard times to many smallholders. New techniques of crop rotation, ploughing, and fertilisation were introduced and accepted. Profits were maximised by the economies of scale which went with large land-holdings. These pressures led to the break-up of traditional forms of land tenure in many parts of Britain. In England the enclosure movement sought the elimination of old communal rights; in Scotland the crofters were ousted from their homes. Those who left out the human factor could argue persuasively that such changes constituted improvement. Although peasants may have a special concern and affinity for the land, they are often reluctant to change or experiment, and cling to practices which damage the ecology. The improving landlord was concerned not only with the productivity of his acres but also with their appearance and conservation.

The advent of modern agrarian capitalism in Britain was far from being an environmental disaster. It created that neat landscape of hedgerows and tidy cultivation often extolled as 'typical English countryside'; the product of that cool, damp climate which the British persist in regarding as temperate. Although the annual rainfall of much of Britain is no more than that of Adelaide, and not as great as that of Sydney, Brisbane or Perth, it is spread very evenly throughout the year. These conditions fostered the dense forests of oak, ash, yew, beech and other deciduous hardwoods which originally covered the British countryside. With the clearing of those forests there still remained a marked seasonal rhythm to the pattern of rural life, and an understandable tendency for the British to regard the characteristic lush greenness of their farmlands as the mark of a desirable landscape. These preconceptions would not be appropriate for the settlers of Australia.

Nor was the pattern of land ownership. Britain in 1788 was dominated by its propertied aristocracy. Twenty-four dukes, over two hundred lesser noblemen, and about three thousand gentry between them owned half the land in the British Isles. In two important respects the British upper classes differed from most of the aristocracies of Europe. They were not a closed caste, but were reinforced continually by merchants, investors and other successful accumulators of wealth who bought respectability by becoming landowners and imitating the behaviour of established families. Nor had they any major political or financial advantage to gain by constant residence close to Court in London. Their sense of national duty was sufficiently stretched by the necessity of attending parliament during the fox-hunting season. They were not under the same temptation to become such lavish consumers and spenders as the French nobility at Versailles or the lesser nobilities among Europe's numerous imitations of Versailles. Instead they tended to concentrate on upholding their position in their own neighbourhood. This often involved exercising a sense of responsibility about the care and improvement of natural resources. Many of the British gentry were among the forefront of agricultural improvers, quick to experiment with new methods of farming and concerned to introduce these methods to their tenants and other neighbouring farmers. This was enlightened self-interest, as it made for better revenues. It also hastened the process by which the British rural landscape was consolidated into the shape we know today.

This was not an unconscious process. Most of the British land-owners of the eighteenth century had a trained eye for comely land-scape. Their poet, Alexander Pope, commended the landlord

> His Father's Acres who enjoys in peace,
> Or makes his Neighbours glad, if he encrease;
> Whose chearful Tenants bless their yearly toil,
> Yet to their Lord owe more than to the soil;
> Whose ample Lawns are not asham'd to feed
> The milky heifer and deserving steed;
> Whose rising Forests, not for pride or show,
> But future Buildings, future Navies grow:
> Let his plantations stretch from down to down,
> First shade a Country, and then raise a Town.[3]

Usefulness and visual pleasure were equally prized by the gentlemen of eighteenth-century England. They planted trees, sometimes in the formal geometric patterns approved by the Dutch, more often with an eye to producing an effect of tamed wilderness. They were great builders, most often copying the models of ancient Greece and Rome. Their opulent country houses were in turn a model and an inspiration for the colonial gentry of Virginia and the West Indies, and for the East India Company's officials in South Asia. Before the British settled in Australia they had come to regard their architecture as suited for export to any climate under the British flag. They took the ideal of the Georgian country house with them wherever they went, and this in time would influence the prosperous squatters and mer-chants of Australia when they came to build for their families in the new country. They also had a vision of the ideal landscape: neither

the wilderness nor the formal garden, but the park, the forest tamed
and cultivated for human enjoyment. It would prove hard to adapt
the Australian scenery to the model of an English park.

Parks were not only ornamental but functional. Often they were
maintained as a habitat for deer and other game. The right to hunt
game was regarded as one of the main marks of a gentleman, and a
law of 1671 restricted the privilege to landowners. Poaching was
considered a gross offence against property.[4] This did not discourage
the bolder among the village poor from venturing out on moonless
nights to help themselves to the squire's deer, pheasants or rabbits.
The landowning class reacted by getting their parliament to pass laws
for the protection of game with increasingly ferocious punishments,
culminating in the death penalty in 1803. Consequently some of the
convicts sent to Australia were criminals only because of the game
laws (though there has been a good deal of sentimental exaggeration
about the number of innocents transported merely for taking a rabbit
to feed their starving families.)

These game laws had a profound effect on the attitude of the first
generation of white Australians towards conservation. Because the
colony was often short of food in its early years, convicts and free
settlers sought their protein from kangaroos, bandicoots and other
native animals. Since Australian fauna seemed plentiful, and were in
any case too bizarre to arouse sentimental feelings, the British in
Australia lacked built-in protective attitudes towards them. Instead it
became a mark of Australia's standing as a democratic society that
the poorest man had the right to kill as many animals as he liked
without interference from the laws or from the power of the rich.
Precisely because Australia was a free and expanding young society
it would reject the notion of conservation of fauna as a hated relic of
the feudal past from the Old Country.

The game laws were the ugly face of British attitudes towards
property; but respect for property also tended to make many landowners into preservers and beautifiers. As a side-effect of maintaining
and improving their estates they developed conservationist attitudes,
organising their natural resources in ways which were not only useful
and payable but also pleasing to the eye. But their sense of what was
pleasing was very much a product of their experience of the British
environment. Their perceptions were not trained to appreciate the
qualities of a landscape as different from Britain as the Australian
bush. The preconceptions which made good landowners in Britain
would make the first generations of prosperous Australians blind to
the virtues of their country. It was possible to ape the British gentry

Panshangar, c. 1831
From Philip Cox and Clive Lucas, *Australian Colonial Architecture*, (Lansdowne 1978)

in life styles, luxuries and architecture, but less easy to adapt for Australian conditions their ideas of how to create a planned landscape.

Nor had many Australian landowners the same sense of attachment to the land which sometimes characterised their British models. Life in the bush was often harsh and brutalising. Little wonder that when they could afford it many Australian landowners chose to live in Toorak or Vaucluse, if not to return to that everlasting 'Home', old England. And of course the structure of political power was different in Australia. 'English landlords were still investing in authority and a social system in the nineteenth as they had done in earlier centuries, and had if anything become more interested in maximizing their returns in that direction than in the pursuit of profit'.[5] Australian landowners never had much chance of exercising that kind of authority, and although some tried to create a rural aristocratic environment for themselves, many others were content with profit.

This left the government as the main source from which initiative in environmental management might be expected. In Britain, where liberty was seen mainly as defending the individual and his property, strong central government was not encouraged. The labouring class, English or Irish, hated all forms of official interference.[6] In Australia, where survival and the maintenance of law and order were the over-riding aims during the early years of white settlement, the pattern was markedly different. Authority was centred strongly on the governor and his supporting armed forces. The rulers were not aristocrats but practical naval and military men, measurers and surveyors whose training taught them to value the useful above the merely beautiful. Some, such as Phillip and Macquarie, would plan with grandeur, but their ability to translate their ideas into action was limited severely by the human means at their disposal and the parsimonious level of British Treasury funding.

Right from the beginning the pattern of government in Australia, and with it the responsibility for environmental management, differed radically from Britain or North America. Unlike those older English-speaking countries Australia began with a strong tradition of government initiative and a necessarily weak expectation—indeed, while the colony remained chiefly a convict settlement, a positive discouragement of grass-roots enterprise. Instead its environmental planning depended on a handful of administrators whose major function was policing: not just in the modern sense of checking crime, but also in the older definition as the regulation of public order and the provision of the essential services of civilisation. Town planning, surveying, road-building could all be seen as outgrowths of military engineering.

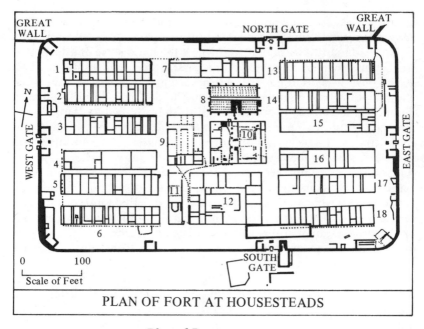

PLAN OF FORT AT HOUSESTEADS

Plan of Roman army camp
From David Webster *The Roman Imperial Army* (Adam & Charles Black, 1969)

Farming and animal husbandry were at first subordinated to the needs of the commissariat. As free settlers arrived in increasing numbers, a deep ambiguity crept into Australian attitudes towards government initiative. Australians inherited the strong British dislike of government interference; but they also formed the habit of relying upon government action to promote economic gain and social welfare.

Later on in the second half of the nineteenth century, when colonial Australia became self-governing, there was no obvious source of either private or public initiative in matters of environmental planning —even at the fairly basic nineteenth-century level of water supply, sanitation, or landscape conservation. No great industrialists arose to impose paternalistic order on the housing of their employees. Such wealth as was made in the pastoral and mining industries tended to be spent either on further capital investment or on the comforts of the rich. Those who turned philanthropist such as Sir Samuel Wilson or Francis Ormond were on the whole institutional benefactors, devoting their largesse to a university or a hospital rather than to improvement of the quality of everyday life.

Municipal government was kept weak by grudging ratepayers who demanded the strictest economy. Nor were the colonial governments of the nineteenth century in a position to impose policies of environmental management. Until the 1880s they were usually the short-lived product of unstable coalitions of factions, lacking the support of a skilled civil service, and constantly under pressure to spend money on developmental public works. Dominated by competing pressure groups in quest of roads and bridges, the colonial parliaments gave little scope for those with a concern for the quality of life. It was only occasionally that a persistent campaigner such as Krichauff in South Australia with his advocacy of good forestry, or a durable statesman such as Sir Henry Parkes with a receptivity to the idea of national parks, could change the direction of policy.[7] Consequently some have seen progress in ecological matters in Australia as depending on the influence of a few enlightened individuals, inspired mostly by their understanding of overseas developments.[8] Yet in many respects the Australian achievement in providing an acceptable and hopeful environment for the common people was second to none anywhere in the civilised world in the nineteenth century. Some of the least satisfactory features of the Australian setting arose because Australians looked too much over their shoulders at overseas developments.

The getters and spenders who dominated colonial society were all too conscious of British bourgeois models. Looking outside their own country for guidance about taste and values, schooled to believe in the overriding importance of money, the British settlers in Australia did not always appreciate and respect the character of their environment. Sometimes they sought to live as second-hand Englishmen, as if Australia were a cool and rainy island off the north-west coast of Europe. The response of the white Australians of the nineteenth century to their environment can be seen in many ways as an initial period of enterprising adaptation followed by a recession into acceptance of imported and sometimes incongruous models.

If Australia's growth in the nineteenth century was influenced for a long time by British preconceptions, it was a period when those preconceptions themselves were changing. Once a mainly rural society, Britain was experiencing that great transformation which historians call the Industrial Revolution. Modern Australia is the offshoot of that dynamic industrial society. Increasingly the economic use of labour and resources was planned in the mass, creating major changes in the relationship between people and the means of productivity. Workers were encouraged to develop specialised skills and to seek their reward through mass-produced amenities. At the same

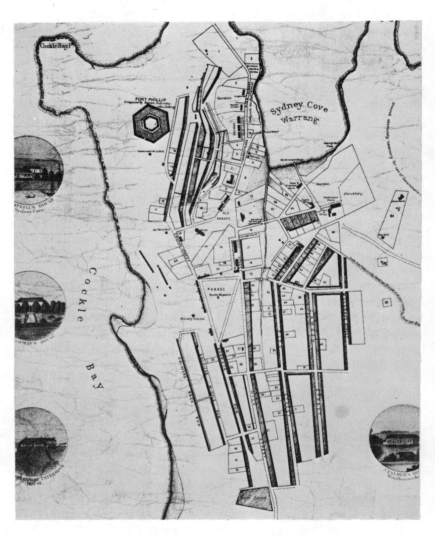

Survey of Sydney 1807 by Meehan

time the population grew at an unprecedented rate. By 1900 the English, Scottish and Welsh totalled over 40 million, three times as many as in 1800. It was different in Ireland, where after reaching 8.5 million in the 1840s numbers were drastically reduced by famine and emigration, stabilising at around 4.5 million. Many of the Irish who left home and many of the excess rural population of England and Scotland moved to the industrial and commercial cities.

Probably most of the migrants who came to Australia were products of city life, lacking any direct experience of rural life and environment. Few grew up in surroundings where they could develop a strong sense of scenic beauty. Britain's industrial cities were improvised, grey, damp, and subject to various forms of environmental pollution. Many employers were frankly on the make, caring for little but maximum profitability. Proclaiming a debased version of the old eighteenth-century belief in the rights of property, they held that any government intervention to improve working-class conditions was an interference with their rights as property owners. Those who emigrated to Australia from such backgrounds could be excused for placing environmental beauty very far down the list of priorities among their expectations in their new land.

Even among those who came to Australia from a rural background, few had the opportunity of exercising choice in the planning of their environment, and most were the products of limited and tradition-bound villages with little in their background which would be of use in adapting to Australian conditions. Often they were worse off than the city workers. Thatched cottages have a picturesque appeal to the modern eye, but in reality they were often appallingly dank and insanitary. For much of the nineteenth century except between 1840 and 1870 British farming was hit by a recession, so that landowners often failed to pay reasonable wages or to improve the farmworkers' living conditions. Most British farm labourers expected little good from rural living, not even adequate warmth and shelter. Those who emigrated to Australia, like their city cousins, were not likely to question their environmental conditions. Yet they took possession of the country with devastating rapidity.

In 1788 when Governor Arthur Phillip arrived with just over a thousand marines and convicts there may have been 300 000 human beings on the continent. By 1888 there were three million, the great majority British in origin, but with minority groups from continental Europe, China, Indonesia, Melanesia and the surviving Aborigines. By the end of World War II the number was over seven million, most of them locally born, but belonging to a culture even more exclusively derived from British origins. In 1980 there were fourteen million Australians, including a substantial injection of European immigrants and a few from South and South-east Asia. By world standards the population was still small. Probably fewer than 100 million individuals throughout the whole of human history have survived early childhood to experience the Australian environment consciously at first hand. This contrasts with the 200 million who at the present moment inhabit the United States, or the more than 800 million who find a living in China, neither of them countries with a land mass more than 20 per cent greater than Australia.

Of course this reflects the great inhospitability of much of inland Australia, but it also suggests that Australians have yet had less collective opportunity of getting to know their environment and learning how to come to terms with it. Because until recently the dominant culture was so overwhelmingly British-based, Australians lacked the stimulus to change which comes of living among the clash and compromise of different ethnic traditions. Because Australians nevertheless saw themselves as a young nation—even today over half the population is under 30 years of age—there was no sense of continuity with a living cultural tradition, but rather pride in capacity to adapt empirically to the needs of the moment. Because Australia grew early into a socioeconomic paradox, heavily urbanised but dependent for its wealth on the export of rural raw materials, it was hard to reach agreement even on the major characteristics of the Australian environment: its capacity to tolerate population increase, the desirable balance between rural and urban growth, the techniques of exploitation and adaptation best calculated to promote social and economic welfare. Throughout modern Australian history the odds have been stacked against the development of public attitudes which would make for enlightened policies on environmental conservation.

The spread of the frontier of settlement was fast even by North American standards. In 1815 most effective European settlement was concentrated within a radius of one hundred kilometres of Sydney, with smaller outposts at Van Diemen's Land (now Tasmania). Fifty years later the pastoralists had taken up almost all the land in eastern Australia that would ever be occupied for economic use, and behind them came miners, farmers and town-dwellers, sheep, cattle and railways: in short, all the features of an outlying province of nineteenth century industrial capitalism. By the 1890s the Northern Territory and Western Australia were also taken up almost to the limits of permanent white settlement. For another half century the arid interior remained for the surviving nomadic Aborigines who kept up a pattern of life continuous with their past traditions. The Second World War and the postwar quest for minerals brought their isolation to an end. Improved road and air transport fuelled by cheap oil imports enabled the present generation of white Australians to bring every corner of the continent within their reach. Seldom were so few people in possession of such power to shape the environment of so much of the earth's surface.

Because of the rapidity with which Australia was taken it was inevitable that its environment would be imperfectly understood by the landtakers. In exploiting natural resources and building urban and rural landscapes the Australians would be influenced neither by the ideals of aristocratic taste nor by the sense of familiarity and appreciation which comes from generations of experience. Yet from the outset some were to be found who responded positively to their Australian surroundings. William Charles Wentworth in Cambridge in 1823, drawing the images for his prize poem from the scenes of his Australian youth, was only the first among the native-born to express a sense of belonging in the newly settled continent. Against the backward-looking yearnings of spiritual exiles from England there were always those who trusted the native experience. One way of looking at the environmental history of Australia is to see it as a conflict between those who exploited the country to serve preconceived economic goals and imported attitudes of mind, and those on the other hand who sought to create a civilisation where human use of resources was compatible with a sense of identity with the land.

3 The Weather

Climate shapes environment, and the climate was one of the first features of Australia's geography to impress itself on British settlers. Some suggested that Australia was dealt a poor hand. It would be a fine country, said a disgruntled English cricket captain, except for the inhabitants and the climate—adding that one could say much the same about Hell. He went on to assert that Australia would be much improved if it were totally immersed for twenty-four hours. Both sneers embody one of the few clear ideas held about Australia by outsiders. The image persists of a parched land of drought, scattered with the bleaching bones of dead cattle while gaunt and thirsty settlers eat their Christmas dinners in temperatures well over the Fahrenheit century. Like all stereotypes it contains a grain of truth. In proportion to size Australia is the world's driest continent. Much of its inland is the 'dead heart', once perhaps fertile but now the harshest of environments. It is easy to agree with the geographer Oskar Spate when he writes that Australia is obviously the oldest continent, as the Creator must surely have made a better job of it with greater experience. If only it had been situated ten degrees further south, so as to take better advantage of the rain-bearing westerlies, or if only it were traversed diagonally by a mountain range on the Himalayan scale, from whose eternally snow-capped peaks great rivers might have brought sustenance to the arid inland . . .

Such conjectures were beyond the imagination of the first European settlers. They knew very little about the climate of the continent which they were preparing to occupy. They were not entirely sure about its size or its shape, of whether it comprised one island or several. Those such as Governor King who took the trouble to consult Aboriginal lore picked up one or two fragments of information, such as the story that about 1780 'a flood occurred that no other Conception of it could be formed than that the Natives who had ascended the highest Trees were swept off—It had then poured in torrents for Nine Days and Nights.'[1] Beyond that the white men learned little. Aboriginal folk memory was notably flexible about the measurement of time, and could give no useful information about the recurrent cycle of seasons. Persistent reports of a large inland sea, if they had any basis at all, must have referred to a period thousands of years in the past; yet the story seemed credible enough to lure Sturt and other explorers into long and difficult searches through the arid inland. The notion of an inland sea also gained strength through comparisons with the Northern Hemisphere, where the Mediterranean suggested an analogy. The ancient belief that the Southern Hemisphere must be a mirror image of the Northern was a long time in dying.

Travellers trying to convey an idea of the Australian climate often sought to make comparisons with European models. Thus Sir Joseph Banks stated that the climate of Botany Bay was very like Toulouse. This may have suggested something to that minority among the educated who had visited the south of France, but to most Englishmen it meant nothing, or perhaps worse than nothing since from reading and report they may have formed a mental image of the Mediterranean climate which was quite unlike reality. Similarly when in 1827 Captain Stirling compared the Swan River with Virginia and the plains of Lombardy, his readers may have envisaged scenery very different from what he meant to communicate.[2] With greater experience British observers grew more cautious. The British in Australia did not find it surprising that the seasons were the reverse of the Northern Hemisphere—Europeans had been visiting and settling in South America and South Africa long enough to expect this—but it was difficult for them to generalise when they were forming their first impressions in the Sydney region where rain may fall at any time of the year. After many months with the first settlement at Sydney Captain Watkin Tench could say about the climate only that it was 'changeable beyond any other I ever heard of'. His senior, Governor Phillip, unhesitatingly declared: 'a finer or more healthy climate is not to be found in any part of the world'.

This verdict was endorsed by others who could not be thought biased. Michael Hayes, an Irish exile after the 1798 rising, assured his relatives that fevers, smallpox and agues were strangers to young and old alike: 'No sickness but from old age and intemperance'. Later generations thought similarly. By 1841 the Presbyterian moderator in Hobart, John Lillie, could assert that:

It is generally allowed that the climate of this country, whether arising from the absence of moisture or from a higher temperature, or from some other cause, is of a much more stimulating and exciting character, and tends to bring on a quicker development of the bodily and mental powers than the climate of Great Britain.[3]

A fine climate for children, and as Lillie was the father of a young family we may take his word for it; but adolescents tended to be less thriving, and Lillie thought this might be due to the maintenance of the traditional heavy English meat diet instead of lighter foods more suited to a warm climate. He might also have added that Australians did not dress to suit the climate. Some adaptability was indeed shown during the early years in New South Wales. Governor Hunter wrote in 1797 proposing that thin canvas trousers should be provided by the Home government rather than the conventional English breeches and stockings, as these were much more desired by the people.[4] Governor Bligh's spirited daughter, Mrs Putland, drew ill-natured comment because of the thinness of the clothing with which she confronted the Sydney summer. By Queen Victoria's day women and men alike had largely succumbed to the unsuitable garb of the British bourgeoisie.

Writing to his sister at the hot New Year of 1857 W.S. Jevons, the very able young North Country Englishman who at the age of twenty-one was the Sydney Mint's first assayer, commented that most Englishmen seemed unable to tell that Sydney was much hotter than London or Liverpool, and

> . . . may accordingly be seen encountering the hottest of hot winds in black cloth suits or clothes, black hats, and everything complete. On the present occasion I luxuriated in a grass-cloth coat as thin as a ladies gauze dress, trousers and waistcoat but a shade from white, and a cabbage-tree hat.[5]

In outback Queensland and Western Australia it was acceptable even for bank officers to be seen without their jackets, and at the Mackay races in the 1880s even the bosses were sufficiently well dressed in moleskin trousers and Oxford blue shirts—only visiting cardsharps from the cities wore coats and hard-hitter hats. But although the bush was free and easy, city dwellers usually conformed to every stifling whim of British fashion. As late as 1907 the recently married young surveyor H.S. Trotman, back in Perth after many months in the bush, 'chafed at the restriction of the collar, tie and city clothes,

> . . . but the fashions which the womenfolk slavishly followed—even in hottest weather—made me marvel at their courage. Those were the days of leg-o-mutton sleeves and sweeping skirts, of feathered, flowered, and fruity hats, and although Maude outshone the rest in my eyes, I remember saying that the whalebone, net and lace contraption that she wore round her neck was an abomination, and that the pad known as a bustle, worn under her skirt, was idiotic.[6]

Australians may have been slow learners about living comfortably but in economic matters a greater responsiveness was soon evident. Climate provided the stimulus for settlers to break out of the Sydney coastal strip and to take possession of the continent. The drought of 1810–12 played a large part in spurring Blaxland, Lawson and Wentworth to find a path over the Blue Mountains to the new country at Bathurst and beyond. A later drought in 1819–20 prompted Governor Macquarie to throw open for pastoral settlement the country south and west of Camden as far as the present Goulburn-Canberra area. 'The publication of this Order on 25 November 1820 marked the real beginning of the great outward spread of pastoralists and graziers which continued into the thirties and forties.'[7] The tracks travelled by those frontier squatters were sometimes fatefully guided by the hazards of climate.

This may be seen by contrasting the experiences of Sturt and Leichhardt when they went exploring in 1844–45. That was the appalling summer when Sturt, questing for his inland sea in the far west of New South Wales, spent several months penned up at Fort Grey in heat which dried the ink in his pen and made the birds fall lifeless from the trees. At the same time the rainy season in what is now the centre and north of Queensland was no more than light to moderate, so that the Burdekin and the big rivers of the Gulf Country at no time rose in flood to render the country impassable. So it was that Ludwig Leichhardt on his first major attempt at exploration spent sixteen months traversing the country between Brisbane and Port Essington without undue privation or delay. When Sturt and Leichhardt returned to civilisation the outcome was predictable. Repelled by Sturt's forbidding account of the country beyond the Darling the pastoralists checked their westward spread for many years, though the country was eventually found capable of tolerably successful occupation. On the other hand Leichhardt's promising report from the north turned the tide of settlement in that direction and so laid the foundations for the colony of Queensland. Had Sturt and Leichhardt gone out in a different season it might easily have ended with Sturt returning with reports of likely grazing country in the far west, and Leichhardt retreating baffled by a heavy 'wet'—if indeed he was not swept away in a flood, which may well be what happened to his 1848 expedition.

With no precedent from the rest of the world to serve them as a model and no reliable records of the past to guide them, the Australians of this pioneering generation tried to discern regular patterns in the coming of good seasons and droughts. E.S. Hall, editor of the *Australian*, suggested in 1830 that the weather of New South Wales followed a seven-year cycle. Perhaps he was influenced by the Biblical precedent of seven fat years followed by seven lean years, but the theory did not stand the test of time. Peter Cunningham, a much travelled ship's surgeon who had spent two years of drought in New South Wales, later asserted that the Australian weather produced droughts at nine-yearly intervals.[8] He based this on a belief that the conditions producing long dry spells followed a westerly circuit around the world, occurring at regular intervals in South Africa, then in South America, then in Australia. Other theorists favoured a ten-year cycle. Dr Edward Day, speaking from a background of Melbourne experience, asserted that no consistent pattern at all could be found in seasonal variations.[9]

W.S. Jevons rejected the ten-year cyclic theory in favour of a twenty-year variation.[10] By his reckoning the First Fleet arrived in the middle of a dry spell lasting until 1798. Next came a run of better seasons to 1821, then two decades of drier weather, and from 1842 a period of generally good rainfall. This pattern suggested that another turning point would be reached in the early 1860s, but few drew this conclusion. Instead the run of good seasons probably fed the optimism with which politicians in the early 1860s whipped up campaigns to throw open the land of the inland for agriculture.

It was of course inevitable that New South Wales and Victoria would seek to retain the tens of thousands of migrants attracted by gold, and perhaps equally inevitable that the easiest way of doing so was to promise the diggers farms carved out of the squatters' sheep runs. Yet such a policy would not have seemed feasible to men of colonial experience such as John Robertson, author of the 1861 Land Act in New South Wales, unless they firmly believed that the inland climate was reliable enough to make farming a fair risk. Nor would the pastoralists, among them the same John Robertson, have thrust so eagerly into the Queensland outback for new runs without sharing the faith that the country could seldom be too dry to run sheep and cattle profitably.

At first Jevons seemed justified in his forecast. Between 1862 and 1868 there were several light seasons in New South Wales, so that the influx of free selectors into districts such as the Riverina was slowed considerably.[11] South Australia experienced drought in 1864–65 and 1866 was poor in Queensland. On the whole, however, the later sixties and the seventies brought a rather good run of seasons in eastern Australia. Pastoralists throve. Australia's sheep numbers rose from 20 million in 1860 to 40 million in 1870 and 100 million by the mid-nineties. This was not simply the result of favourable seasons, because in good years when feed was plentiful on the stock routes more sheep and cattle found their way to market so that the rate of increase seems sometimes to have been fastest during mediocre seasons. Wool was nevertheless a main prop of the long boom which lasted until the end of the eighties, during which Australians came to enjoy and expect one of the world's highest living standards. Poorer seasons would have dimmed perceptibly the lustre of Australia as working man's paradise.

In those years a great optimism grew up about the likely improvement of the Australian climate. This was nowhere more marked than in South Australia, a colony which lacked gold and was obliged to mend its fortunes by wheat growing. By a happy accident the two great indentations of Spencer Gulf and St Vincent's Gulf placed much of its best farming country within easy reach of ports. Wheat could reach the bakers of Melbourne and Sydney more easily on coasting vessels from South Australia than by road or rail from their own hinterlands. Early success and the fear of competition from California spurred a demand in South Australian farmers for more land. Following the drought of 1864–65 the surveyor general, G.W. Goyder, was commissioned to find out the limits within which rural settlement could reasonably be attempted. Goyder's line was founded on a study of rainfall and vegetation by a careful and experienced observer who stressed that even within the line crops might sometimes be at risk from hot northerly winds.

Nevertheless, as usual, the practical farmers thought they knew better than the expert. It took only one or two good seasons around 1872 for Goyder's line to be thoroughly discredited. The settlers poured north to Hawker, to Quorn, even to the unpromising country east of Lake Torrens, their optimism fortified by a freakish run of good seasons. On all sides the theory flew that the breaking up of the soil, by facilitating the absorption and evaporation of rainfall, would increase the moisture in the atmosphere and so bring more rain. Old colonists were sure they could remember the same thing happening on the Adelaide Plains in the 1840s. The reckoning came in the summer of 1879–80. That was the first of a run of dry years which vindicated Goyder but spelt tragedy for many of the pioneers. A large number of northern farms were abandoned, leaving a few sagging lines of fencing and ruined stone farmhouses as the only mementos of the great surge forward of the frontier. Ten years earlier than its eastern neighbours South Australia lapsed into a prolonged recession from which it would not emerge until after the turn of the century.[12]

The South Australian object lesson was not taken very seriously. Elsewhere in Australia politicians continued to speak and legislate as if the Australian climate could be tamed. Irrigation or artesian water

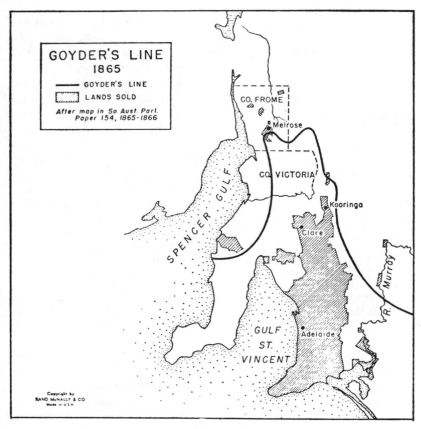

Goyder's Line
From D.W. Meinig *On the Margins of the Good Earth* (Rigby, 1970)

could compensate for any deficiencies in the rainfall. In much of eastern Australia, however, the droughts began to come more frequently during the eighties. There was a bad year in 1884 and another, the driest so far known in Sydney, in 1888. In 1892 the young Henry Lawson, carrying his swag through the Darling country between Bourke and Hungerford, saw those harsh and mournful images of drought which would influence the view of the bush in so much of his writing.

Worse was to come. The years which culminated in 1902 went down in Australian history as the 'king' drought of all time. There were illusory breaks in the sequence—1894 was a reasonable year in much of eastern Australia, and 1899–1900 brought enough rain to keep hope alive—but for many outback pastoralists the overall impact was ruinous. They were already deeply indebted for investment capital and they were reeling from an eight-year drop in wool prices which bottomed in 1894 and recovered only slowly afterwards. Poor markets led to overstocking, and pastures were eaten bare long before the drought broke. It may be that in Queensland the seasons were no worse than in the great modern drought of 1957–67, but modern technology and better prices for wool and beef cushioned the blow to some extent in the 1960s, whereas the 1890s disaster was beyond palliatives. One large cattle station in the channel country of south-west Queensland had nearly 30 000 cattle on its books at the beginning of 1900 and mustered 818 survivors in June 1901. 'Mulga that died during that drought is still standing in some areas', wrote F.H. Bauer in 1963, 'and graziers have told me that some plants common before the drought did not reappear until as much as fifty years afterwards'.[13]

> Droving that year, Charleville to the Hunter,
> nineteen-one it was, and the drought beginning;
> sixty head left at the McIntyre, the mud round them
> hardened like iron; and the yellow boy died
> in the sulky ahead with the gear, but the horse went on,
> stopped at the Sandy Camp and waited in the evening.
> It was the flies we seen first, swarming like bees.
> Came to the Hunter, three hundred head of a thousand
> —cruel to keep them alive—and the river was dust.[14]

It was not only the inland that suffered. In Sydney the native street-trees died in many suburbs. Even in Tasmania the churches prayed for rain.

The long-term effects of the drought have yet to be fully assessed.[15] In Victoria and southern New South Wales it stimulated an increased interest in irrigation, illustrated within the next decade by the planning of the Burrinjuck dam and the Murrumbidgee scheme. In Western Australia the dry years 1894 and 1895, coming as they did immediately after the discovery of the Coolgardie-Kalgoorlie goldfield, probably nudged the Forrest government into taking its successful gamble on the construction of C.Y. O'Connor's great pipeline bringing water nearly 600 kilometres to the goldfields; but in general the West suffered a great deal less than the rest of the continent from the drought. Because of the dry years William Farrer of Queanbeyan turned aside from his researches on the elimination of rust in wheat—a problem mostly associated with high rainfall districts—in order to concentrate on the breeding of drought-resistant varieties. It took six years to perfect the dry wheat 'Federation' in 1901, the first of the new varieties which were

Drought
From *People* 21 June 1950

to be the making of the inland wheatbelts of New South Wales, Western Australia and the Mallee.

Perhaps one further legacy of the nineties drought is the Australian Labor Party. If a run of good seasons had enabled pastoralists to weather a period of low prices and to respond less uncompromisingly towards trade union demands over pay and conditions, there might have been an end to the confrontation between bosses and men which produced the strikes of the early nineties. As in Canada, the Labor Party might have failed to establish itself; certainly without a strong base among the bush workers Labor would have found it much harder to entrench itself in colonial parliaments. As it was, by the time recovery came with good seasons, Labor had been long enough in politics to stimulate the coming of the arbitration system, after which its future was assured ... But probably this is carrying the effect of climate on history further than is justified.

That the long-term study of climate was a government responsibility was fully accepted by 1900. As early as 1803 the government approved Sydney *Gazette* published meteorological reports. Victoria, South Australia, and New South Wales maintained government meteorologists from as far back as the late 1850s. The meteorologists of these three colonies and New Zealand met in Sydney in 1879 to discuss co-operation and the pooling of information. The initiative does not seem to have been the result of any particular concern about the long-term tendency of the Australasian climate, but followed the availability of communication by telegraph. Two further conferences were held in Melbourne during the eighties, during which the other Australian colonies appointed meteorologists.

The most energetic compaigner for Australia-wide co-operation in identifying major trends in the weather was Queensland's Clement Wragge, who for nearly two decades after his appointment in 1886 busied himself with endeavours to improve the science of forecasting throughout the whole of eastern Australia. He gained a great reputation among farmers, and it would be interesting to know whether his work helped to influence the framers of the Australian constitution in includ-ing meteorology among the powers to be taken over by the federal government in the new Commonwealth. But Wragge was not to be the first Commonwealth meteorologist. Too many colleagues had been annoyed by his irascible temper. Besides, his reputation suffered when in September 1902 he tried to bring about an end to the great drought by a rainmaking experiment at Charleville, invoking the old Aboriginal notion that persistent noise attracted rain. Throughout the whole of one afternoon the unresponsive skies were bombarded with the noise of six Italian cannon firing at intervals worked out by Wragge; but no rain fell. So Wragge went off to New Zealand, leaving his disciple Inigo Jones to carry on the work as purveyor of long-term forecasts to farmers and graziers.

Official meteorologists for many years tended to avoid as unpro-fitable speculations on the long-term trends of the Australian climate, and the consequent effects of climate on the environment. Yet the land had been long enough settled by white Australians for the observant to notice some tendencies which required explanation. In the Northern Rivers district of New South Wales winter frosts were encountered increasingly in valleys which in earlier times were considered virtually frost-free. The change came, old residents said, after the hillsides were cleared of trees; there was now nothing to hinder the cold mountain-top air from moving down into the valleys and lowering the temperature more than formerly. This was a new twist to an old argument. As early as 1864 the American writer, G.P. Marsh, was arguing that trees exercised a significant influence on attracting rainfall[16] and in 1868 von Mueller was also making this point.[17] Around the same time a number of Australians were asserting that the climate would be affected by the wholesale clearing of forests, and other Australians were refuting them vigorously. It is odd that so little scientific research was undertaken into the question, since of all the human activities which might have been thought to affect the climate and environment of nineteenth century Australia, few were carried out more zealously than the cutting down of trees.

4   They Hated Trees

Of Australia's pioneers a noted Australian historian wrote:

> The most precious possessions of Australia are her rivers, whose even flood is protected by the forests which stand around their mountain sources and the trees which line their banks. The invaders hated trees.[1]

The first European arrivals in New South Wales may well have been oppressed by what they saw as the vastness of its forests. Many of the earliest drawings of the Australian bush tend to exaggerate the size of the trees and to dwarf the human figures among them, and this probably reflects the way the newcomers felt about their new surroundings. But it did not take long for those with a scientific and commercial eye to measure the potential of the native timber. In 1791 Surgeon John Harris wrote: 'the Red Gum tree is the only vegetable production that seems to thrive here, I wish I could say beneficial to Brittain but am sorry to add that the wood is not fit to be wrought into any material and the gum is so acrid and disagreeable to the stomach as not to be palliated'. The yellow gum, he said, had some reputation as a remedy against 'chronic fluxes': 'I myself have taken it to the quantity of 2 drahms in a little rum and water as a substitute for milk punch as it is possess'd [of] a grateful flavour.'[2]

To most settlers the trees were simply a nuisance to be cleared to make room for building or farming. It was not long before the part played by indiscriminate tree-felling in causing soil erosion came to be recognised. As early as October 1803 Governor King issued a proclamation forbidding felling along the banks of rivers and water-courses. He stated his motives clearly:

> From the improvident method taken by the first settlers on the sides of the Hawkesbury and creeks in cutting down timber and cultivating banks, many acres of ground have been removed, land inundated, houses, stacks of wheat, and stock washed away by former floods which might have been prevented in some measure if the trees and other native plants had been suffered to remain ...

The grammar becomes complicated but the sense is clear. Despite the threat of heavy fines, despite the encouragement of replanting, King's proclamation seems soon to have become a dead letter. At any rate in 1826 James Atkinson was damning the 'ignorant, indolent and improvident' Hawkesbury settlers who choked the rivers with fallen trees and so contributed to the spread of flooding.[4]

In any case King's proclamation referred only to the cutting of trees in river valleys. For the most part he, like every other man of his time, saw Australia's native timber as an asset for the economy. A few months before his Hawkesbury proclamation he issued an edict requiring government permission for the cutting of timber fit for naval and ship-building purposes and of a variety of commercially useful species, including she-oak, swamp oak, red gum, blue gum, blackbutt, springy-bark, ironbark, box, mahogany, cedar, lightwood and turpentine.

Cedar was the timber most in demand for export. An experimental cargo was shipped to India as early as 1795. From 1804 convict gangs were cutting out cedar on the Hunter and by 1820 they had to go more than a hundred kilometres upstream to find workable stands. The exploitation of Illawarra and Shoalhaven cedar began in 1811, and during the 1820s and 1830s the axemen moved into new districts— Port Stephens, Port Macquarie, the Manning, Brisbane Water, the Clarence and by 1842 the Richmond—pressing ever northwards in their eagerness to get first choice of the unspoilt timber.

For the strong and poor cedar cutting was an attractive occupation, because although hazardous the life was remote from the hand of authority and required little capital. By all accounts the cedar cutters enjoyed an independence and a mateship very like that of the future diggers' camps on the goldfields. There was no policing the methods of the cedar cutters, and a great deal of waste took place; but by 1829 timber stood third among the list of exports from New South Wales, and in 1836 the total sent away exceeded a million and a half feet. The idea of Australian timber as a commercial asset became strongly entrenched in men's minds. John Hart, a future premier of South Australia, droving in a dry season about that time from New South Wales to Adelaide, was moved to comment as he followed the Murray Valley: 'Nothing struck me so much on this river as the splended timber that grows on its banks; I never saw anything equal to it for ship-building purposes'.[5]

Until the gold rushes of the 1850s the destruction of timber was confined to the coastal valleys of New South Wales, and mainly involved taking timber for commercial purposes or in clearing farms. The boom in town building after 1851 boosted local demand greatly.

Cutting out Australia's forests
Reproduced with permission from Forestry Commission of NSW

At the same time improved shipping facilitated the export of Australian hardwoods. Thus from the late 1860s an export trade grew up in the Western Australian jarrah blocks which beneath the bitumen pave many of the streets of the City of London. Mounting demand from many sources sent the timber getters searching further afield for new stands, until by the 1880s cedar cutters on the Atherton Tableland were logging their timber down the Barron River in the far north of Queensland. At the same time older established districts enjoyed boom conditions. In one day in September 1873 nineteenth schooners loaded with pine sailed from the Richmond river, and in one week a million feet of pine and cedar were sent away from the district. Each year in the early 1870s the Richmond produced 5.5 million feet of pine and ash and 3.5 million feet of cedar.

Most Australians were so overwhelmed by the sheer quantity of bush timber that they took its inexhaustibility for granted. Perhaps they were influenced by official estimates such as the calculation that nearly half of New South Wales, 92 million acres in all, was timbered country; Victoria, according to a report of 1861, was covered for over 90 per cent of its area by open timbered country, mountain woodland, or dense mallee scrub. Restraint seemed unnecessary. When the Burra copper mines were opened in 1845 the *South Australian Register* saw no problem about fuelling the new industry, since there was enough wood to 'meet a vast consumption for generations to come, even if we discover no coal of our own'.[6] The district is today classed as a tussock grassland.

Commissioner Fry of the New South Wales Lands Department informed an official inquiry in 1847 that the Big Scrub in the Richmond river cedar country could not be cleared for five or six centuries.[7] Within thirty years selectors were farming the same country, stripped of its timber by the muscle and the three-kilogram axes of the cedar cutters. Despite these examples the old optimism died hard. As late as 1892 when an earnest member of the Western Australian parliament spoke up for timber conservation he gained little support, and the main Perth newspaper confidently asserted that the jarrah and karri forrests were sufficient for many centuries in the future.[8] To the men who had the job of chopping down the Australian forests the task no doubt seemed dishearteningly immense. To armchair experts it was agreeable to think that one of Australia's natural resources was inexhaustible.

Another argument for as much clearing as possible was put forward in the middle of the nineteenth century by William Howitt. Usually one of the most sensible observers of south-eastern Australia, Howitt

went astray when he tried to apply scientific theory to his environmental studies. Australia, he wrote, was

> ... with very trivial exception, one huge, unreclaimed forest. Now,
> I do not believe that any country, under any climate in the world,
> can be pronounced a thoroughly healthy country, while it is in this
> state. The immense quantity of vegetable matter rotting on the
> surface of the earth, and still more of that rotting in the waters,
> which the new visitants must drink, cannot be very healthy. The
> choked-up valleys, dense with scrub and rank grass and weeds, and
> the equally rank vegetation of swamps, cannot tend to health. All
> these evils, the axe and the plough, and the fire of settlers, will
> gradually and eventually remove; and when it is done here, I do
> not believe that there will be a more healthy country on the globe.[9]

Others thought less harshly of the native trees. Sir William Macarthur, speaking with the authority of a native-born son of one of
Australia's landowning families, held the view that the virtual absence
of malaria in Australia was due to the health-giving influence of the
eucalyptus. Before the discovery at the end of the nineteenth century
of the role of the anopheles mosquito as a carrier of malaria it was
thought that such diseases were provoked by the unhealthy miasma
which arose from decomposing plant material. The eucalyptus was
thought to counteract these unhealthy influences because of its power
of absorbing moisture through its root system and because of some
physicochemical action of the distinctive aromatic oil in its leaves. For
such reasons medical practitioners worried by outbreaks of typhoid
and dysentery sometimes urged the planting of native street-trees as
a health measure as well as for ornament.

These theories were taken up enthusiastically by Joseph Bosisto,
who in 1852 began to distil oil from eucalyptus leaves for medical
purposes, and who exhibited commercial eucalyptus oil at seventeen
major exhibitions between 1854 and 1891. Eucalyptus oil was found
to have medical and industrial uses, and was even in demand for per-
fumery. In the 1880s it was the only distinctively Australian substance
in the British Pharmacopoeia. Bosisto gathered oil from the eucalypts
of coastal districts during the summer months and from the mallee
country of north-western Victoria in winter. He calculated that in a
good season nine litres of eucalyptus oil could be distilled from two
tonnes of rough-cut mallee branches, and since from 1865 Victoria
built up a thriving export trade in the commodity, the pioneer axemen
who worked for Bosisto must have cleared a formidable amount of
scrub.[10] At the same time other entrepreneurs developed a trade in
wattle bark for tanning, and this contributed further to the exploita-

tion of Australia's forests. 'While money is to be made', wrote W.S. Jevons in 1856, 'trees will never in Australia be spared for mere ornament'.[11]

The main enemies of Australia's trees were the pastoralists. From about 1860, seeking clear grazing for their sheep, they went in for ringbarking on an enormous scale. The origins of this practice have not been completely traced. It is thought to have been developed in North America, although history records at least one example of a disgruntled English farm labourer who annoyed his landlord by destroying some of his prized trees by ringbarking.[12] The landlord was Benjamin Disraeli, and the year was 1869, so it may be that the unknown axeman was an Australian expatriate; for the practice was known in New South Wales many years earlier. Atkinson writing in 1826 noted stump felling and ringbarking as the two main methods used in clearing land for farming, but added that only the wealthiest pastoralists could afford to clear for grazing. There was a good deal of debate about the usefulness of the practice, but Atkinson thought it made for sweeter grass.[13]

During the 1830s the first generation of Swan River colonists experienced great difficulty in clearing the local hardwoods. Some took to ringbarking and burning off. Because of their inexperience the fires often got out of control with calamitous results.[14] In the fear of bushfires lay the beginnings of wisdom. In 1847 Western Australia legistlated that any person wilfully or carelessly setting fire to any vegetation between 1 September and 1 April would be fined a maximum of £50—or, if an Aboriginal or a boy under sixteen, given a public flogging of up to fifty lashes.[15]

Other parts of Australia were also coming to see the need for some form of fire control. Alfred Howitt thought that scrub and undergrowth were running wild in many parts of Gippsland because the country was no longer regularly burnt off by Aboriginal fires.[16] Major Mitchell believed that the omission of periodic burning and the consequent growth of thick scrub was a main cause of the disastrous 'Black Thursday' of February 1851. On that day the whole of Victoria from Gippsland to Mount Gambier seemed ablaze, and the captain of the *Henry Edward* tacking through Bass Strait reported: 'The fire flew above the vessel in large flakes which caused to burn the running gear, so that the sails fell down on the deck'.[17] Such holocausts were a powerful argument for clearing.

In 1860 Thomas Hungerford, a colonial-bred Hunter Valley landowner, decided to go in for ringbarking and fencing paddocks on a bigger and more systematic scale than any previous attempt. In the

Ringbarking

post-gold-rush era of high prices for labour he soon found a host of imitators. Ringbarking was cheaper and simpler than clearing, and brought pastoralists a gratifyingly quick increase in their acreage of grazing land. In a number of districts gangs of travelling Chinese, no longer able to make a living from alluvial goldmining, offered their services as cheap and hard-working contractors for ringbarking. They met with little competition from white axemen, for such monotonous work.

It was some years before the disadvantages of ringbarking became apparent. In such districts as the Lachlan and Mudgee after the opening of the country by the 1861 Land Act it was found that the clearing of eucalypts was followed by a takeover of pine scrub. In the Illawarra country south of Sydney tangles of scrub took over in many places where the blackbutts were cut out for mining timber, and some observers believed that clearing and overgrazing led to erosion and in wet winters to landslides.

Soon some were questioning the wisdom of the sweeping devastation caused by ringbarking. Believing that trees influenced rainfall, men such as the clergyman-geologist W.B. Clarke feared that wholesale clearing would bring about greater aridity. Such warnings were echoed by experts in South Australia when the 1879 drought brought ruin to the farmers beyond Goyder's Line. The forester Ednie-Brown explicitly blamed the bad seasons on the absence of trees. Practical men would have none of this talk. In 1880 W.E. Abbott, speaking from the experience of twenty years of ringbarking in the Hunter Valley, gave an address to the Royal Society of New South Wales which was accepted for many years as the decisive word on the matter:

> The very rapid spread of ringbarking in spite of the opposition of all the lovers of fine scenery, and of so many scientific men . . . proves that there must be a clear gain to the graziers in getting rid of the timber.[18]

Nothing could have put more bluntly the conflict between economy and ecology; but Abbott did not leave it there. On the basis of practical experience he stated that since clearing the creeks and watercourses usually retained water throughout the summers, whereas previously they were dry by December. Hence it was unlikely that ringbarking reduced rainfall or had any adverse effect on drainage and runoff. Abbott's confidence was bolstered by a run of good seasons, and we do not know whether he later changed his mind, but his printed words remained authoritative enough to be consulted for at least thirty years afterwards.

There were plenty to echo him a year later when the New South Wales parliament debated the implications of a Supreme Court judgement defining ringbarking as an improvement for the purposes of valuing an occupier's equity in his land. The issue was raised by J.E. McElhone, the maverick member for Upper Hunter and a great spokesman for the free selectors. Ringbarking, he stated, certainly improved the value of pastoralists' lands. They could carry a sheep to an acre (0.4 hectare), four or six times as many as previously. By ringbarking they could improve the value of their land from five shillings an acre to ten, at a cost of no more than a shilling an acre. But vast forests were destroyed indiscriminately, and selectors were finding it difficult to get timber. One or two other speakers drew attention to the absence of forestry legislation, but most stoutly asserted the value of ringbarking. J.P. Abbott followed the family line in claiming that clearing did not affect the rainfall. W.A. Brodribb asserted that 'Springs were found gushing up where they had never been known before, because the water had been absorbed by the trees'. J.S. Farnell told the House that 'We should not have heard a word about ringbarking had it not been a bar to free selection'. Only old Philip Gidley King, the governor's grandson and a landowner of lengthy experience, stood out in insisting that the rainfall would in fact diminish after excessive clearing, and urging that surveyors should recommend large timber reserves.[19]

Debate continued while the trees fell. H.C. Russell told the Australian and New Zealand Association for the Advancement of Science that although widespread ringbarking and clearing had no influence on rainfall, there might be some effect on temperature and runoff.[20] In 1892 A.G. Hamilton estimated that 9.5 million hectares of New South Wales forests had been destroyed by clearing or ringbarking, a little more than a quarter of the total area which was under forest when the white men came a century earlier.[21] In his view comparatively little of this loss was due to the commercial exploitation of timber for export. Clearance for farming and ringbarking for grazing were the major agents of destruction.

The mining industries were also greedy for timber. In a suspiciously exact display of statistics, Hamilton calculated that 51 942 trees had been felled by the end of 1891 to provide the coal mines of New South Wales with pit props at the cost of a pound for a hundred. He could not produce any such figures for the gold mining industry, but it too was a formidable user of timber. Within eight years of the discovery of gold at Charters Towers in 1872 local editors were commenting on the bareness of the surrounding countryside; every tree too stunted for use in the mines was either burnt for fuel or stripped and nibbled by the troops of goats kept by the miners' families for milking. In Western Australia in 1902 an experienced mine manager estimated that the mines of Kalgoorlie were burning 47 000 tonnes of firewood a month to fuel their steam engines and crushing machinery: 'the wood has to be good . . . it is mostly salmon gum and some harder woods'.[22] He made the statement a few days before the Legislative Assembly debated the construction of sixty-four kilometres of railway from Coolgardie to tap the timber reserves to the south, closer supplies being virtually worked out.

Besides the demands of major primary industries, further inroads on the country's timber resources were made by the demands of railway construction. A big red gum could produce as many as three hundred sleepers but contractors usually took the nearest timber to hand, thus helping to clear the land for pioneer farmers. Timber was also needed for domestic firewood to fuel kitchen stoves, bath heaters, and sitting-room fireplaces. I have not found an estimate of demand earlier than 1925, but in that year, when gas and electricity were available in all major cities and brown coal briquettes were coming into common use in Melbourne, it was calculated that New South Wales and Victoria between them consumed a million tonnes of firewood each year.[23]

Australians were finding that foreigners seemed to value the eucalypt more than they did. Until the 1850s Australian trees were planted overseas mainly as a botanical curiosity, establishing themselves in regions as far apart as Scotland, the Crimea, and Peru.[24] Then the botanist Ferdinand von Mueller saw the implications of the theory that the eucalyptus was an enemy of malaria. If Bosisto could develop a thriving commercial trade in eucalyptus oil, could not the trees themselves be transplanted with benefit to those parts of the civilised world where malaria was a hazard to life and industry? As early as 1856 von Mueller was encouraging a French visitor, Prosper Ramel, to attempt the acclimatisation of eucalypts in France and in the French colony of Algeria where malaria was crippling development. This initiative succeeded so well that by 1877 there were nearly a million blue gums in Algeria.

Old William Howitt, by now living in retirement in Rome, was persuaded to change his ill opinion about the value of Australian trees. He befriended the monks of the Tre Fontane monastery at the scene of St Paul's martyrdom just outside Rome, and finding them plagued with malaria advised them to start eucalyptus plantations, consulting his son Alfred in Gippsland about their importation.[25] Soon the Pontine Marshes were studded with rows of young eucalypts, which were additionally appreciated for their ornamental qualities and their use as windbreaks.

Meanwhile the forty-niners who poured into California for gold were dismayed to find that the malaria had got there twenty years earlier, and they too looked to the eucalyptus for salvation. Between 1856 and 1860 a nurseryman named William Walker made several plantings in San Francisco. His example was followed by a number of others, so that by the 1870s the planting of blue gums was 'almost a mania', and over seventy species of eucalyptus were introduced into California. It was not long before most Californians came to regard them as a native species, and at times complaints have been voiced— unjustly on the whole, it would appear—about their prowess in invading abandoned orange groves and otherwise competing with the local flora.[26] Between 1855 and 1875 plantations of Australian trees were also made in Portugal, Spain, Brazil, Argentina, and Hawaii. So, although malaria was not eradicated, foreign nations fostered the eucalypts while Australians strove for their destruction in their native land.

Australia's slowness to practise enlightened forest husbandry was to a large extent an attitude inherited from the British, who with comparatively little remaining of their original forests lagged far behind their neighbours in Western Europe in the art of reafforestation. Since the Napoleonic period France and much of Germany practised strict control over private forests, the Prussian authorities even repurchasing private estates for tree planting. The main centre of scientific forestry in the British Empire was India, and in later years the officers of the Indian forestry service were to provide a helpful influence on developments in Australia.

It was a German settler who took the first significant initiatives in Australia. Heinrich Krichauff was a Schleswig-Holstein man from the same part of the country as Ferdinand von Mueller. Having carried a banner in the 1848 rising in Berlin, he departed for South Australia later that year, and after a short spell of partnership on the land with von Mueller settled down to a useful and honourable career in politics. It was no surprise that South Australia should first feel the need for an enlightened forestry policy, since its timber resources were markedly smaller than those of the other colonies. When in 1870 Krichauff moved in the House of Assembly for a report on the creation of forest reserves in South Australia he found a ready ally in the curator of the Adelaide Botanical Gardens, Robert Schomburgk, who had long lamented 'the wasteful destruction of our forests'.[27] Schomburgk urged that municipal councils should be encouraged by government subsidy to plant vacant lands, and with a fine eclecticism recommended not only local natives such as she-oak and blackwood, but also jarrah, tuart and sandalwood from Western Australia and European evergreens such as elms, oaks and poplars.

In the next session of parliament on Krichauff's motion, Schomburgk was authorised to circulate a questionnaire among a number of prominent citizens and local authorities. This sought advice on new primary industries which might be started in their districts, as well as asking for specific recommendations on the planting of forest trees and the choice of desirable localities. The response was disappointing. Few were as blunt as John Robertson, a justice of the peace of Teatree Gully, who answered 'That the House of Assembly had no business to interfere or to ask those questions', but apart from J.H. Angas, who saw tree planting as a constructive use of exhausted wheat land, few answers gave evidence of serious thought. Although most agreed that the supply of native timber was fast diminishing, only a few councils urged an active policy of planting blue gums or jarrah. At least as many favoured exotics such as oaks, walnuts and Spanish chestnuts. Flax, olives and mulberries for silk were seen as the most likely candidates for commercial planting.

Largely due to the initiative of a few enthusiasts such as Krichauff, Schomburgk and the surveyor general G.W. Goyder, the South Australian parliament acknowledged the need for a coherent forestry policy, and in 1875 an act was passed setting up a board of management under Goyder's chairmanship. Its main achievement was the introduction of the Monterey pine, *Pinus radiata*, as an import designed to make good South Australia's lack of commercially useful softwoods; a constructive initiative in its time and place, but the forerunner of what was later to be an excessive zeal for the planting of pines. In 1882 a government department of woods and forests was set up, and three years later a conservator was appointed. Victoria passed a forestry act in 1876 and in 1884 appointed a Conservator of Forests. But forest reserves continued to be exploited for agricultural settlement, particularly among the beech and mountain ash forests of the Otways. Although two eminent overseas experts were invited at different times to advise on forestry policy a royal commission of 1898 still remarked that 'The destruction of mountain ash and spotted gum in some parts is simply appalling', and it was not until 1907 that legislation provided for a Forests Conservatory Board. In New South Wales Sir Henry Parkes created a position of inspector general of forests, but used it as a piece of literary patronage to provide a living for the poet Henry Kendall. Kendall died soon afterwards in 1882, and the job then went to the South Australian forester Ednie-Brown, who attempted to bring professional standards to his work but found himself frustrated by a lack of adequate finance and resources. Tasmania appointed a conservator of forests in 1885. Queensland and Western Australia, the colonies with the biggest area under timber, made no effective steps towards setting up a forestry administration until the end of the century.

Even in those colonies where officials had been entrusted with responsibility for forestry policy it was not possible to provide either the trained personnel or the resources to carry out any adequate program of reafforestation. As the South Australian inquiries had shown, the public still viewed the idea of tree preservation with apathy, if not with downright hostility. Few were yet aware of the desirability of conserving Australia's timber as a renewable economic resource; fewer still were convinced of the ecological or aesthetic arguments for restraint with the axe. At the end of a century of white occupation the destruction of Australia's forests seemed likely to be checked only by the influence of a few well-informed officials and professionals, and by the gradual dawning of the realisation that the supply of good timber was not after all limitless.

5 The First Generation

Trees were not the only victims of the spread of European settlement across Australia. So many animal species were hit by the impact of two centuries of colonisation that in the mid-1960s, when Professor Jock Marshall and his colleagues produced a book on the subject, they called it *The Great Extermination: a Guide to Anglo-Australian Cupidity Wickedness and Waste*.[1] It is a fine angry title, and although the book is now out of print it played its part in raising the level of awareness of conservation among some Australians. But it does not tell quite the whole story, since after the coming of white settlement some Australian animals managed to breed as never before. Naturalists disagreed strongly about the extent of the changes which took place during the opening up of the Australian inland, but few seem to have remarked that the first major slaughter of Australian wildlife did not take place on the mainland at all. It began, together with the most successful off-shore oil industry ever developed in Australia, on a fine spring day in 1791, and the man who started it was Captain Thomas Melville. A seasoned whaling captain who had sailed for Enderbys, Melville was commander of the *Britannia*, one of the five transports of the Third Fleet carrying convicts to New South Wales. As his ship coasted before a brisk southerly about seventy kilometres out of Sydney Harbour, Melville was greatly cheered to see 'Sperm Whales in great plenty'—more, he thought, in one day than he had observed off the coast of Brazil in six years:

> We sailed through different shoals of them from 12 o'clock in the day till sunset, all round the horizon, as far as I could see from the mast head. In fact I saw very great prospects in making our fishery upon this coast and establishing a fishery here. Our people was in the highest spirits at so great a sight, and I was determined as soon as I got in and got clear of my live lumber to make all possible despatch on the Fishery on the Coast.[2]

It did not take him long to persuade Governor Phillip to permit a trial run among the whales, in company with another experienced captain, Ebor Bunker of the *William and Ann*. Squally weather hindered their operation, so that although they killed seven whales they recovered only two, but the experience was enough to whet their appetites for the future.

It was no coincidence that the Third Fleet included so many skilled whalers. Following the loss of the American colonies and the spread of Nantucket whalers into the oceans of the Southern Hemisphere, British firms such as Enderbys and John St Barbe had been clamouring for the opportunity to operate in the unexploited waters around Australia and New Zealand. As with so many other areas of commerce in this region, the whaling masters had to contend against the prior rights of the East India Company. By making vessels available for convict transportation they gained a legitimate opportunity for spying out the southern waters. Whereas the first two convict convoys arrived at times when there were few whales to be seen off the coast of New South Wales, the Third Fleet happened on the great seasonal migration when the southern whales, having cruised north to winter in the latitude of the Barrier Reef, were returning to the colder seas towards Antarctica.

To a seafarer of Melville's generation this was as exciting as the discovery of a gusher would be for the modern petroleum geologist. Whale oil was the lubricant on which many of Western Europe's infant industries depended. It was also in demand as a source of lighting and illumination and the urban growth of the late eighteenth century guaranteed a growing market. The whale population of Spitzbergen and Greenland having been hunted to near extinction, and the seas off Canada offering falling returns, the whaling fleets were ready to exploit the southern oceans.

Seals were prized even more than whales. Unlike whale oil, seal oil burnt in a bright pure flame without smell or smoke, and was required for candles of better quality. Seal oil was also colourless and free from any rancid taste, so it could be used in food processing. Around 1750 the Chinese developed a method of separating the soft, luxurious underfur from sealskins, thus stimulating a fashion among the richer families of Chi-en-lung's empire for seal fur. And if this was not enough, the fine gentlemen of London in the 1790s took to wearing the so-called 'beaver' hats for which seal fur was the main material.

No sooner had the enterprising men of Sydney found the means to build a few small boats than they were eager to take advantage of these demands. By 1798 two or three parties were finding their way to the islands of Bass Strait where seals collected in vast numbers to breed. Captain Charles Bishop of the *Nautilus* stayed on Cape Barren

Island long enough to grow crops of peas and potatoes for his crew, and they brought back 9 000 skins. Captain William Reid claimed to have been through the strait ahead of Bass and discovered King Island; he certainly found a tempting colony of sea elephants, three metres long and full of oil. Where these men led many followed. Sealing, though a dirty job, offered more prizes than whaling, and was less hazardous and difficult because the breeding seals were, as one well-informed writter stated, 'almost innumerable':

The beach is encumbered with their quantities and those who visit their haunts have less trouble in killing them than the servants of the victuallers have who kill hogs in a pound with mallets.[3]

In the first rush of exploitation so many seals were clubbed to death that as early as 1802 the French explorer Nicolas Baudin warned Governor King that the species would be in danger of extinction on King Island. He was a good prophet, for the sea elephants have long since vanished from Bass Strait, and will not be found any closer to Australia than Macquarie Island. The traffic drew aggressive adventurers from the United States who met with keen competition from Sydney merchants. Sealing was one of the few good investments available in the struggling colony, and plenty of hardened ex-convicts were ready to sign on as crew. By the end of 1805 King reported difficulty in finding enough labour to harvest the colony's food supplies because of the greater attractiveness of sealing. In six years after 1800, 133 000 seal skins passed through the port of Sydney, and they represented only a portion of the total kill.[4]

Before long the sealers were faring as far afield as Kangaroo Island; some eventually reached New Zealand, others the south-west coast near the future site of Albany. Many made permanent camps on islands and remote parts of the coast, persuading or seizing Aboriginal women to live and work with them. By all accounts they were a rough lot, careless of human or animal life. Hunting for food, they soon brought the emu to extinction on both King Island and Kangaroo Island. Seal numbers dwindled, since they were particularly easy to slaughter during the breeding season. By the time permanent white settlements were established along the south coast of Australia in the 1830s there were not enough seals left to make the industry worth attempting. New Zealand still offered good returns for the sealers, but here too the habit of slaughtering during the breeding season soon spelt disaster.[5]

Whaling lasted longer, playing a particularly notable part in the early history of Hobart. In 1804, a year after the arrival there of the first settlers, Parson Robert Knopwood, boating up river to take service at Risdon, was obliged to keep close inshore for fear of the numerous whales in the Derwent.[6] Bolder colonists soon found equipment to start a modest but thriving whaling industry. It is said that Lieutenant-Governor Collins, vexed at the oily taste of the pork served at his dinner table, found it due to the feeding of pigs from the scourings of the try-pots in which whales were boiled down. (Another yarn has it that he was kept awake at night by the snoring of the whales in the Derwent.) Competition from American whalers did nothing to discourage local enterprise. The first generation of currency lads took to whaling with the same skill and enthusiasm as their modern descendants show in surfing. By the 1820s the Hobart press was confident that 'the exertion of our enterprising youth has done much for the colony'—though, again like modern critics of youth, complaining that the young men spent too much on liquor.[7]

The abolition of port duties in 1829 gave a new boost to whaling in both Hobart and Sydney, and in the next two years it produced more export income than wool. On the south coast of New South Wales a number of entrepreneurs went in for bay whaling (in which the operations are carried out from a shore base rather than entirely from a whaling ship). In those days the port quarter of Sydney stank so pervasively from whaling operations that Archibald Mosman and others were persuaded to set up their works on the unsettled north shore of the Harbour. As for Hobart it was described as 'enriched with oleaginous spoils'. 'In 1848', wrote Thomas Dunbabin, 'Hobart, with 37 deep-sea whaleships, manned by 1046 men, was the greatest

Salamanca Place, Hobart
From C.J. Lloyd, *The National Estate: Australia's Heritage*, (Cassell, 1977)

whaling port in the British Empire'.[8] The bluestone pubs and warehouses of Salamanca Place, now treasured by conservationists, are relics of that raffish era of prosperity.

It did not last. The practice of killing females at the time of calving soon caused whaling to dwindle, just as it had with the sealing trade. In Sydney the best days of the trade were already over before the 1851 gold rush provided an even more powerful lure for seekers after wealth and adventure. By 1857 even that dogged old speculator Robert Towns was trying to dispose of the remnant of his whaling fleet which, as it swung listlessly at anchor off Moore's Wharf, earned the name 'Rotten Row'. In Hobart the decline was not yet quite so apparent, but after 1860 it accelerated. Those were the years in which whale oil began to give place to petroleum, first exploited commercially in Pennsylvania in 1859 and soon valued as a cleaner and more versatile source of energy. Whalers continued to slip out of Hobart and range the Southern Ocean until the very end of the century, but their importance grew steadily less, and other opportunities beckoned.

Whale bones at site of old Norfolk Island Whaling station
From *People* 13 Sept 1950 p. 45

In the Derwent where the great schools of whales once alarmed Parson
Knopwood there was seldom a whale to be seen from one year's end
to the next. Those who survived and still made the annual run from
the Antarctica to the Barrier Reef tended to be the humpback whales,
containing less oil and so less often harpooned. Their turn would
come later.

None of the fauna on the Australian mainland lent themselves to
exploitation on the same scale. Want of protein and a desire to conserve
their own sheep and cattle sent the first generation of settlers hunting
after native game, and between 1806 and 1813 the commissariat of
Van Diemen's Land offered payment—at times as much as a shilling
a pound—for kangaroo meat. The hungry pioneers were willing to
eat almost anything. Governor Hunter wrote in 1795 that kangaroos
provided good mutton 'although not so delicate as that which we
sometimes find in Leadenhall Market'. Matthew Flinders considered
the wombat 'resembled lean mutton in taste, and to us acceptable
food'. That much-travelled ship's surgeon Peter Cunningham thought
that 'bandicoot tastes somewhat like a suckling pig, and makes a
delicious dish with a well-prepared pudding in its belly'. Even the
echidna was not safe from the cooking pot: 'it is exceedingly fat, the
flesh has a somewhat aromatic taste, and was thought delicious'.[9]
The bilby, a common type of New South Wales bandicoot, tasted
like the finest rabbit. Emu eggs were valued for their protein, and
white cockatoos made good soup. Only the galah became a byword
for uselessness, the old bush recipe advising that to cook galah it
should be placed with a stone in a billy of boiling water and boiled
until the stone is soft.

As well as hunting for food, the colonists also enjoyed hunting for
sport, and in addition soon found that kangaroo and platypus skins
were acceptable items on the export market. The inevitable result was
that in the longest settled districts the wildlife soon dwindled. The
platypus, comparatively common in the river pools of the Blue Mountains in 1815, had almost vanished by 1850. The naturalist Gerard
Krefft, working along the Murray between 1852 and 1862, noted that
on the Victorian side of the river many species had become almost
totally extinct within twenty-five years of white settlement.[10] Practical
men who enjoyed their hunting confirmed this. About 1850 Captain
Foster Fyans, old soldier and magistrate, complained:

> Emus and kangaroos on our arrival were plentiful in all parts of
> the Western district; also bustards in large flocks of from 10 to 30
> or 40, or perhaps more. The bustards now are scarce, and only
> met with in distant places. The kangaroo and emu are nearly

extinct in the district; the country is almost void of game. Quails in years gone by were plentiful, but I think are fast disappearing; snipe we have in the season, but not in the same abundance as in other countries, also various small ducks . . . black swans—useless and ugly; snakes of many descriptions, and some exceedingly bold—more so than I have known them in India . . . For an idler or a sportsman this country affords nothing and for a military officer it is the most damnable quarter in the world.[11]

Fyans the military officer and Krefft the naturalist at least both agreed that the fauna was fast decreasing in number, but the remedy was hard to find. When in 1846 the Legislative Council of Van Diemen's Land passed an act for the restraint of kangaroo hunting by a system of licensing it was intended not for the protection of native fauna, but to check the spread of sheep stealing by marauding gangs of ex-convict kangaroo hunters. The Attorney-General went to some pains to point out that he was not suggesting anything resembling the English game laws.[12] Yet the ravages of kangaroo hunting were obvious enough to visitors such as Captain John Lort Stokes, who wrote in 1849 of the Western Australian trade in kangaroo skins:

. . . Sixteen thousand of these were the produce of last year, in the vicinity of Albany only, and although the animal exists in vast herds upon the wide grassy savannahs of the interior, no increase can bear up against this wholesale animal slaughter . . . This the more to be regretted because its flesh forms the chief sustenance of the wandering people of the soil, who have no means of resisting this flagrant invasion of their hunting grounds.[13]

He suggested checking the evil by levying a tax on the export of kangaroo skins, but such Utopian notions had no chance of acceptance in colonial society. However between 1853 and 1878 licenses were required to shoot kangaroos except on one's own property. This measure was introduced after Western Australia became a convict colony, and apart from protecting Aboriginal hunting served as a measure of social control. Many observers nevertheless agreed with Stokes that the passing of the Aborigines resulted in a great increase in numbers among animals previously hunted for food.

A parable of ecological chance was told by the Reverend Peter MacPherson, who, travelling regularly on his rounds from Geelong to Ballarat between 1862 and 1874, noticed that a fine stand of eucalypts at Bruces Creek north of Meredith was gradually dying off until only the gaunt skeletons were left. He sought an explanation. Drought, bushfires, poor soil and swampy ground were each considered and discarded as not squaring with the evidence. Then the local Aborigines

told him the reason: 'too much big one possum'. In the days before
white contact the Aborigines had been in the habit of catching something like two hundred possums a day for their food. As MacPherson
chose to put it, 'the tooth of the blackfellow operated on the opossum,
and the tooth of the opossum operated on the leaves of the eucalypt'.[14]
As soon as white settlement drove the Aborigines from their own
pattern of food gathering, the possums bred to unprecedented numbers,
and their attacks ravaged the foliage unhindered. 'The new disturbing
factor was the white man, the resistless white man, before whom
disappear all obstacles that come in his way, whether black men,
opossums, or eucalyptus forests.'

Not that the newcomers showed much sensitivity in their approach
to the ecology. As conservers of the environment the first generation
of small farmers left much to be desired. Often they lacked both the
financial resources and the education even to adopt good farming
practices, let alone to cherish their new environment. Commissioner
Bigge in 1820 summed them up:

> They constitute the middle and lower orders of settlers in the colony
> and having in general begun with very limited means they have
> been obliged to depend solely upon the return of produce of their
> land. It is through these means therefore that the great quantity
> of grain has been produced for the consumption of the colony, and
> it is also through their want of means and their want of capacity
> that the productive powers of the soil, that is not generally a fertile
> one, have been exhausted by repeated cropping.[15]

James Atkinson in 1826 went even further in condemning the 'slothful
and negligent' farmers of New South Wales. 'Men of this description',
he wrote, 'were but little calculated to improve and beautify the face
of the country and to develop its agricultural capabilities; accordingly
their farms exhibit to this day nothing but a scene of confusions,
filth, and poverty'.[16] For many years this pattern persisted. The
banks which grew up in Australia after 1817 were not interested in
such petty clients, so that the farmers found it hard to scrape together
the investment capital for good husbandry. Peasant fashion, they
depended on their wives and children for cheap labour and flogged
the country bare.

The pastoralists had a much greater impact on Australia's inland
scenery. As early as the 1820s perceptible regional differences could
be seen between the pastoral districts of New South Wales—the tough
practicality of the Goulburn run-holders wresting quick profits out
of harsh country, the conviviality of Bathurst's squireens, the simul-
taneous development in the Hunter Valley of vineyards and sheep-

walks—but it was not until the 1830s that wool growing firmly established itself as the main aim of Australian grazing. In that decade improved shipping, increased British investment and the winning of an assured place in the Yorkshire wool market fixed wool growing for a century and a half as a staple of the Australian economy.

Merino sheep are dainty feeders. Where grazing takes place intensively over a number of years they tend to eat out the sweeter grasses, leaving the tougher, less nutritious and more deeply rooted botanical communities. The first generation of pastoralists may not have recognised this fact because of their surprise and delight in finding that sheep also took to the native saltbush and mulga, and so could be grazed in regions of comparatively little water. It took some time for sheepmasters to realise that once a piece of land had been regularly nibbled and trodden by their flocks, it could not revert to its original condition even if spelled for a period. Thus the carrying capacity would be steadily reduced after the first generation of settlement unless artificial pasture grasses were introduced or new watering places developed. There was no going back to the earlier balance of nature.

The majority of first-generation pastoralists probably did not see themselves as founding permanent estates in the Australian interior. Many frankly intended to return to England as soon as they made money. Others, aware of the way in which the Australian climate swung from drought to plenty, thought it sensible to maximise profits in good seasons so that they might survive bad. Disease was rife in those early decades. An epidemic of catarrh killed many sheep in 1841. Scab was common in New South Wales, Victoria and South Australia until the mid-1860s, and survived in Western Australia until the 1890s. When flocks were liable to such losses, overgrazing was the only way to stay solvent.

Until 1847 few pastoralists enjoyed security of tenure over their licensed grazing lands, so that investment was often kept to a minimum. There was little incentive to fence paddocks or to outlay capital on extensive clearing. At least until the gold rushes of the 1850s most pastoralists managed their flocks by shepherding, using relatively cheap convict or ex-convict labour. 'Even a prosperous squatter would be content to live in a collection of slab hovels, with hurdles moving from place to place as each become filthy, and with the inevitable heaps of sheep dung and sheep bones piled everywhere. It was a sordid, filthy existence.'[18] No doubt it was worse for the shepherds and the stockmen.

From the Aborigines the rural settlers learned the uses of stringybark and she-oak. The first homesteads were usually bark huts or humpies built of weatherboard slabs. William Howitt described one in 1852:

> We are lodged in a slab hut, roofed with broad sheets of the stringy bark, which are tied to the rafters by thongs of bullock hide, and still more secured from the force of the winds by poles, which are fastened along the outside of the roof . . . there is a broad verandah on the sunny, that is the north side of the house, and the whole has a rough and picturesque aspect. At each end there is a chimney, built externally of wood, and lined some four or five feet high in the inside with slabs of granite to prevent the wood catching fire . . . In the room where we were first located, the bare wood of the walls had no lining, and the chinks between the slabs were often wide enough to put your hand through. There was no ceiling, but all open to the roof. We soon removed to the room at the opposite end of the building, which was still lined and ceiled with canvas, but where the floor was still mud, and an old table or two, and a few broken-backed chairs, the only furniture, except an old-fashioned sofa.[19]

Often every tree within range of the station homestead was cleared. This may have been done in some cases for fear of ambush by Aborigines, but it was more usually recommended as a firebreak. Not everyone shared this attitude. George Fletcher Moore, erecting a homestead in Western Australia in the 1830s, said of his building site: ' . . . to avoid injuring the appearance of the place I have cut down but one large tree, and not above a dozen shrubs or smaller trees, preferring to fell the timber necessary for building, at the distance of quarter of a mile.'[20] But Moore, who was able to define the Swan River district as possessing the character 'of an interesting landscape rather than of sublime or grand scenery' was perhaps unusual in his eye for appearances.

Casually destructive, the first generation of land takers in inland Australia were restricted in their impact on the environment by their technology. From the 1850s gold, railways and wire fencing would greatly hasten the transformation of the countryside, producing the landscapes which later generations would regard as 'typically Australian'. But even before 1850 the majority of Australians were town dwellers, and the most characteristic Australian environment was a raw new town. We must now consider how the Australian urban landscape came into being.

6 Urban Beginnings

When Governor Phillip arrived at Sydney Cove in 1788 he left behind
a Europe which prided itself on its recent advances in town planning.
Rejecting the crooked and crowded streets of earlier ages, the planners
of the eighteenth century favoured the creation of spacious urban
landscapes whose inhabitants might take pleasure in their surroundings. Wide streets elegantly varied by crescents and squares were the
hallmarks of Bath and Bloomsbury. Of course this was an aristocratic
ideal, and less attention was paid to the accommodation of the poor.
Most new subdivisions were made in the expectation that they would
house at least the respectable middle classes. As a rule the poor in
preindustrial towns took possession of an area only when it was
aging and run down.

When the British settlers in democratic North America carved out
new towns in the wilderness they brought with them this preference
for geometrical symmetry. Phillip in his turn carried the eighteenth-
century ideals to New South Wales. His first plans for Sydney were
designed on the grand scale. The main streets were to be about 60
metres wide, and town allotments would have a minimum size of
about 20 × 45 metres. 'This will preserve uniformity in the buildings,
prevent narrow streets, and the many inconveniences which the increase
of inhabitants would otherwise occasion hereafter', he wrote. Later
commentators were less sure. 'It was a magnificent idea', admitted a
writer in 1909, 'in keeping with the spaciousness of his surroundings,
but as he boldly ran his streets straight from Sydney Harbour over
the ridge . . . to Darling Harbour, regardless of grades, the superses-
sion of his plan was the lesser of two evils'.[1] Well, maybe; but San
Francisco, Sydney's opposite number across the Pacific, was built on
a grid plan imposed on an even more sensationally hilly terrain. As
it was, the human resources at Phillip's disposal were limited, and other
pressures proved more imperative than town planning.

The Sydney that struggled into existence between 1788 and 1810
was a makeshift collection of huts and tenements strung out along

the valley of the Tank Stream from Sydney Cove towards the inland. Nevertheless several of the permanent features of the Sydney of the future were already in evidence. Because Sydney was built on a peninsula most of its traffic was carried by a few main streets along its north–south axis. Congestion was bound to result as the town grew. The lands on the eastern side of Sydney were set aside as the government reserves which would later become the Botanical Gardens, the Domain and Hyde Park. Expansion in that direction was discouraged, thus confirming the town's sprawl along the north–south axis. Because Sydney's site was chosen by a naval man looking for good anchorage and fresh water, no thought was given to future problems of easy access to the hinterland, and the formidable barrier of the Blue Mountains ensured that traffic between port and inland would be squeezed into a small number of access routes coming in from the west and passing along that north–south axis.

Sydney's unplanned growth had its importance not only as setting the character of Australia's oldest city but also as a model to be avoided by subsequent towns. Not that it was seen as beyond redemption by improvers such as Macquarie. When he took over from Foveaux in 1810 his predecessor warned him that the streets of Sydney were almost impassable and the main roads and bridges leading out of it dangerous and neglected. When he left in 1822 he boasted that he had caused 442 kilometres of public roads to be built. In Sydney old streets had been remade with stone and gravel, provided with footpaths and raised in the centre to carry off waste water in drains and sewers.[2] But Macqurie was not able to check the growth of an incipient slum district. In the western streets of the city on land difficult for development there early grew up that warren of cottages inhabited by ex-convicts and the labouring poor which gained notoriety as 'the Rocks'. Nor could Macquarie manage entirely to straighten the streets as they followed the banks of the increasingly polluted Tank Stream. Even in the smaller settlement of Hobart, founded in 1803 and laid out at the end of 1811, Macquarie allowed some major modifications in the basic grid plan so as 'not to interfere with many Houses which are now erected and which if disposed of in a regular plan, must be entirely destroyed'.[3]

Such concessions were grudging. As an officer brought up in the traditions of military engineering Macquarie favoured the grid plan in town building. He was happiest with an entirely new settlement such as Port Macquarie where this could be imposed. In 1829 that strict disciplinarian Governor Darling gave official standing to the rectilinear grid as the standard street plan for Australian towns, but

Panorama of Brisbane in 1880s

Sydney and Hobart were past correction. When in 1834 Governor
Bourke proposed a program for the formation, improvement and
alignment of Sydney's streets he was chillingly rebuffed by the Colonial
Office and told not to spend money 'for the mere embellishment of
the Town or in any other mode not of immediate and indispensible
necessity'.[4] Such penny-pinching encouraged Sydney's authorities to
turn a blind eye to the haphazard sprawl of town growth.

Such an attitude was not good enough for the English migrants
who in the 1830s were planning to found cities for colonies of free
settlers. Perth and Fremantle, established in 1829, produced modest
variations on the grid plan because of local topography, but both
for many years languished in backwardness. Brisbane's grid plan was
tilted to fit a meander in the Brisbane River, but otherwise admitted
few variations except on the ridge of Wickham Terrace. Government
parsimony forced its streets into a narrower width than its original
planners intended. The same thing happened at Melbourne, where
the original grid of 1836 was characterised by wide main streets and
smaller parallel lanes meant to afford rear access to properties on
the main streets. Not only was the width of the main streets restricted,
but the needs of local tradespeople ensured that Little Collins Street,
Little Bourke Street and the others became thoroughfares in their
own right, eventually adding to the congestion of the city block.

Adelaide, laid out in 1836–37 by Colonial William Light, presented
the most successful adaptation of the grid plan to Australian conditions. Light provided not only for a wide central thoroughfare and
strategically located squares, but also for a reserve completely surrounding the city—the original 'green belt'. Geoffrey Dutton has
suggested that Light was influenced by his recollections of classical
descriptions of the layout of Roman army camps; but Dutton also
praises Light's practical achievement. 'If Adelaide is lacking in my-
stery', he writes, 'so is the light that beats upon it and the plain that
bears it'.[5] Most South Australians enjoy the results of Light's vision,
but his contemporaries grumbled about his choice of town site. Until
the 1850s they were not above using the town reserves for dumping
rubbish, grazing stock and even attempting the alienation of choice
pieces for private use. Nevertheless Adelaide retained enough of its
original plan to become later in the nineteenth century a shining model
to other Australian cities of the advantages of forward planning.
This was largely because Adelaide grew more slowly than Melbourne
or Sydney. Economic stagnation promoted environmental conservation.

The design of these new towns may have been admirable, but in early years they were no pleasure to live in. Looking back in old age on the state of Adelaide's streets in 1839 J.C. Hawker called them 'wretched':

> Parties sinking cellars were allowed to throw the earth from excavations into them, as it was plausibly stated that holes could thus be filled up and the streets raised. The effect, however, was disastrous. Vehicles, chiefly bullock-drays, continually passing along them cut the surface into the finest dust in summer and a regular bog in winter.[6]

In such roads drays bogged axle-deep and pedestrians floundered in gluey holes while unsympathetic bystanders asked 'if they had been turning up their little finger too often'. 'Brickfielder' winds blew clinging grit into the wooden houses in summer and made them almost uninhabitable. One other notable feature of Australian life was also present from Adelaide's first summer:

> The common fly also is here a perfect pest. When we first landed they exceeded in numbers and audacity anything you can conceive. I do not say that a leg of a duck would actually be taken from your plate while eating it, but I do assert that it was impossible to eat it without slaying some, or to eat it without including others.[7]

Melbourne in its early years was no better. Alfred Howitt in 1852 found the streets infested with starving dogs and flies battening on the dead horses and cattle left in the streets to rot. There were few gardens, and most houses were built on small blocks. By contrast his uncle's house and garden at the east end of Collins Street were an oasis, if to his eyes a bizarre one: 'a date palm and several tufts of English primroses are all flourishing together'.[8] George Russell identified a long-lasting drawback to the Melbourne environment when he complained of the hot northerlies which stirred up the dust in the principal streets and made them disagreeable for walking.[9] 'There is no pavement of any description', complained another visitor in 1852:

> . . . so that in winter the streets are several inches deep in mud, and in summer the dust is horrible, completely obscuring the sun and rendering objects a few yards off indistinct and hazy.[10]

These circumstances explain why, despite a climate often described as Mediterranean, Australian town dwellers failed to imitate Spaniards and Italians in using their streets as open promenades where friends and neighbours could meet and chat. The pavement café, the ornamental fountain were not to enliven Australia's city centres. Instead, from an early date, Australians became a nation of vehicle owners, emerging from their private homes to use the road for pleasure driving—and for showing off their possessions. Long before the invention of the motor car this trait was noted by Dr John Dunmore Lang. In the 1840s a good road ran from Sydney along the sandstone heights to the lighthouse on South Head, and around four o'clock in the afternoon, wrote Lang:

> ... all the coach-house doors fly open simultaneously, and the company begin to take their places for the afternoon drive on the South Head Road. In half an hour the streets are comparatively deserted; by far the greater portion of the well-dressed part of the population being already out of town. In the meantime, the long line of equipages—from the ponderous coach of the nominee Member of Council, moving leisurely and proudly along, or the lively barouche of Mr Goldfinder, the merchant, to the *one-horse-shay* in which the landlord of the *Tinkers' Arms* drives out his blowzy dame *to take the hair arter dinner*—doubles Hyde Park Corner, and arrives on the Corso; while ever and anon some young bachelor merchant, or military officer, eager to display his superior skill in horsemanship, dashes briskly forward along the cavalcade in full gallop.[11]

Where such attitudes prevailed it was unlikely that high priority would be given to developing the urban environment as a source of pleasure for the pedestrian and the bystander. Then as now, most of the inhabitants of Australian towns were prepared to put up with inconvenience in public places, preferring to concentrate their energies on acquiring and maintaining a home of their own.

Here too the environment began to impose its constraints on building styles from the earliest times of settlement. British housing favoured, and still favours, the two-storey house, often in a terrace row or semi-detached. This is intelligible in a country with a high population and limited land. The Australian tendency towards single-storey building began before 1791 when Governor Phillip reported: 'The want of limestone still obliges us to confine our buildings to a certain height, for although the clay is of a strong, binding nature we cannot with safety carry the walls of those buildings more than twelve feet above the ground, as the rains are at times very heavy—should they come on before the clay is thoroughly dry, the walls would be in danger from the great weights of the roof'.[12]

The veranda was from early days a distinctive feature of the better houses. Probably introduced from India by way of the south of England, verandas provided cool surroundings for Australian homes

Elizabeth Farm
From Mitchell Library

at least from the time that John Macarthur and his wife built Elizabeth Farm in 1795. Building was at first held back by want of suitable timber, but the she-oak and the cabbage tree were soon found useful, and by the first decade of the nineteenth century excellent building timbers were discovered in the Hawkesbury and Illawarra districts.

Brick was not at first used extensively because of the difficulty of finding lime for mortar, but by 1820 Sydney could erect a brick church, St James's, capable of lasting over a century and a half. The next two decades saw an improvement in building materials in most Australian settlements. Hobart in 1820 was a town in which a visitor could find only twenty houses worth the name. 'The remainder, in number about 250, could only be classed as huts, being constructed of various materials, such as split palings, wickerwork bedaubed with clay, and log and turf cabins of all orders of low architecture'.[13] Times improved, and by 1841 71 per cent of Hobart's 2350 houses were of brick or stone, with shingle roofs predominating over slate. By this time the pioneer phase was beginning all over again in Melbourne, where huts, cottages and shops were built mainly from spars of the local ti-tree with grass thatches. The transition from such vernacular materials to brick or stone was coming to be seen as the usual march of progress in an Australian town.

Men in authority began to feel the necessity of controlling building materials. By 1837 Governor Bourke was contemplating the prohibition of timber roofing in Sydney because of its fire risk. In that year he wrote to the British government requesting permission to use imported slates for roofing public buildings, pointing out that tiles were heavy and inferior, while shingles did not last and constituted a fire hazard.[14] On 1 January 1838 the New South Wales government banned the use of shingles, bark or thatch for roofs in town areas. Unhappily the same legislation prevented the construction of verandas or timber shutters, stating that timber could not be used for construction closer than ten centimetres from the face of a building. Protests from builders and the public secured some modification of this law in 1845, but the effect was to turn Sydney's dominant building material into brick with zinc-coated iron roofs. The quality of colonial architecture was also affected by the gradual mechanisation of the timber industry following the introduction of steam saws in 1838 and milling machines in 1846.[15] This may have lowered the standards of colonial craftsmanship, but it brought building materials within the reach of a wider range of users and thus powerfully boosted Australia's urban growth.

Already the bush was yielding to the towns as the place where most

Athlone Place, Sydney, late nineteenth century

Australians lived. As early as 1840 Sydney contained a third of all the inhabitants of New South Wales. With growing freedom of choice this tendency increased. It was not just that most British immigrants were either urban souls who chose to linger in their port of arrival or else so accustomed to a different style of rural life that they found the bush repellent. Many more migrants found their way to the United States during the nineteenth century, and yet New York and Boston retained a far smaller proportion of the intake. The fact was that the United States could offer much more land for farming and many more job opportunities on its frontiers of settlement than Australia. Most skilled workers in Australia gravitated to a metropolis. The Australian coastline is not plentifully supplied with good harbours commanding easy access to the inland, so that even without the pressure of vested interests from capital cities it made sense to centralise the economies of New South Wales, Victoria and South Australia respectively on Sydney, Melbourne and Adelaide.[16] Brisbane's role in Queensland was for a time an exception, because other ports such as Rockhampton and Townsville took significant percentages of the colony's trade, and Brisbane was not even connected to Queensland's railway system until 1875. Hobart and Perth stagnated for most of the second half of the nineteenth century. But Melbourne, Sydney and Adelaide set the pattern for Australian urbanisation.

As settlement moved inland surveyors followed to mark out town sites. The need for speed and economy discouraged innovation, and they took the grid plan with them everywhere: grids facing river frontages in the coastal valleys of eastern New South Wales, grids spread out on the level plains further inland. Squares or marketplaces were included in some of the older town sites such as Maitland and Bathurst, but otherwise there was no variation.[17] Towns sometimes grew up ahead of the surveyors. Sometimes the whim of fate intervened: Winton in central Queensland is said to have originated around the place where a dray carrying rum and other supplies broke down. The Hunter Valley towns were first sited so that settlers could load their produce on to river craft with the minimum of difficulty, but in time the townspeople grew tired of annual flooding in winter and a major inundation every few years, and shifted the town centres to higher ground. A cynical South Australian newspaper editor jeered at the foolishness of poor planners:

> Avoid all sites that are naturally high and dry and possess natural facilities for easy drainage. If there be a gentle slope, sheltered by friendly upland, avoid that also; eschew any elements of the picturesque, and select rather the flattest, most uninteresting site possible;

if a flat with a creek running through it and subject to overflow, by all means get on the lower bank of the creek and peg away. If a running creek be not available get in the way of a storm channel. A mangrove swamp with sinuous cozy channel is a combination of favourable conditions too good to be often hoped for, and if subject in addition to direct tidal overflow, consider it perfection.[18]

Few country towns during their first generation of existence showed much to charm the eye. Consider Alfred Howitt's thumbnail sketch of Albury in the early 1850s:

> The town is one short street of slab houses—two or three Hotels, a few tradespeople—stockyards—pigsties—dirty hovels—stumps sticking out of the ground on all sides—natives—dogs—goats— some old women—dirty children—a bullock dray with a driver making pistol reports with his whip ... paste up several glaring yellow posters about the 'Gold Escort'—imagine the whole on a scorched-up flat—with the external round-backed Australian hills behind and miles of lagoons and giant gum trees in front and you have Albury.[19]

The country towns languished in the first half of the nineteenth century because except as administrative and service centres they had no other role. In an economy where most primary production was aimed at the overseas export market they had little scope for growth as market towns. Lacking railways and resources, few showed the slightest promise for the development of local industries. Nor could it be expected that their comforts and amenities would match those offering in the coastal cities. Some had churches; all had pubs.

But between the 1840s and the 1880s two great developments came to speed the transformation of both urban and rural landscapes in Australia. Gold was discovered in New South Wales and Victoria in 1851. And in the ensuing prosperity railways were built to tether the bush to the metropolitan ports. The impact of the European on the Australian environment before 1850 would seem puny compared with what came after the gold rushes.

7 After Gold

The first impact of the gold rushes was almost entirely destructive. Of all Australian country towns mining settlements were usually the most makeshift and unkempt. Spawned wherever a patch of good gold brought prospectors, storekeepers and their families for more than a few weeks at a time, mining townships were often abandoned after a brief and hectic life. Although most of the finds in New South Wales and Victoria took place in wooded, hilly country there was little encouragement to care for the environment until a field showed some hope of permanence. By that time it was usually hopelessly ripped and scarred. Early gold mining created a voracious demand for timber, so that the country around a mining town was usually levelled bare, leaving no shelter against wind or dust. At Mount Alexander in 1852 the *Argus* correspondent reported:

> ... such trees as have escaped the axe are dusted to an unnatural brownness, and look more like the desperate attempts at vegetation made by the stunted shrubs of a Hackney roadside villa than the giant growth of an Australian forest.[1]

This was to be the prototype for many more mining settlements.

Equally detrimental to the environment was the disposal of waste sludge after the sluicing and puddling of gold-bearing dirt. The Goulburn river in Victoria, until 1860 a notably clear stream, was milky with sediment for miles below Woods Point after the discovery of gold along its banks. At Ballarat, 'Horse-driven puddling-machines slobbered acres of yellow slime, blocking the rudimentary drains, and were so thirsty that they had to be served by networks of crude water channels ending in loathsome stagnant dams'.[2] An English visitor, Louise Meredith, thought the result 'more irredeemably hideous than the blackest mining village in any English coal or iron district'. There was a curious combination of filth and elegance, since the two-storey wooden hotels and shops on Ballarat's Main Street were often given classical façades of some pretension. And yet—with these unpromising beginnings—within twenty years Ballarat had become a model for other Australian country towns.

Ballarat was blessed by an unusually fortunate combination of circumstances. Its wealth was evenly distributed and consistently accessible. Diversification came because Ballarat gained its railway early and was well suited to light industry. It was also one of the towns which found a role as a service centre for the farmers who appeared after the gold rush. A temperate if not cold climate encouraged planting. By 1871 its elegant town hall, its tree-lined main streets, perhaps above all its parklands around Lake Wendouree provided a mellow and well groomed setting to excite the surprise and admiration of visitors such as Anthony Trollope. In contrast to earlier mining centres Ballarat enjoyed a very high level of home ownership: 73 per cent of all houses were owner occupied in 1867, 63 per cent as late as 1890. Over 90 per cent were built of wood. This compared very favourably with older centres such as Burra in South Australia, where because the management insisted on retaining the land on which miners built their cottages, the quality of these buildings

Scarred country around Lithgow Iron Works, c. 1880
Reproduced with permission from the Public Transport Commission of NSW

was often crude and makeshift. For some years many Burra mining families lived in holes in the ground.[3]

Ballarat's achievement served as a model for later mining towns across Australia. Charters Towers, Broken Hill, Kalgoorlie all probably owed part of their civic pride and their willingness to plan and build generously to the knowledge that Ballarat had shown that a pleasing environment could be created on the ruins of a mining camp. The tradition of home ownership was also strong. In 1889 75 per cent of Broken Hill's housing was owner occupied, and the fall to 50 per cent in 1895 and 33 per cent in 1908 was a sure index of the deterioration of working-class conditions and industrial relations on the field.[4]

In Australia's major cities, the gold rush boom of the 1850s strained every facility. In the ten years after 1851 Sydney's population leaped from 54 000 to 96 000, only to be outstripped by Melbourne's growth from 29 000 to 125 000. The demand for labour and materials ran hot. Few building workers stayed on the job, and those who did demanded such high wages that builders tended to cut corners by economising on materials and workmanship. Following a pattern already emerging before 1850, speculative builders who put up properties for rental ran up rows of terrace houses. In this way the maximum number of dwellings could be crammed on a strip of land. Frontages of under five metres were not uncommon. Except for brick partition walls such terraces were often built cheaply of wood. There was little privacy and crowding was frequent. In Sydney's Brougham Place each of the twenty-six four-roomed cottages held an average of sixteen inhabitants.[5]

Others built more solidly, embellishing the balconies of their terrace houses with cast-iron screens and ornamentation, the product of the local iron-founding industry which developed from the middle of the century. These have been the terrace houses which have tended to survive into the later twentieth century and to be sought after in areas such as Paddington and Carlton. It has been said that the terrace house was the nineteenth-century equivalent of the flat, and there were as many varieties and qualities of terrace house a century ago as there are of flats today.[6] But as the nineteenth century wore on terrace houses came to be associated in the public mind with the crowded inner suburbs. As street traffic increased the public came to prefer houses with a front garden setting them back a little from the dust and noise of the road. Terrace houses fell out of favour, giving way to forms of subdivision which made less economical use of land.

For those who did not like or could not afford terrace housing there

Surry Hills housing, now inner city Sydney, dating from c. 1850
Photograph by Max Kelly

was always do-it-yourself. Patches of makeshift housing erupted around the edges of Melbourne and Sydney. Collingwood in 1853 was a 'motley collection of tin and packing-case shanties' with 'partitions formed of calico, covered by a cheap tawdry paper, flapping backwards and forward in every breeze'.[7] Jevons, surveying the inner suburbs of Sydney in 1858, found houses of every conceivable material: logs, slabs, palings, weatherboards, canvas, corrugated iron, plain iron, lath and plaster, rubble, ashlar stone, and even glass bottles. 'As Australian second or third class suburb would not be taken for a permanent part of a town at all', he asserted, 'it more resembles the wooden huts of a military encampment'.[8]

Behind this sudden spurt of urban growth public amenities lagged alarmingly. Water supply and sanitation were critical problems. Sydney's past record on this score was not reassuring. Until the 1830s its water supply was drawn from the increasingly polluted Tank stream, supplemented by public rainwater tanks, private wells and supplies brought in barrels from neighbouring swamps and lagoons. The most valuable real estate tended to be that which was situated closest to the public pump. John Busby proposed in 1825 to pipe water to a reservoir at Hyde Park through a four-kilometre tunnel from the Lachlan Swamps (now the site of Centennial Park). Although the Colonial Office would have preferred the work to be undertaken by private enterprise permission was given and work began in 1830; but the elderly Busby was an inefficient supervisor of convict labour, and costs and criticisms mounted. 'Busby's Bore' was not completed until 1837. The quantity and quality of water from this source was not good enough to meet the demands of the 1850s, and when a fresh supply was provided in 1858 by piping from the Botany Swamps, the citizens of Sydney showed their gratitude by erecting a handsome obelisk. The new scheme provided only a short-term answer, though it enabled Sydney's politicians and government engineers to evade for another twenty years the bigger question of bringing a supply from the Blue Mountains.[9]

Melbourne responded to growth by securing the completion of the Yan Yean reservoir between 1853 and 1857. But until these schemes came into operation both Melbourne and Sydney underwent several years during which the lack of piped water bore hard on migrant and working-class families. Women and children often had to spend long hours queuing at a public pump or waiting for the municipal water cart, and cleanliness was hard to achieve. Nor was it easy to lay the dust of inner-suburban streets without a piped water supply. Even after the completion of the new schemes, there often followed a lapse of some years before the poorer areas were connected to them.

Water shortages made for poor sanitation. In most suburbs as in most country towns nightsoil was disposed of in a cesspit in the backyard, often at no great distance from the kitchen and from the well where the family drew its water. In Melbourne refuse was often channelled into the open gutters along the streets, from which it ran into the Yarra or accumulated in stinking heaps in low-lying quarters of the town. Such unhygienic practices were thought to give rise to the spread of typhoid. The wealthy sought to avoid 'the unhealtry miasma' by moving to residential districts on high ground. This did not render them immune, but the majority of typhoid victims probably came from working-class districts, and as Bernard Barrett has said, the nineteenth century accepted deaths by typhoid with much the same fatalism as we accept the road toll today.[10] 'Society tolerates it', wrote the *Sydney Morning Herald*, 'and they look upon it as their inheritance—it was so in the old country'.[11]

The smaller towns in warm climates, such as Brisbane and Perth, probably offended the nose most with their lack of sanitation, but Melbourne and Sydney excelled in other forms of pollution. The Yarra, once a stream of notable clarity and purity, was notable from the 1850s as the receptacle of household filth and industrial waste— though it was remarkable that as late as 1886 a platypus was sighted near the Johnston Street bridge between Kew and Collingwood. While citizens from the more affluent suburbs sometimes complained about the deterioration of the Yarra most of the riverside property owners staunchly defended their right to use the stream as their rubbish dump, triumphantly clinching their argument by stressing the expense of alternative arrangements.[12]

Sydney was no better. After years of complaint about the emptying of human waste into open drains, the Sydney City Council in 1859 completed five sewer mains discharging into Sydney Harbour, and more were added later. By 1877 this practice led no fewer than 3 900 citizens and property owners in the neighbourhood of the Harbour to complain that its shores were 'disgustingly offensive' and a health hazard. Many parts of Sydney remained unsewered. Cesspits sometimes flooded and overflowed into low-lying residential areas, so that in the poorest part of Redfern it was stated that 'The whole of the subsoil of the low ground appears to be saturated with sewage, giving out the most offensive fumes. Many of the houses have been constructed in what are now green foetid fields, and complaints of illness and mortality during the hot weather . . . were general'.[12]

The problems did not end when sanitary contractors were employed to collect human waste at night, since if they sold the nightsoil to market gardeners it provoked complaints from neighbouring householders, and if they dumped their loads on vacant land (even the front of the Sydney Cricket Ground was used for the purpose), the consequences could be worse—as when the Sewage and Health Board in 1875–77 found that faeces were polluting Sydney's piped water supply. Perhaps one of the worst corners was Blackwattle Swamp Creek, where the sewage of Chippendale and Glebe ran into a large mill dam above a distillery, collected the waste from that operation, and then oozed into the creek where it was mixed with the offal from the main city slaughterhouse. From there the mixture was pumped out again into water carts and spread in the city streets to lay the dust. Jevons in 1858 described the colour of the creek as a light coffee brown, and added: 'The foul mud deposited in the channel, giving off a fearful stench, renders this place as unhealthy and disgusting to all the senses as can possibly be imagined'.[13] Forty years later the slaughterhouse was still operating in the same way.

In country towns the nuisances were on a smaller scale but they made their presence felt. A Mansfield newspaper editor complained in 1890:

> The noble horse, the useful cow, the sturdy bullock, the fleecy sheep, the amorous and bleating goat, divide the highway and streets of Mansfield between them . . . The animals like the footpath as well as lordly man and being . . . great depositors—they render the pathway a most unsavoury place to use.[14]

The streets, he asserted, were either like the scene of a ploughing match, or like an Irish bog, or else like a Tasmanian school for stone breakers. He wrote shortly after having fallen over a sleeping cow while going home late on a winter night; but his experience was not unusual. Even in South Australia, where the example of Adelaide's green belt persuaded the surveyors of country towns to surround town sites with substantial reserves, the outcome was unfortunate. The parkland usually remained a weed-infested waste. In those towns which grew beyond their reserves settlement was dispersed, creating excessive costs in street maintenance, drainage systems, and water supply services.[15] And in most country towns, dependent for their rates either on local tradesmen or on the neighbouring farmers and graziers, there was nobody to advocate municipal spending on anything beyond the most unavoidable necessities.

If local councils were too tightfisted to spend much on advancing the appearance of public building, colonial governments were mindful

Albury railway station, opened 1881
Reproduced with permission from the Public Transport Commission of NSW

of elections and the benefits of investing substantially in schools,
railway stations and post office. A.J. Rose contends that such public
buildings, whether rural or suburban, were built to a standardised
pattern with little regard for variations in the local physical environment. In his view this stresses the uniformity of Australian culture.[16]
Major private investors such as the banks also showed little interest
in architectural experiment. But colonial builders were gaining in
experience and confidence, and their results were often pleasing. The
New South Wales government in the late nineteenth century, for
instance, went in for a fashion of pseudoclassical court houses which
materially improved the appearance of the main streets of such towns
as Gundagai and Yass. The Queensland National Bank's surviving
buildings show an opulent use of cedar panelling which must have
impressed its customers. The large hotels boasted flourishes of ex-
uberant style. The use of cast iron on balconies and verandas gave
main streets in towns such as Wagga Wagga a touch of elegance
which later generations were too insensitive to cherish. Gradually
during the second half of the nineteenth century the country towns
of eastern Australia mellowed in appearance to provide what promised

to be the foundation of a distinctive provincial environment.

Some showed initiative in providing amenities. Bega started Australia's first municipal gasworks in 1885. Tamworth's streets were lit by electricity in 1888, several years before any of Australia's big cities. In Thargomindah in the far south-west of Queensland they tapped an artesian bore to provide hydroelectricity in 1893—two years before Launceston began what was to become the Tasmanian speciality of generating electricity by water power. This lively sense of enterprise among Australia's country towns was the more surprising because critics had often been in the habit of accusing rural Australians of technological backwardness. It may be that visitors such as Anthony Trollope, who travelled the Australian colonies in 1871–72, exaggerated Australian shortcomings, failing to remember that scythes and sickles were still in use in many parts of the British Isles. Nevertheless in the absence of a developed Australian engineering industry, technology was often primitive. Even flour mills, the pivot of farming technology, were often home-made. As for the notion of spelling the land or attempting to restore its productivity by the use of fertiliser, many selectors simply lacked the capital. William Evans, the Welsh swagman, noted censuriously in 1869 that 'Smeaton district, once considered the garden of Victoria, is now a ruinous area from continued exhaustion of the land. The farms are overrun by weeds. There are numerous deserted homesteads'.[17] More than once in his travels around Ballarat and Maldon he commented on the failure of selectors even to clear their land.

South Australia, depending on wheat exports to a much greater extent than any of the other colonies, had the best reputation for innovation. Admittedly in the 1860s wheat growers in the Mount Lofty region were still using the traditional English single-share plough, often the handiwork of a local blacksmith. They ploughed across the contours in long furrows, seeded immediately after ploughing, and heaped up the land in broad ridges to improve drainage much as their English ancestors had done.[18] But the opening of new lands inspired new technologies. The invention of the stump-jump plough in 1876 marked a major advance. This was followed between 1883 and 1888 by H.V. McKay's evolution of the combine harvester. But it was one thing for innovations to become available, another entirely for farmers to use them. 'So long as virgin soil is to be obtained at £1 per acre, so long will the average South Australian farmer prefer to spend the money on the purchase of new land rather than in the improvement of what has been impoverished'.[19] Perhaps it was unfair to blame only the farmer. After the coming of the railways the standard

of milling improved, so that in many country towns the proprietor
of a steam-driven flour mill became the main local capitalist. Such
men advanced money to selectors on the security of their crops and
dominated their lives when they ran into debt. They seldom operated
on a big enough margin to grubstake farmers with advances for
improvements, so that in many districts technological change remained
slow.

And yet there was often much to praise in the created landscape
which emerged after the first generation of settlers had dug in. Even
that critical young man W.S. Jevons, travelling the Hawkesbury
district between Wilberforce and Penrith, allowed that:

> In this part the country might have had the homelike appearance
> of your English fields and meadows, but for one or two striking
> differences, viz. hedge rows and trees. Ditches are not at all required
> in this country since there is seldom any excess of water to drain
> off except during our regular heavy rains when your ditches would
> go for nothing and hedges which are the natural accompaniment of
> ditches are replaced here by the universal three-rail fence . . . [20]

He was still judging the country with the eye of an Englishman, but
he was able to see merit in the works of Australian settlers—including
the wives:

> The houses were either small farm houses or very neat comfortable
> cottages generally of wood. They are often distinguished for very
> pretty little gardens filled with rose trees, oleander bushes, orange
> trees, and all the ordinary garden flowers, while passion flowers
> and other creepers cover the walls or verandah with almost too
> great luxuriance.

Then came the disparaging postscript: 'Too much credit must not
be given to the Colonials for this care and tastefulness, considering
that the plants once set, grow almost without further care'.[21] This
was carping. It had required a good deal of hard work and adaptability
for the ordinary rural settler in New South Wales to create a comely
home environment.

As urban demand grew during the 1850s and 1860s a modest prosperity spilt over into the farming districts, and accommodation
improved. Verandas became universal. Shingles remained the main
roofing material until the later 1850s, when imported galvanised iron
began to replace them. Not only was the new material less laborious
to use, but it was also more effectively waterproof than shingles. Its
main drawback was a tendency to retain heat in summer, and various
home-made forms of insulation were attempted with mixed success.

As the extension of railways eased the problems of freight, galvanised iron became the ubiquitous roofing material of rural Australia. It was soon found that rainwater from iron roofs could be stored in iron tanks, and the tankstand became a standard feature of country houses. During the 1860s timber companies began the large-scale manufacture of weatherboards, and as transport improved their use became common throughout much of rural Australia. Only in the western districts of New South Wales and Queensland, beyond access to the railways, was much experiment attempted with the use of local pisé and adobe, and although effective and durable buildings were constructed with these materials they demanded too much labour for general use.[22] As a general rule the use of indigenous materials gave way in the second half of the nineteenth century in rural Australia to mass-produced weatherboards and galvanised iron; but because of the homogeneity of these materials and because bush housing was often attractively sited such buildings soon came to fit comfortably into their surroundings.

In the forty years following the discovery of gold in 1851 a generation came to maturity among whom the Australian-born were for the first time in an adult majority. They enjoyed a greater sense of familiarity with their surroundings. Prosperity brought confidence, and their buildings reflected a determination to put down roots and live as comfortably as they could. But in both rural and urban Australia there was still much to be learned.

8   The Pastoral Impact

Gold may have brought the squatters of New South Wales and Victoria a troubled time of labour shortages and political demands for the unlocking of the land, but it also gave a great boost to the pastoral industry. In the years of prosperity ushered in by the 1850s many pastoralists in Victoria and New South Wales were able to afford improvements on a scale beyond their earlier imagining. The pastoral frontier took a great leap forward to reach the western border of Queensland by the mid-1860s and to encircle Australia by the mid-1880s. None of the exotic invaders that ran wild across the country, not even the rabbit, brought about such profound transformation of the Australian environment as beef cattle and merino sheep. At the beginning of 1788 no hoof had ever been imprinted on Australian soil. By 1860 the continent was carrying twenty million sheep and nearly four million cattle, mostly in its south-eastern quarter. By 1890 there were over a hundred million sheep and nearly eight million cattle pastured in every part of the country except the desert interior. Their spread was accomplished in a hundred years, and in that space of time the original Australian bush gave way to a landscape and environment created very largely in the interests of the flocks of sheep, the herds of cattle and the men and women whose economy depended upon them.

The rural landscapes created by the pastoral industry were accepted as 'typically Australian', even though most Australians were town dwellers. The scenery celebrated by Banjo Paterson and Will Ogilvie and painted by artists such as McCubbin and Roberts still dominates many Australians' view of their country. From Paterson's vision splendid to the fantasies of Marlboro country pastoral Australia serves as an archetype. One element of this archetype is the station homestead, and here a discrepancy sometimes creeps in between myth and reality. The homesteads which have caught the popular imagination, and which form a staple item on the National Trust's bill of fare, tend to be the more opulent specimens of their kind: the

House outside Moss Vale c. 1890
Reproduced with permission from the Public Transport Commission of NSW

adaptations of the English country house built by the Campbell, Rutledge and de Salis families on the Southern Tablelands of New South Wales between Queanbeyan and Cooma, or the baronial grandeur attempted by the 'men of yesterday' of Victoria's Western District. More typically homesteads were rambling single-storey buildings surrounded by deep verandas and sheltered under a pitched galvanised iron roof, with the kitchen as a separate lean-to. Out-buildings, shearing sheds, branding yards and men's quarters made up the community. In the last quarter of the nineteenth century a few luxuries came in: a tennis court, deck chairs (an innovation taken from the steamships which plied the Suez route from England to Australia), perhaps a piano. But sound managers frowned on too much expenditure around the homestead, preferring to plough back their profits into improvements on the property. Thus the station homestead never exercised much influence on the design of Australian housing in general.

Among these improvements fencing played a prominent part. Contrary to what has sometimes been asserted, the old system of shepherding was not immediately brought to an end by the gold rushes. Although squatters had their moments of anxiety about losing their workmen to the enticements of gold they managed to prosper throughout the 1850s and the early 1860s without embarking on large programs of paddocking. When fencing began to spread in the Western District of Victoria and the Riverina after 1860 it was in part a response to competition against free selectors for secure possession of the land; but it was also an attempt to practise better husbandry, by taking advantage of the recent introduction of wire fencing. Previously the usual form of enclosure was the traditional post-and-rail fence, using stringybark or messmate. In parts of Victoria brush fencing was used, and in one or two suitable areas such as the region between Camperdown and Colac the old British technique of dry-stone walling was tried. All these methods were too labour intensive for large-scale paddocking. Improved transport facilitated the introduction of wire fencing. By 1860 riverboats from South Australia plied up the Murray as far as Albury and the Darling as far as Walgett. Another line of access was provided by the railway from Melbourne to Echuca completed in 1864.[1]

The Riverina pastoralists usually began by fencing the outer boundaries of their runs and then subdividing internally. Often as they did so they sank wells or cut irrigation channels so as to open up the back country away from the river frontages. Elsewhere in New South Wales fencing hardly got under way until a boom in the early 1870s, and there the practice was usually to fence outward from the homesteads without troubling about the demarcation of station boundaries. The achievement of the 1870s and 1880s has been summed up thus:

> A population of less than one million people, most of them urban dwellers, had, in the course of twenty years, strung ten million miles of wire around the New South Wales countryside; had felled and split trees to yield roughly half a million miles in overall length of fence posts; and, in erecting fences, had excavated the equipment of 8,000 miles of railway track. This activity was not designed primarily for purposes of legal enclosure of landed property but in order to provide the basic equipment for a new and highly-productive technology.[2]

This massive spread of station fencing accompanied the great attack on ringbarking timber described in an earlier chapter.

This transformation of much of inland Victoria and New South Wales into a cleared and paddocked landscape went with marked changes in the native vegetation. Sheep prefer to graze not more than five kilometres from water, so that as flock numbers increased they tended to concentrate on favoured areas along the rivers and natural watercourses. This sometimes led to complete defoliation. The constant padding of sheep's feet on soil which had never before felt a hoofed animal made for erosion and the creation of dust. It took about twenty years of grazing before erosion was noticeable enough for concerned comment among pastoralists, but sometimes the effects of stocking could be discerned much more rapidly. Thus the Burdekin valley in North Queensland attracted a rush of pastoralists with sheep in 1861, only to be abandoned or turned over to cattle before the end of the decade. The retreat came because as the nutritious pasture grasses were eaten they were quickly replaced by the cruel spear grass which penetrated the sheep's hides and 'worried the condition off them'. Perhaps this development was hastened because the northern squatters burnt off their holdings annually to promote regrowth. In this they were simply following Aboriginal custom, but the Aborigines had no sheep and cattle to eat out the finer grasses.[3]

Yet even on such evidence it was hard to generalise. In 1866 an experienced squatter, looking back on grazing in the Clarence, Richmond, Logan and Burnett districts, claimed that it was common knowledge that the quality of native pasture diminished rapidly after initial stocking. A similar deterioration was noted in the Peak Downs

Serrated tussock grass flourishes in area which has been over-stocked
Reproduced with permission of the NSW Department of Agriculture

district, with star grass coming to predominate. Yet when the King Sound pastoral company went to the Kimberleys in the 1880s they fenced about 4050 hectares of a much larger sheep run. 'Within three years', according to that experienced naturalist W.W. Froggatt, 'the enclosed land, though very lightly stocked, was transformed into a different and better class of country from that outside the ring fence, which was poor and thinly grassed.'[4] The surface hardened and the rough feed was eaten off. Of course 'though very lightly stocked' may have been the crucial phrase.

Overgrazing brought its nemesis. In the Riverina during the 1860s the original feed of old man saltbush and cotton bush was giving way to a mixture of coarser feed. Unlike cattle, sheep eat saltbush bare to the stump, and the pastoralists were unable or unwilling to spell the country for regeneration. When the country beyond the Darling was taken up and fenced after 1878 the same thing happened. As a veteran inspector of stations for Dalgetys described events:

> ... In its virgin state with the saltbush and other edible bushes in their prime, there was hardly a limit, except as regards water, in the opinion of settlers there to what the country would carry, and in many cases it was stocked accordingly, but they forgot in doing this that they were eating the haystack, and there was no crop growing to building another. Then the rabbits came along.[5]

Then the rabbits came along ... Even before that dire calamity the native grasses were being overtaken in many places by introduced species. It was not just that the grazing of livestock suppressed seedling regeneration, so that nutritious natives such as the kangaroo grass (*Themeda australis*) gave way to poorer species, but also that they yielded to introduced plants. Some, such as the buffalo grass and the white clover, were attractive and nourishing. Others were of little use of man or beast. It has been estimated that over 1300 plants have been introduced to Australia during the last two centuries, including all the sown pasture plants and some of the worst weeds. Undisturbed plant communities can usually repel the invasion of aliens, but along the stock routes, the sheep camps and the river frontages where the ground was heavily trampled and manured, exotics throve.[6]

It was remarkable how even in the days of sail the pests of the English countryside such as nettles, Scotch thistles or horehound could survive the long voyage across the world to proliferate in Australia. Their spread was encouraged by pastoral overlanding, particularly during the booms of the 1830s and the early 1860s. Thus Scotch thistles, presumably introduced by accident along with other forms of fodder, were a serious enough nuisance to warrant acts of parliament in South Australia in 1851 and Victoria in 1856. South Australia legislated again in 1862 and a third time in 1871, but paper laws were no match for thistles. In 1871 a landowner near Montacute claimed that large quantities of thistles were filling all the rich gullies in his district. Their only use was as fodder for cows in summer when nothing else grew.[7] But some graziers praised thistles as fodder, and while such attitudes persisted the chances of eradication were poor.

Other weeds followed. Bathurst burr, an exotic first noted in New South Wales in the 1830s, followed the stock routes north to the Darling Downs and south across Victoria to reach South Australia about 1859. Three years later Surveyor-General G.W. Goyder was asserting that it could be eradicated for a cost of not much more than £500 a year; but nothing of the sort happened. Apart from the normal amount of human apathy, it often happened that many failed to recognise a weed when it was first acclimatised. Thus the Bathurst burr was often mistaken for New Zealand spinach. The 1860s also saw the spread in South Australia of the aster, alias the stinkwort, an inedible annual which destroyed grass, owned no nutrient value, and had only limited use as a manure. In the same year the Riverina was becoming infested with Cape clover as it took over the river frontages eaten bare by the flocks of 'Hungry' Jimmy Tyson and his neighbours. Later comers among Australia's noxious weeds included blackberries, a relic of English sentiment, and St John's wort. This greedy feeder on plant nutrients in low fertility soil was a source of wasting and dermatitis in cattle, and might have been ousted by the native kangaroo grass in country left ungrazed; but no such action was taken, and from its original establishment at Bright in the Ovens Valley of Victoria it spread tenaciously.[8] Skeleton weed began to assume importance with the expansion of wheat growing around the turn of the century.

Worst of all was prickly pear. This was in use as a cheap and ornamental hedge at Scone in the Hunter Valley as early as 1839. Although growing wild in Queensland in the 1860s it was not considered serious enough to be classified as a noxious weed until the 1880s when both Queensland and New South Wales legislated against it. These acts provided special lease arrangements for badly infested land together with compulsory destruction clauses, but the failure rate was very high. Neither poison nor drought nor experiments in its commercial use deterred the pear's inexorable spread.

Most of Australia's plant invaders arrived accidentally. Its animal pests were mostly introduced with deliberate and often painstaking

Bathurst Burr (*Xanthium spinosum* L.)

Blue Weed, or Paterson's Curse (*Echium plantagineum*, I.)

Stinkwort (*Inula graveolens* Desf.)

St John's Wort (*Hypericum perforatum* L.)

effort. There was no limit to the willingness of nineteenth-century settlers to improve on the Creator's arrangements for peopling Australia with animals by introducing exotic newcomers and eradicating the native fauna. It was only after a hundred years of white settlement that the realisation dawned that the indiscriminate release of new species was not always desirable and that the preservation of Australian natives was not always undesirable. By that time it would be hard to reverse many of the changes in the balance of nature in Australia.

Of all the exotic species introduced by European settlers the most destructive to native fauna, and the ones about whose impact least is known, were probably the domestic dog and cat. The wild descendants of domestic dogs have probably done more damage to sheep and native fauna than the dingo.[9] Feral cats were the contribution of those hundreds of householders who, too squeamish to drown unwanted kittens and too mean to pay others to do the job, abandoned them to fend for themselves. They throve everywhere in the bush, developing a taste for small birds and marsupials and often growing to considerable sizes. As early as 1868 the Tasmanian parliament passed a law fining anyone who dumped cats in the bush; but on the mainland in the 1880s New South Wales and Victoria legislated to protect cats because they were thought to check the spread of rabbits, and in general little has been done to curb this pest at any time since.

Most of the domestic animals introduced by Europeans have gone bush. Sometimes the results were fortunate; in the early years of New South Wales most of the good grazing country seems to have been discovered by stray cattle with enough enterprise to escape from the government herds. Horses, as a more valuable item, were better protected, but brumbies have run wild in many parts of Australia; however their environmental impact was localised to regions such as the mountainous areas of New South Wales and Queensland. Pigs were a greater nuisance to crops, but at least provided sport. Pride of place for destructiveness probably went to the goat. A mainstay of mining districts and railway construction gangs in regions where it was difficult to keep cows for domestic milk and butter, goats were a major hazard for all growing vegetation. Towns such as Charters Towers and Kalgoorlie were stripped bare for miles around, the larger timber being required for mining purposes and the grass and smaller saplings devoured by goats. The miners' familes suffered the heat and dust arising from a lack of greenery.

More exotic species included the alpacas introduced into the Monaro district of New South Wales in the 1860s, the angora goats bred for mohair in Western Victoria at the same time, and the ostriches farmed in the Wimmera and South Australia during the late Victorian era when their plumes were sought for ladies' hats. Their impact was less troublesome than the camels and the donkeys who, having been used as beasts of freight in the dry outback of central Australia, Queensland and Western Australia were released to run wild when motor transport superseded them. But they were not as destructive to the pastoral industry as the Indonesian water buffalo. Intended as a source of meat for British garrisons and Australian mining communities, several colonies of buffalo escaped to acclimatise themselves in the Northern Territory. Overlanders in the 1880s found the buffalo herds a tempting source of hides for marketing; Paddy Cahill and his mates are said to have taken 80 000 hides from the Alligator River herds between 1885 and 1910. But the buffaloes had their revenge, as they were carriers of the cattle tick (*Ixodes bovis*) which infects domestic cattle with red-water fever. Between 1894 and 1896 the entire North from Wyndham to Townsville was infected, and many cattlemen lost between a third and a half of their stock.

Sportsmen also contributed to the infestation of Australia. Deer were popular; as early as 1808 John Harris introduced some Indian spotted deer to what is now the St Marys district near Sydney, though they did not last long. The sambar and the fallow deer were established in the forests east of Melbourne between 1863 and 1870, and throve so well that a later generation declared them vermin. Axis deer from Ceylon (Sri Lanka) were released successfully near Charters Towers in 1886. Aspiring fox-hunters found it more difficult to acclimatise their quarry, and until the 1860s the young bloods who donned hunting pink in New South Wales and Van Diemen's Land had to be content with dingoes and kangaroos. But in 1864 Melbourne had its hunt club, and improved shipping enabled foxes to be established in Victoria and South Australia by the 1870s. By 1885 they were at home over an area of 12 000 square kilometres, and from 1893 their depredations on lambs and native fauna led a number of shire councils in Victoria and New South Wales to place bounties on their heads. But until 1910 they were confined to the three south-eastern states, and as pests for the pastoral industry they were not in the same league as the rabbit.

Yet it took many years for rabbits to make themselves at home. In the early years of settlement they represented a convenient and nutritious source of food for a population hungry for meat. Hutch-bred rabbits were kept in considerable numbers and released on various islands around the coast and even on the mainland. A Tasmanian newspaper of 1827 speaks of rabbits in thousands in the bush.[10] And

yet they do not appear to have become a plague. Perhaps there were
still enough native predators to keep them in check.

Samuel White of Wirrabeen in South Australia reputedly introduced
a colony of rabbits in 1855, but for more than a decade their numbers
showed no sign of getting out of control. It was left for Thomas
Austin of Barwon Park near Geelong to earn himself an unenviable
niche in history as the man who introduced the rabbits. The Austins
were a family of Somerset yeomanry not far removed from peasantry,
who prospered as squatters in the Western District of Victoria and
yearned to live like gentry. Thomas Austin's brother returned to
Glastonbury to set up as a local squire and to spend a good deal on the
restoration of its sacred sites. Thomas remained in Australia and
sought his recreation in hunting. Having the countryman's shrewd
eye for essentials he knew that it was no use releasing hutch rabbits
if one wanted good hunting and a landscape dotted with warrens.
Instead his English agent went to some trouble to locate two dozen
of the authentic English wild grey rabbits, but in the end had to make
up the number for shipment with a few hutchbred rabbits. That was
the particular crossbreed which acclimatised so fruitfully in the
Australian environment. Once released in the vicinity of Geelong, they
never looked back.[11]

At first the damage was confined to the west of Victoria. By 1865,
six years after introducing them, Austin had 20000 rabbits on his
property. Fifty kilometres west at Colac the Robertson brothers,
having prosecuted a man who was fined £10 for taking a rabbit on
their land, were soon obliged to spend £20000 on the eradication of
the pest. They imported Scottish professional trappers who dug out
some burrows and bricked up others; 'in the end the Rabbit had to
give way to the Scotchman'.[12] By 1874 rabbits were spreading north
into the Horsham district, and before the end of the decade, reinforced
by escapees from Samuel White's colony, were ruining the graziers
along the South Australian border.

Of four stations carrying a total of 125000 sheep in 1877, one was
abandoned and the others reduced within three or four years to 21000,
almost entirely because of the competition of rabbits. By 1880 the
rabbits were over the Murray and heading north across New South
Wales at the rate of more than 100 kilometres a year, and by 1886
they were authentically reported in Queensland. Hares were also
spreading in Victoria, though in lesser numbers. The Welsh swagman
William Evans wrote in 1884: 'Four years ago a jugged hare was a
delicacy, but now they are so numerous as to be unwanted'.[13]

If acts of parliament could have stemmed the invasion, the tide should have turned by 1880, when Victoria and New South Wales followed the lead of Tasmania (1871) and South Australia (1875) in passing Rabbit Destruction Acts. Various attempts were made to import the rabbits' natural enemies from Britain, but it was found that ferrets were unable to stand the Victorian winter, weasels destroyed other fauna, and foxes soon developed a taste for lamb. Dogs were enthusiastic hunters, but grew tired of catching rabbits long before the numbers were endangered. Nor could government action claim to do better than private enterprise. Between 1884 and 1886 the government of Victoria spent £30 000 on a campaign of eradication, partly through poisoning and partly through a bounty, but although claims were made in respect of 1 884 000 rabbits in two years, the rabbits continued to flourish. There were too many trappers who found an easy living in claiming the bounty or in marketing skins for export—in one year in the mid-eighties more than four million skins left Victoria—and these men took good care that enough breeding does were left to keep them in business.

One of the main obstacles in checking the spread of the rabbit was the fact that their eradication was a headache only for big pastoralists and farmers and their political representatives. Poorer people valued the rabbit for a cheap meal, if not for the earnings to be made from the sale of skins and carcasses. From the early 1880s canneries were established in the Western District of Victoria and in the 1890s Victoria exported 1500 tonnes of rabbit meat annually. For a surprisingly long time too there were sentimentalists who deplored any move against the bunnies. Thus in 1880 when the Queensland Legislative Council debated legislation to prevent the introduction of rabbits for breeding, the cantankerous W.H. Walsh, a veteran squatter who should have known better, asserted:

> ... To provide that the whole population of a colony containing millions of acres should be debarred from introducing one of the most domesticated and certainly one of the most innocent of animals, is far too absurd.[14]

Such attitudes would have received short shrift in New South Wales during the eighties as the rabbits entrenched themselves. One retired squatter, C.G.N. Lockhart, went in print to claim that if the rabbits were not utterly subdued the colonists would have to evacuate the inland entirely and withdraw to the Sydney side of the Blue Mountains, there to await the elimination of the pest by starvation or other means.[15] The New South Wales government took the problem seriously enough, spurred by a report to the Legislative Council which stated with curious precision that, by the end of 1883, 7 843 787 rabbits had been destroyed at a cost of £361 492. The Rabbit Nuisance Act of 1883 obliged landholders to take all possible steps to eliminate the rabbits on their properties, and on the Riverina poison, phosphorised grain, yarding machines, netting fences and other resources of technology were mobilised against the invaders. In one year on Tyson's Tupra station 92 000 rabbits were killed.[16]

Amateur theorists launched eagerly into debate about the best means of controlling the pest, and some remarkable ideas came forward. William Rodier, of Tambera near Cobar, informed the Zoological Society in Britain that he had found the answer: after trapping a considerable number of rabbits, the females were slaughtered and the males released, when they competed so ruthlessly for the few remaining females that the does were worried to death and the frustrated males died without progeny. The Society thought well enough of the idea to award it the honour of publication in its scientific journal.[17]

In 1887 the government of New South Wales determined to attract the best brains in international science to the problem. A reward of £25 000 was offered for a sure means of eradicating rabbits. No less a figure than Louis Pasteur entered the field. In a series of controlled experiments on the Pommery champagne-growing estates in France he showed that chicken cholera swept through rabbit colonies with a fearful mortality.[18] When his nephew sought permission to introduce specimens of the virus into New South Wales the authorities hesitated to grant permission. They feared that poultry, sheep and even horses might be infected if the chicken cholera virus got away. They were not persuaded by the claims of one Miller Christy who was said to have identified from Canadian experience a safer strain of rabbit cholera which would not attack other fauna. As Professor H.A. Strong sagely remarked: 'After all, a continent overrun with mad Rabbits would not be a very cheerful place of abode', thus anticipating an idea which would be put to good use by a modern Australian novelist.[19]

This antiscientific bias persisted for many years. In 1906 a Polish-French scientist, Dr Jan Danysz, was brought out by the New South Wales government to conduct experiments on Broughton Island. It was an ill-starred venture. Danysz went down with food poisoning. He could not produce a virus strong enough to affect rabbits. His work met with bitter hostility from many quarters. Billy Hughes, champion of the working-class population of Sydney who relied on the 'rabbit-oh' for cheap meat, launched a scorching attack on Danysz in the House of Representatives. One of the most persistent critics, an Adelaide editor named Giddings, was appointed to a federal commission of inquiry on his researches. The *Bulletin* said his work was 'utterly unreliable', and even the staid Melbourne *Age* wrote:

> It had to be admitted that there was something frightfully repulsive about a wholesale propagation of disease even though it were only a rabbit plague. To cover the sweet earth with a filthy virus which living animals are to communicate to one another is a horrible idea.[20]

So various prejudices combined to reject Pasteur's original insight that rabbits might be brought under control by the propagation of some suitable infection. It would be half a century before the coming of myxomatosis.

The outer colonies of Queensland and Western Australia sought their salvation through fencing. In 1885 the citizens of Charleville urged the erection of a rabbit-proof fence south of the Roma railway, and in the following year the Queensland parliament voted £50 000 for the construction of a fence from Haddon Corner at the south-west boundary of the colony to a point about 25 kilometres west of the Warrego. When the fence was completed in 1891 boundary riders were appointed to patrol it, and an Act was passed creating local authorities with power to proclaim and levy infested areas. These boards were later given power to supply netting at a low rate of interest and to carry out programs of poisoning. The northward spread of rabbits was indeed halted in Queensland after about 1900, but this may have been due not so much to this legislative activity as to the severity of the 1895–1902 drought at a time when the rabbits were reaching the limit of their natural habitat.[21]

In Western Australia the Nullarbor served for a time as a barrier, but in the late 1890s the rabbits followed the hundreds of cyclists and foot travellers who in good seasons flocked to the Coolgardie and Kalgoorlie gold fields. It was thought that the invasion began when a prospector carried a nest of young ones in a billycan and liberated them.[22] Having tried the futile experiment of releasing 160 cats to catch the rabbits, the Western Australians also turned to fencing. Between 1902 and 1907 a major effort was made to put up a rabbit-proof fence along the outer limits of rural settlement, stretching 1800 kilometres from Starvation Harbour on the south coast to Pardoo in the North-West. No fence is proof against fools who leave gates open, and the rabbits were soon at large in the fertile south-west of Western Australia, though their numbers do not appear to have reached plague proportions until the 1920s. In the West also,

WA Rabbit Proof Fence
From *Journal and Proceedings of WA Historical Society*, vol. 2, 1939

despite rumours of rabbits as far afield as the Kimberleys, they failed to establish themselves in the tropics.

The rabbits had spread prodigiously in the half century since Samuel White and Thomas Austin released the first few pairs. Although some regions such as Gippsland and New England were less infested than others, the rabbits had taken over every major pastoral and agricultural district south of Capricorn. It was estimated that their presence almost halved the value of Australia's woolclip. By eating out native grasses and stripping bark from young saplings they made a formidable contribution to ecological change, as well as competing effectively for natural resources with the sheep and cattle who were themselves exotic invaders of the Australian environment. Many pastoralists have been improvers, and the pastoral contribution to the Australian landscape and environment has been profound. But the sheep and the rabbit have ensured that we shall never see the waving plains of Mitchell grass or the rich and diverse native herbage that the Aborigines knew and worked.

9   Towards Conservation

In the prosperous years following the gold rushes of the 1850s some citizens began to grasp at the possibility of remaking the Australian environment into a harmonious and orderly background for the new communities which were thrusting into maturity. Acclimatisation societies came into being in New South Wales and Victoria in the early 1860s. Their aims were stated clearly, if a little floridly, by that annual report of the New South Wales group which spoke of:

> . . . stocking our waste waters, woods and plains with choice animals, making that which was dull and lifeless become animated by creatures in the full enjoyment of existence, and lands before useless become fertile with rare and valuable trees and plants.[1]

A noble aim; but how could they have thought the Australian bush dull and lifeless?

In Victoria these views had an untiring spokesman in Edward Wilson, editor of the conservative *Argus*. A bachelor of prodigious energy, Wilson took the initiative in the founding of a Zoological Society in 1857, which was responsible for Australia's first important zoological gardens at Royal Park. Wilson's influence also brought into being the Acclimatization Society in 1861. His strongest enthusiasm was for the introduction of English songbirds. He argued that soft-billed English birds would be more effective than the local variety in cleaning up Australia's numerous insect pests. He rejoiced when a colony of skylarks was successfully released near Geelong, and looked forward to the day when nightingales and canaries would warble in the Australian bush.[2]

Others shared his enthusiasm. In 1862–63 G.W. Rusden introduced sparrows from China and England. From Melbourne they spread in ten years as far afield as Mansfield. Then controversy surrounded them. Farmers accused them of damaging crops and fruit. In 1880 a correspondence raged for weeks in the *Argus* as Melbourne citizens complained in discreet but unmistakable terms about the droppings which sparrows were apt to let fall on streets and pedestrians.[3] In 1890 the import of sparrows was banned.

Edward Wilson was also a strong lobbyist for the Imported Game Protection Act passed by the Victorian parliament in 1860. This piece of legislation sought to encourage and protect the acclimatisation of grouse, partridges, pheasants, bustards and other species which might in time prove attractive to well-bred sportsmen. It was perhaps as a spin-off from this legislation that a concern began to arise among Australians for the protection of some of their own more distinctive birds and animals. This may simply have been an imitation of mid-nineteenth-century British initiatives to give the force of law to traditional closed seasons, such as the convention that grouse should not be shot in Scotland before 12 August. But it may also show a dawning appreciation of Australian fauna.

Tasmania was the colony which in those years took the most active initiatives towards fauna protection, perhaps because working-class prejudices against game laws were less powerful and gentry attitudes stronger and more responsible. In 1860 the Tasmanian parliament legislated to protect black swans and their eggs, wild duck, teal, quail, emu, plover, bittern and bronze-winged pigeons for eight months of the year during spring, summer and early autumn. When in the following year a similar proposal was brought before the Victorian parliament the working-class representative for Colling-wood, C.J. Don, attacked it as a move to establish what he termed 'the evil of the game laws in the mother country'.[4] If the animals of the colony could not protect themselves, he argued, they were unfit to live in the country. The legislation nevertheless passed early in 1862 in a watered-down form covering a short breeding season from 1 August to 10 November.

A similar debate took place in New South Wales in 1865 when a bill to establish a closed season for various Australian birds passed the Legislative Council but was attacked in the Legislative Assembly by Henry Parkes, again showing the fear of the emigrant English workers that the aristocratic game laws of old England were about to follow them out to their new country. On this occasion the opposition managed to talk the bill out.[5] It passed in a modified form in 1866, but the strength of anticonservation feeling was still evident.

It was left to the Tasmanians to make the running. In 1868 a greater variety of native birds was brought under protection and a more flexible approach taken to the definition of 'closed seasons'. In 1874 protection was extended to brush and forest kangaroos, which could not be hunted between 1 August and 30 January. This was a re-

markably enlightened step at a time when the mainland colonies such
as New South Wales and Queensland were passing legislation to
compel land-holders to exterminate kangaroos and wallabies on their
properties.

In the outcome the adoption·of sensible policies of fauna conservation depended on arousing the awareness of urban as well as rural
Australians to the need for action. This would necessarily be part of
that wider process by which the colonial-born came to terms with
their changing environment and began to value those aspects of it
which they saw as distinctively Australian. Perhaps this was a response
to urbanisation. In 1880 as in 1980 residents in the suburbs were often
the most insistent in calling for the conservation of those distinctive
features of the Australian environment which could no longer be
found in the suburbs.

It was in Victoria, the most highly urbanised of the Australian
colonies, that the first initiatives were taken to encourage the popular
study of Australian wildlife. The Field Naturalist's Club of Victoria
came into being with fifty-six members in May 1880, and soon established high standards of amateur research. A similar club was formed
in Brisbane in 1886. In New South Wales a Natural History Association was started in 1887 in association with the Sydney Mechanics'
Institute. By the end of 1888 there were 348 members, mostly under
eighteen, including members in five rural and suburban branches, and
the *Sydney Mail* gave two columns weekly to its activities.[6] By 1891
each of the mainland colonies supported such a society. It was because
of the activities of such groups, largely suburban in the origins of
their membership, that in 1893 the Australasian Association for the
Advancement of Science was calling for government subsidised closed
reserves for the protection of native fauna and flora. Meanwhile the
Tasmanian bird lovers who started an ornithological society in 1888
inspired a movement which by 1901 led to the formation of the Royal
Australian Ornithologists Union. It was partly as a result of this
pressure group that New South Wales passed a Native Birds Protection Act in 1893, but much still remained to be done. In 1909, encouraged by Count Birger, the Swedish consul general, a group in
Sydney founded the Wildlife Preservation Society, which pressed for
the creation of sanctuaries for native fauna and flora.

If around 1900 some naturalist had attempted a summing up of
the impact of white settlement on Australian fauna, he would have
found considerable carnage among the smaller species, but the larger
marsupials showed little trouble in surviving and adapting. In some
cases it could even be that the partial clearing of the forests by pioneer

axemen improved the habitat for such animals. The red-necked scrub
wallaby of Tasmania, for instance, probably became more numerous
after clearing. In the semi-arid lands of northern and western Australia
the yuros and some other larger kangaroos prospered as pastoralists
improved the back country with bores and dams. Squatters along the
Fitzroy River in the Kimberleys were heard to grumble that they
were pasturing ten roos to every sheep. But the smaller wallabies and
rat kangaroos were decimated with the gradual destruction of their
native habitat. Some, such as the broad-faced rat kangaroo, may
have already been in decline before European settlement began, but
others vanished in the last decades of the nineteenth century when
the trees were ringbarked to make way for sheep pastures and wheat
fields. Droughts, overstocking and rabbits all played their part in
hastening the extermination.

By 1900 the brush-tailed rat kangaroo, once very abundant in the
mallee country of Victoria and the Riverina, was extinct except in
Western Australia. Leseuer's rat kangaroo was wiped out in New
South Wales, and except for a few colonies on offshore islands its
days were numbered in Western Australia. Gaimond's rat kangaroo
was extinct on the mainland. Gilbert's potoroo, an inhabitant of the
wet coastlands of the South-West, was gone. The brown hare-wallaby,
once very common, was gone by 1890, and the banded hare-wallaby
was last recorded in 1906. Among the nail-tailed wallabies the brindled
variety were on the verge of extinction and the crested species destined
to precarious survival in some of the most remote corners of Central
Australia. The parma wallaby's future depended almost entirely on
a colony founded at Kawau Island in New Zealand. Even in the face
of such a record, it was not always wise to write off a species. Thus
the plains rat kangaroo of South Australia, considered rather a rarity
by 1900, suddenly turned up after a few unusually good seasons
between 1931 and 1935 in large numbers over about 15 000 square
kilometres of the Channel Country north-east of Lake Eyre, only to
dwindle again as the feed vanished. Unfortunately many of the smaller
macropods reached a point of no return which even the most bountiful
of seasons could not undo.[7]

This destruction went largely unregarded. There was no menace
of extinction for the large red and grey kangaroos, and these were
the species of which most Australians thought when they sought an
emblem for their federal coat of arms and their first Commonwealth
postage stamps. Pademelons, yuros, scrub wallabies, spectacled hare-
wallabies, rock wallabies, and the rufous rat kangaroos had all
demonstrated their ability to coexist with sheep and cattle and to

THYLACINE
Thylacinus cyanocephalus

BRIDLED NAIL-TAILED WALLABY
Onychogalea fraenata

KANGAROO RAT
Bettongia penicillata

Extinct and endangered species

compete all too vigorously for pasture. But some varieties still plentiful in 1900 survived only because their habitats were not yet required for agriculture. The initial impact of closer settlement was often devastating. Thus when the railway came through the Williams district in Western Australia it was estimated that between May 1887 and December 1891 a million and a half kangaroos were destroyed.[8] The tammar, common in South Australia at the turn of the century, almost disappeared during the next twenty years as more land came under the plough, and now survives only in two small colonies (though a significant number still remain in Western Australia). Very little attention was paid to the fate of the smaller marsupials; there was little outcry when the last of the bilbies in New South Wales was shot by a sportsman near Wagga Wagga in 1912, and yet a century earlier the bilbies were probably the commonest form of native game for feeding hungry pioneers.

Greater concern was shown about the killing of Australian fauna to meet the dictates of fashion. It may have been somewhat exceptional when a European lady of fashion appeared at court in a dress trimmed with 150 breasts of Queensland riflebirds.[9] But the trade in platypus and koala skins went on for many years. Lady Tennyson, wife of the Australian governor general, in 1903, wrote:

> Hallam has given me the most lovely platypus rug of 20 guineas, so expensive because the poor little creatures have been so killed they will soon become extinct, but I am going to send it back. It is too much to give me, and I am working now at Premiers and Governors to get them to arrange a universal close season all over Australia for all these native animals, opossums, wallabies, platypus, kangaroos, which otherwise will soon be extinct. We must have furs, I suppose, but not when the animals are with young.
>
> The Premier, Mr Irvine, agrees with the proposition, but writes that not many skins are exported from Victoria only 243,000 annually!![10]

In the same year the government of New South Wales passed a bill protecting kangaroos, wallaroos, possums, koalas, wombats, platypuses and echidnas for two years, then retaining the ban on platypuses and echidnas and maintaining a closed season on the others from 1 July to 31 December. Victoria and Western Australia both tightened up their Game Acts in 1912, and in 1918 New South Wales placed under protection all native birds not specifically excepted.

It was one thing for parliament to pass legislation; it was quite another to police it effectively. Country justices of the peace were often local landowners whose favourite Sunday recreation was a day's shooting, and if a policeman was zealous enough to launch prosecutions against any of the Bench's friends, he often found it hopeless to expect a conviction. For the rural worker who disliked taking a wages job, trapping offered an independent living, and city-made laws had little force. Accurate statistics are hard to come by, but it has been calculated that between 1919 and 1921 Australia exported over five and a half million possum furs and 208 677 koalas described as wombat.[11] Another estimate claims that two million koala pelts were exported in 1924.[12]

The test case was the protection of the koala. Because of its dependence on a highly specialised eucalyptus diet this marsupial was more threatened than most by the destruction of habitat. Its appealing appearance made it a general favourite with the public, a process which may have been hastened by the publication in 1919 of Norman Lindsay's *Magic Pudding*. In Queensland in 1909 a closed season was declared on killing koalas, and with two short breaks was maintained for the next decade. In 1921 the government passed a comprehensive Animals and Birds Act protecting all fauna not specifically named and providing for the licensing of trappers and dealers.

Black possum with friend
By 1924 when this photograph was taken on the Albert River, Southern Queensland black possums were rarely seen.

Then in 1927 the government lifted the ban on killing koalas. It was a period of growing unemployment and industrial unrest, and the move was probably intended to enable the government's working-class supporters to earn some extra income without cost to the Treasury. Protests poured in from within and outside Queensland, but the acting premier, William Forgan Smith, behaved with that deaf obstinacy habitual in politicians when they have decided to do something discreditable. The slaughter lasted for five months. It took years for the koala colonies of Queensland to recover, and did not even earn the government dividends in the form of cheap popularity. They lost the next elections, and although this probably had very little to do with the killing of the koalas, no subsequent government has chosen to raise the ban. The episode made a point which would be reinforced during the next fifty years: that there was no point in a government courting unpopularity by flouting conservationist sentiment for short-term economic gains. Only the hope of major economic gain justified taking major ecological risks.

Allied with the movement for wildlife conservation was the growing demand for large areas of bush to be set aside as national parks for public recreation. There is still a good deal to be found out about the origins of this idea of reserving open spaces on a large scale for public use. J.G. Mosley has pointed out that from the 1860s Australian governments made a practice of reserving the coastal foreshore and the banks of lakes and streams for public use, showing foresight in a generation not much given to the use of the beach for pleasure.[13] And in 1866 the New South Wales government declared a reserve at Jenolan Caves. Maybe such policies found encouragement in the example of the United States government, who at much the same time resolved to reserve as national parks such outstanding natural features as Yellowstone and Yosemite. But the provision of open spaces for town dwellers was largely neglected.

Sydney, Melbourne and Adelaide each inherited some fine parks from their founders, but later suburban developers, greedy for every pound of profit which could be made from subdivision, left no unbuilt acres for recreation. With the growth of suburban railways one possible outlet was the provision of national parks in the areas of relatively unspoilt bush closest to the cities. In 1879 the New South Wales government declared 73000 hectares south of Sydney as the Royal National Park, 'for the use of the public forever'. This in practice meant a mixture of uses, ranging from bushwalking to family picnics, without any clear understanding of the impact of such use on the bush; in fact the government cherished notions of introducing deer and other exotics to the Park as added attractions. All the same, it was a constructive initiative, and soon found imitators.

In 1887 the government of Victoria set aside about 167 hectares at Ferntree Gully, later increasing the reserve to more than double that size; this became a notable sanctuary for lyrebirds and other birdlife. After several years of agitation, a group of interested citizens in Adelaide secured the reservation of the old government farm at Belair as a national park in 1891. Meanwhile, New South Wales also set an example of inner-city planning by the establishment of Centennial Park in 1888—arguably still Australia's best example of a multi-purpose recreational park serving an area of high population density. This was meant to be the first of a series of open spaces serving the expanding eastern suburbs, but most of the other intended sites were converted to such uses as race courses or sports grounds. Perth profited from its belated growth by reserving in 1894 Kings Park at the city's western edge, but although this was frequently extolled as a farsighted decision to preserve 'a thousand acres of natural bush' near the heart of the city, it must be admitted that the bush was all secondary growth after the clearing of the original jarrah, and that it remained in this condition only because the park's trustees could never afford to convert it into a Europeanised botanical garden after the Melbourne pattern.[14]

Gradually a more constructive attitude was emerging towards Australia's native forests. Commissions of inquiry in Tasmania and Victoria in 1898 and in Western Australia in 1903 stressed that forests could not be regarded as in the past as a limitless resource, but should be managed and harvested so as to allow for renewal and regeneration. Although forestry commissions were set up in every state except Queensland between 1907 and 1920 this enlightened attitude did not always find expression in official policy; indeed the Western Australian Forests Act of 1918 stated that the commercial production of timber was the major legal responsibility of forestry policy. Certainly the Conservator of Forests appointed to administer this legislation, C.E. Lane Poole, suffered many frustrations at the hands of politicians besotted with the notion of clearing the forests to make room for dairy farms. After his resignation in 1921 his friend Kingsley Fairbridge told him: 'You are beating the air. There will be no forestry in Western Australia until the last mature jarrah tree has been milled or hewn into sleepers and the last pole and pile cut down and sold'.[15]

Other states took a more enlightened view. Victoria set up a school of forestry at Creswick in 1910, and the University of Adelaide followed suit in 1911. The Adelaide school was transferred to Canberra in 1926 to form the nucleus of the Commonwealth school of forestry under Lane Poole. Meanwhile in 1920 an interstate conference on forestry recommended that in order to ensure national self-sufficiency in hardwoods each state should preserve an irrevocable minimum of permanent forest lands. This was accepted by a premiers' conference later in the same year, but where states had already fallen below the desirable minimum it took them a long time to catch up; Victoria, for instance, achieved its target only in 1956.

Queensland took the lead in linking forestry with the deliberate retention of wilderness areas as national parks. In 1906 its parliament passed a State Forests and National Parks Act which not only upheld the guiding principles of conservation and renewal, but also empowered the government to proclaim national parks in areas without enough marketable timber to warrant protection as forestry reserves.[16] (Of course this meant in some cases only that the valuable timber was already cut out.) Although Robert Philp, leader of the opposition, thought the bill 'only fit for wrapping sausages in', it passed without dissent. Under the inspiration of an experienced bushman, Romeo Lahey, the National Parks Association of Queensland built up close co-operation with the departmental foresters, and thus helped to make Queensland the first Australian state to set aside a new kind of national park where the bush would be deliberately retained in an undeveloped condition. Between 1909 and 1913 steps were taken to reserve rainforest on Tamborine Mountain, and in 1915 the Lamington National Park was proclaimed near the New South Wales border, with facilities for bushwalking but none for vehicular traffic.

In 1915 also the Tasmanian government went even further by passing the Scenery Preservation Act, the first of its kind in Australia. This set up a board with responsibility for permanent reserves in regions of outstanding scenic merit, and was followed in 1921 by the reservation of 64 000 hectares as the Cradle Mountain-Lake St Clair National Park. Such initiatives were perhaps to be expected in an underdeveloped state mindful of its tourist potential. No other state passed such thorough legislation, though New South Wales, Victoria and South Australia between 1898 and 1914 all passed acts for the reservation of national parks. These were intended for public recreation rather than the preservation of wilderness in its pristine state.

It took longer for the state governments to legislate for the protection of wildflowers. The great expansion of farming between 1900 and 1930 resulted in the clearing of land so that many varieties grew perceptibly scarcer. It was gradually borne in on the official mind that wildflowers were an incentive to visitors and tourists. Naturalists, as well as expressing concern over native fauna, were also deeply interested in Australia's plant life, and this awareness of botany extended to a minority of farmers and their wives, who were in the best position to note changes in the wildflower population. Responding to these influences the government of New South Wales passed legislation for the protection of native plants in 1926, followed by Queensland and Victoria in 1930, the Commonwealth and Western Australia in 1936, and South Australia in 1939.

The movement towards conservation between 1880 and the 1930s was paradoxical. Most Australians lived in an urban or suburban environment. Among rural Australians most saw their task as transforming the environment to maximum productivity. Yet during that period nearly all the movements for environmental conservation had as their object neither the suburban nor the cultivated rural environment but the undeveloped bush. Where nearly all Australians of the early nineteenth century saw the bush as a potentially hostile environment which must be tamed into conformity with their economic goals, an increasingly vocal and influential minority by the early twentieth century were stressing the uniqueness of the Australian landscape in its presettlement condition, and fighting to ensure that some parts of it should be preserved. In arguing for the recognition of a system of land use which was not developmental in its aim but aesthetic and perhaps even spiritual, the conservationists seemed to fly in the face of Australia's ruling ethos. Yet they gained their share of successes, and in that way prepared the ground for those who wanted an even wider recognition of environmental factors when decisions were taken about the shape of the Australian future.

This attraction for the bush was an acknowledgement, if only indirectly, that the everyday environment in which urban Australians lived and worked left something to be desired. But the men in office were slow to tackle the problems presented by the inner-city slums, the increasing congestion of city traffic, or the beginnings of industrial pollution. Especially during the slump of the 1890s few wished to find pretexts for additional government spending. So it would be left to the lonely voices of a few dedicated reformers to spell out the need for better town planning until about 1900 a number of events combined to awaken Australians to the need to clean up their cities.

10　Suburban Spread

Many families migrated to Australia in hopes of founding a rural estate, but most soon settled for the dream of owning the roof over their own heads and a patch of garden in which to express themselves. In his travels around Sydney's inner suburbs in 1858 Jevons made an observation which many would echo:

> Almost every labourer or mechanic here has his own residence on freehold or leasehold land, and unpretending as it is to any convenience or beauties it yet satisfies him better than the brick-built closely-packed rented houses of English towns.[1]

This was an exaggeration, but a justifiable one. In proportion to population the Australian achievement in providing owner-occupied homes was at least twice as good as the United States, and four or five times better than the British average.[2] Yet home ownership in Australia's major cities fell far short of such prosperous mining settlements as Ballarat or Broken Hill in its early years. Most estimates reckon that in the last quarter of the nineteenth century between 30 and 40 per cent of the houses in Melbourne and Sydney were owner occupied, though it also seems that the typical landlord was not the grasping tycoon of fiction but a local businessman or artisan—often a builder or stonemason, or later his widow—who invested in a few properties in his own neighbourhood as security for old age or bereavement.

Nevertheless the myth of home ownership was powerful. 'Not to have your own home is unpardonable in a country like Australia' trumpeted the *Australian Financial Gazette* in 1890, ' . . . the first, the paramount duty of a working man is to acquire a home'.[3] The advice came from an interested party, but many heeded it. Australian labourers were probably the best paid in the world in the second half of the nineteenth century, though individual pockets of poverty were neither few nor temporary. Although banks were sometimes slow to see a flourishing source of business in the urge for home ownership, building societies came to the fore from the 1840s as a means of redressing the balance. Acquiring land was far easier in Australia than in Britain, where the complex system of land title based on ground rent made conveyancing a lawyers' delight. From the 1850s the Australian colonies, beginning with South Australia, adopted the Torrens system of a single transferable title to land. This made subdivision and sale easier and cheaper. All that was required was an inexpensive and reliable public transport system, and Australia's cities would be ready to put on their middle-aged spread of commuter suburbs.

These suburbs were the most characteristic feature of the environment in which the majority of the Australian-born spent their formative years. Although their origins can be discerned in the 1850s their development belongs to the last thirty years of the nineteenth century, and particularly to the public transport revolution which came after 1880. Combining many of the features of the country town with a strong sense of identity with their parent city, the Australian suburbs summed up the Australian ethos: the yearning for private ownership taking precedence over either individualism of taste or a great sense of concern for the shared amenities of the community.

Suburban development was balefully influenced by the weak and lopsided system of local government which grew up from the middle of the nineteenth century. The franchise for local government favoured property, and most councils were dominated by local businessmen—real estate agents were often prominent—whose main aim in life was to keep the rates low. In Melbourne, Sydney and to a lesser extent in the smaller cities the inner suburbs very soon sought to break away from the central city council and to form their own municipalities, fearing that otherwise they would lose trade to the big shops and businesses of Bourke Street or George Street. But the inner suburban municipalities were too small, and their inhabitants and ratepayers were not rich enough to spend much on public amenities. These suburbs were often the least well provided with water, sanitation, open spaces or freedom from pollution, and they had the least capacity for self-improvement.

Conscious of their lowly place on the social scale, their councils were given to overcompensating by erecting expensive town halls—Paddington in Sydney and Collingwood and Fitzroy in Melbourne are outstanding examples—and although such buildings were splendid advertisements for local pride, they absorbed a great deal of ratepayers' money which might have been spent on improving the quality of everyday life. Meanwhile the more affluent suburbs were able to

Inner city in decay
Photograph by Max Kelly

equip themselves with amenities without inflicting excessive rates on their householders. They therefore tended to resist any suggestion of amalgamation with the less prosperous municipalities, or of proposals that the central government drawing taxes from the population at large should take over some of the functions of local government in order to improve conditions in the poorer areas. Thus the inner suburbs drifted inexorably towards slum status.

Before suburban growth could spread further than walking distance from the city centres, there had to be a cheap public transport system. At first colonial governments had no very decided ideas on whether private enterprise or the government should enter this field. The first railways in New South Wales (Sydney to Parramatta, 1855) and South Australia (Adelaide to Port Adelaide, 1856) were each begun by a private company, but in both cases the high cost of labour and materials thwarted the enterprise and the government was obliged to take over. But in Victoria the Hobson's Bay Railway Company enjoyed greater success because of the very rapid growth of Melbourne. Between 1854 and 1860 its network of lines extended from the city to Port Melbourne, St Kilda, Williamstown, Brighton, Hawthorn and Essendon, thus providing Melbourne with the nucleus of Australia's best suburban railway service.

The more costly and hazardous business of rural railway building was left to government funding, and this told against the towns. Colonial governments were more ready to spend money on country railways, thus appeasing the rural vote and playing up to the public faith in developmental projects, than to find amenities for the 'unproductive' city dwellers. Apart from Melbourne, Australian cities in the 1860s and 1870s relied largely for public transport on a service of privately owned horse-omnibuses. Unlike later tram and bus services the horse omnibuses were flexible about routes and timetables, often diverging from their standard runs if customers required it. Employers at that time must have had a more easy-going attitude about punctuality among their workpeople. But the horse omnibuses became unpopular because they were thought to overcharge. Similar complaints about the Hobson's Bay Company at length caused the Victorian government to buy it out in 1878, stimulated by the need to connect major country lines to terminals in the city.

Government ownership did not make for orderly or rational planning. Even in Melbourne, where the appointment of a commissioner for railways was intended to remove the planning of new lines from the influence of political log-rolling, it was notorious that the land boomers of the late 1870s and the 1880s had little difficulty ın encouraging the construction of lines which greatly increased the value of their subdivisions. In most Australian cities—even in remote and backward Perth—the routing of government railways in suburban districts was influenced by interested landowners. Between the railways tramlines provided feeder services and access routes for the built-up suburbs where no railway was provided. Horse trams were introduced to Adelaide in 1878 and to Brisbane in 1885. Sydney's tramway service, a marvel of modern technology in 1881, was steam driven. Its introduction was bitterly but unsuccessfully opposed by a lobby of produce merchants who feared for the impact on the hay and corn industry. In Melbourne after some initial delay through the opposition of inner-suburban municipalities fearing loss of trade, a network of cable trams proliferated between 1885 and 1891.

Then the subdividers got to work. Except for one or two main roads following the tracks of the old overlanding bullock-wagons (such as the Dandenong Road and the Sydney Road) Melbourne's planners stuck to the grid plan with monotonous fidelity. But they did not even leave Melbourne with the advantages of the grid plan, since neighbouring subdivisions seldom attempted any continuity from one

Steam tram
From Mitchell Library

to another: 'The long straight streets began at nothing and ended at nothing'.[4] Much the same could be said of Adelaide, where for some reason suburbs tended to be much smaller than in other Australian cities. If Sydney and Brisbane showed a little more variation in their street plans, this was only in concession to their hilly terrain, and not a sign of greater enlightenment among the subdividers. Brisbane however benefited from some remarkably advanced thinking by the Queensland parliament, which in 1885 passed an act insisting that no block should be smaller than one-eighth of an acre (about 500 square metres) and prescribing minimum widths for streets (17 metres) and lanes (7 metres). The Queensland Legislative Council, seldom a body given to radical ideas, wanted to make a quarter acre the minimum size for a block, but was persuaded that this might bear hard on working-class developers.[5]

The Australian suburban sprawl by its nature could not expect to inspire high standards of design and craftsmanship. During the years of buoyant growth from the 1850s to the early 1890s there could not possibly have been enough skilled tradesmen to cope with demand. In any case high wages for building labourers placed this option out of the reach of most families below the middle-class and professional levels. Instead many houses, including a great number which would now be promoted by real estate salesmen as 'distinctive colonial cottages', were built on the do-it-yourself principle. Others were run up in batches by speculative builders who lacked means or incentive to spend unnecessarily. This meant that there was little encouragement for experiment and innovation in the design of houses, and little attempt was made to adapt the layout of houses to the requirements of the climate.

The basic plan consisted of a central passage with bedrooms on one side, a sitting room on the other, and at the back, possibly as an outhouse or a lean-to, the kitchen. Bathrooms tended to come later, after piped water. The privy was the classic brick or timber sentry box at the end of the back yard. There was almost always a front veranda on which the family might sit on summer evenings; it was sometimes pressed into service as a sleep-out for the older boys in large families. The front garden boasted a lawn and English bulbs or annuals; the back yard was given over to one or two fruit trees and often a fowl run—for even in the inner suburbs of Fitzroy and Collingwood a third of the householders contrived to keep a few chickens. The poorer classes in Australian cities eked out their budgets by a number of such expedients left over from their small country-town origins. Until the city council in 1886 forbade the practice many Perth families kept a

pig in the back yard as a form of edible garbage disposal.[6] The back
yards were bordered by picket fences, over which neighbours might
talk. This was often almost the only recreation for suburban housewives, as the houses were hard to keep clean and the wood-fired
kitchens and wash houses needed a great deal of time and attention.
Housewives who wanted to maintain decent standards of cleanliness
were sentenced to lifetimes of hard labour. But they were expected to
find solace in the thought that their families enjoyed greater opportunities to become householders than their cousins who remained
in old England.

The choice of building materials varied markedly from city to city.
From an early stage Sydney showed a strong preference for brick.
Even among the crowded slums of the central city area only 1603 of
13 783 completed houses in 1871 were of weatherboard or 'inferior'
materials, and by 1891 the proportion dropped to 1225 out of 21 117.
The remainder, whatever their other faults, were at least built of solid
brick. This preference continued as new suburbs grew, fostered by
the building regulations formed by a number of municipal councils to
ensure that only desirable 'brick areas' sprang up within their
boundaries. The same restriction was in force among some Victorian
suburban municipalities, one or two of which, such as Camberwell,
sought further respectability by banning pubs within their boundaries.[7]
Much of Melbourne's pre-1890 building was in weatherboard and
iron, and when the great slump came the demand for housing lagged
severely, so that rows of cottages in Coburg and Brunswick stood
vacant for years. As a result it was not until the modest resumption
of suburban growth about 1905 that a perceptible shift could be noted
towards brick or brick veneer, although the use of brick was already
viewed as a desirable sign of affluence.

Brisbane remained unashamedly a town of timber; originally slab,
then weatherboard and chamferboard. Brisbane residents found that
hardwood timber was more plentiful than brick; it was said to suit
the climate, it lent itself more readily to do-it-yourself home-building,
and at least until the middle of the tweentieth century it enjoyed clear
advantages in terms of cost.[8] While the first generation of settlers
usually resorted to ironbark shingles for their roofing, galvanised iron
made its appearance by 1856, and between 1860 and 1880 took over
almost completely. Although iron roofs made hot houses, they cooled
off quickly at night and had the great advantage of cleanliness for
water storage. Most Queensland houses were flanked by a stand
with a corrugated iron tank, householders understandably preferring
a cheap and copious supply of rainwater to the uninviting town

water. Equally characteristic of Queensland residences was the custom of raising houses on stilts. A variety of advantages were claimed for this arrangement. White ants were deterred; a space was provided for storage; and it made for draughts which eased the sticky humidity of the summer months.[9] Adelaide and Perth, like Melbourne, built in both weatherboard and brick, the latter conferring more prestige. In Adelaide and the surrounding districts a considerable number of houses and public buildings were constructed of bluestone.[10]

Each of the major cities was shaping its own distinctive character. Melbourne struck visitors as a brash and bustling city, teeming with a crude plebeian energy. Civic pride was fuelled by the rapidity with which the city had grown from a settlement in the wilderness. Only one or two American cities such as Chicago or St Louis could match such an achievement. Sydney in those decades seemed by comparison a genteel backwater—Boston as against Melbourne's New York—but even there the pace of environmental change quickened. Mary Gilmore, looking back on a girlhood in Phillip Street in the 1870s, may have idealised it:

> There were oak-trees and grass on the footpath in Phillip Street when I first lived in it, and bananas, or rather plantains, flowered in a garden in Elizabeth Street near Foy's present shop. Hay-carts passed up and down the main streets, and pigs squealed under nets as they came up from the Quay. There are no pigs in the streets now; and no householder today finds straw on his door step, or chaff on his window-sill. The nose-bag is gone from the heart of the city along with the wool team and the rich smell of the hay-and-corn stores.[11]

But it must have been a noisy city, and with the large number of drays, carts, horse trams and carriages there could have been plenty of flies swarming over the horse droppings.

Adelaide, despite its promising beginnings, was an unhealthy city with an infant mortality rate which at 188 per thousand in 1879 was probably Australia's highest. On the other hand the civic leadership set an example to the rest of Australia. Neither Sydney nor Melbourne produced a lord mayor to match the energy of the brewer Edwin Smith, who after an apprenticeship in suburban municipalities became lord mayor of Adelaide in 1878–81 and 1886–87, and of whom it has been written:

> The squares were enclosed with iron railings in place of dilapidated wooden fences; Victoria Square was beautified and in 1894 received his gift of the bronze statue of Queen Victoria. The Torrens River was converted into a lake, while Rotunda Lawn (Elder Park) and

Victoria Drive were formed. City streets were asphalted, gas-lighting replaced kerosene lamps, deep drainage was laid and public baths were opened. He had trees planted in the Park Lands and also actively promoted the horse-drawn tramway system.[12]

Geography set the patterns of social class in the suburbs of most Australian cities. Thus in Sydney the Harbour, which before 1788 marked a boundary between two different groups of Aborigines, now served as an even stronger line of demarcation between two classes of white Australian. Because the North Shore was not readily accessible by public transport except by ferry it was out of range of the clerk or the working man requiring cheap and easy transport to work every morning. Instead it attracted the professional classes and the better-off merchants and executives who could afford time for the pleasant daily voyage and a brisk stroll along Pitt Street. South of the city lay the old, improverished, inner-city districts from which many of the workers were moving out, and also the reclaimed areas of swamp on which new factories were beginning to arise. Thus the suburbs south of the Harbour—unless they commanded Harbour views or sea breezes—tended to attract the less affluent, and so to assume a self-perpetuating underdog character.

In Melbourne the Yarra was the line of demarcation; north and west for the less prosperous, south and east for the better-off. Fitzroy and Brunswick, originally well-regarded suburban addresses, were overtaken by St Kilda and Brighton as early as 1860. It was usually considered that the south and east were favoured because they were more elevated and commanded a higher rainfall, but this view has been challenged.[13] Before the provision of good drainage and sewerage, lower rainfall may have been seen as an asset, and the fertility of the soil is in general better in the western suburbs. But for those without private transport access to the city was easier from its northern and north-western fringes than from the south-eastern districts beyond the Domain and the Botanical Gardens; and this· may have set a pattern which, once established, continued to reinforce itself. In flat Adelaide and subtropical Brisbane the better-off citizens chose to live in the higher portions of the suburbs, and in Perth access to the sea breeze and the Swan River tipped the balance in favour of the western suburbs.

The better suburbs demanded improved public amenities, and these were not always within the means of a single local authority. Bigger organisation was needed: either private enterprise (but such projects seldom lasted long) or else the government or a government-backed statutory corporation representing all the metropolitan municipalities, such as the Melbourne and Metropolitan Board of Works which was founded in 1888. Adelaide was the first of Australia's major cities to start a waterborne metropolitan sewerage system in 1879, and Melbourne followed in 1880. Sydney had to wait until 1890 after the completion of the Upper Nepean supply scheme—just in time to meet the droughts of 1888 and the nineties, a narrow escape which ever afterwards caused Sydney's planners somewhat to overestimate the city's needs. Affluent suburbs such as Woollahra and Waverley were given priority for sewering. Hobart and Perth did not get round to having functional schemes until 1912, and Brisbane, despite suburban sprawl and a subtropical climate, remained unsewered until 1923 because of municipal squabbles and engineering difficulties.

Even when these schemes were in operation problems remained. It often took some time before the less affluent working-class suburbs were connected, and in some areas, such as the limestone on which much of Sydney is built, it was difficult and costly to lay pipes. Outflow was also a problem. Melbourne had a particularly efficient sewage farm at Werribee, but in Sydney it was (and still is) discharged into the

Circular Quay Sydney, 1914
Old gaslight stands side by side with electric light.
Reproduced with permission from the Public Transport Commission of NSW

ocean at no great distance from popular beaches, and in Perth it went into the Swan river until after years of protest an outlet was found in the ocean—again not far from the beaches. Given the distances which had to be serviced by Australia's metropolitan water and sewerage schemes it was unrealistic to expect that the public money could be found to bring them to maximum efficiency.

Other utilities gradually enhanced the attractions of suburban life. Gas was in use in Sydney as early as 1841. Hobart and Melbourne followed in 1857, and it was used for street lighting in all the cities and major country towns in the later part of the nineteenth century, though in out-of-the-way places such as Perth whale-oil streetlamps remained until the 1880s.[14] Electricity gained on gas in the 1890s, particularly after the metropolitan tramway systems, beginning with Brisbane in 1897, converted from horse-drawn to electric trams. Neither electricity nor gas was much used for household appliances.

Technological change made its presence felt in the urban landscape in a number of ways. From the early 1880s poles heavily festooned with telephone wires crowded the view in almost every city street. In Sydney in 1883 the *Town and Country Journal* deplored 'the effects produced on our fine buildings by the elephantine poles and their network of wires. The ordinary spectator mentally asks himself... whether at the same rate of progress the sky will be visible in two or three years'. A few years later in Perth the wires were welcomed as a portent of urban sophistication.[15] Although gas mains were located underground it was thought too expensive to treat electricity in the same way, and from the 1890s the increasing number of suburbs served by electricity drew their supplies from overhead wires slung on timber poles tarred at the base against white ants.

Such humdrum portents of change went largely unnoticed compared with the dizzying heights to which city building aspired. After the introduction of passenger lifts in 1880 it was possible to leave behind the old four-storey maximum height for city buildings, and office blocks of eight or nine storeys began to thrust upwards in Collins Street and Pitt Street. Because of the economics of load-bearing masonry walls the Melbourne City Council imposed a limit on the height of buildings in 1888, but even within that restriction the building boom of the eighties endowed Melbourne with a skyline of tall ornate office blocks which put the rest of Australia to envious wonder.

Though suburban dwellers of the late nineteenth century shared in the excitement of vigorous urban growth, they were not overwhelmed by it. They still enjoyed easy access to the bush, even in Melbourne. In 1869 four youths on a bird's-nesting expedition could meet and kill a brown snake on the city side of Malvern, and subsequently admire the 'millions of vernal flowers of every variety of hue peeping through the rich sprouting grass' of the country around Caulfield.[16] Even after two decades of boom town expansion a short trip by train or bicycle could take the members of the Victorian Naturalists' Club in 1890 to the pretty village of Oakleigh from which they could ramble through the heath across to the coast at Sandringham 'between hedges of *Acacia amata* loaded with fragrant flowers' or pause to identify a new species of orchid near the market gardens of Cheltenham.[17] Masses of orchids could be found among the neglected orchards of the Mount Waverley district, and although some tracts of country around Burwood and Oakleigh had been cleared to make way for violet farms—an interesting by-product of late nineteenth-century taste—there were still areas towards Moorabbin where the original ti-tree scrubs were standing until the First World War, and where ruthless boys trapped finches and other small birds to sell in the city at fourpence a dozen. Most of the Australian-bred generation who came to maturity between 1875 and 1890 fitted comfortably into their environment, and for the majority this was a suburban environment with access to the bush. As well as making them a receptive audience for the painters of the Heidelberg school and the writers of the *Bulletin*, this sense of acceptance and affection led them to take a lively interest in their country's fauna and flora.

As the nineteenth century drew to a close with the promise of Australian federation, articulate voices were also raised with ideas about the environmental quality of the new nation. Some demanded improvements in the quality of urban living. Others came to see that there was something unique and irreplaceable in the wildlife of their country, and began to challenge those other Australians who took for granted their right to kill and trap whenever money, sport or the whim of the moment suggested. The spoilers of the Australian environment would not cease their activity, but increasingly they would no longer have things entirely their own way.

11 Planners and Improvers

One of the marks of a colonial society is its inability to recognise its own social problems or to set about finding remedies for them without waiting for a lead from some higher authority overseas. Australians were apparently incapable of seeing the possibilities of urban reclamation or town planning until late in the nineteenth century when news arrived of British precedents to guide them, just as in the mid-twentieth century it took American models to awaken them to the problems of environmental pollution and conservation. This may simply mean that, despite the presence of some vile slums, the majority of town dwellers were pleased with the quality of their accommodation and its environment. If after 1890 there was a growth of social conscience about the environment of the underprivileged, this may have arisen from fear of disease spreading from slum regions.

It was left to a recent arrival from Britain, the architect John Sulman, to begin preaching the gospel of town planning in Sydney in the late 1880s. He was influenced by a strong contemporary movement in the British Isles, led by such publicists as William Morris and Ebenezer Howard, who reacted against the ugliness of industrialisation by insisting that imaginative planning and a more generous provision of open spaces could do much to improve the urban environment. By this they meant not only a setting which would be pleasanter and cleaner to live in, but also one in which it would be easier to produce healthy and well-integrated citizens.

If such thinking could gain ground in the Old Country it was easy to hope that the new cities of Australia were not beyond redemption. Sulman called for reforms which would eradicate slums and traffic congestion in Australia's established cities, but he also urged that in the planning of new suburbs and towns there should be an end to the grid system which had dominated street layout monotonously since Governor Darling's time. Instead streets should curve in harmony with the contours of the land. His values were 'convenience, utility, and beauty', and he hoped they could be achieved by thoughtful planning instead of the greedy improvisations of the past.

It was hard to communicate this message to Australian getters and spenders. Sulman threw a lot of energy into the formative stages of the Australasian Association for the Advancement of Science—also, as we have seen, an early advocate of fauna protection—and in 1890 was enabled to give the Association a memorable address on 'The Laying Out of Towns'.[1] This established town planning as a discipline worthy of serious attention. But Sulman found, as many have found, that in boom times demand runs too hot for practical men to have time for innovations, and in recessions nobody can afford them. The slump of the 1890s provided a convincing pretext for inaction, despite glaring social problems. It was in vain that in 1896 Archdeacon F.B. Boyce complained that Sydney's slums were equal in dirt, vice and crime to anything in London, and urged that the inhabitants should be encouraged to move out to healthier areas in the outer suburbs as a preliminary to slum clearance.

It was not that the New South Wales government of the day was totally unsympathetic to reform, for in the same year it at least got round to passing a Public Health Act to regulate such nuisances as polluted water supply, substandard food, and the control of infectious diseases—ten years after Tasmania and Western Australia, twenty years after South Australia and Queensland, and over forty years after Victoria. But slums were seen largely as a problem for the municipal authorities to handle, and the Sydney City Council was of a mediocrity to win the scorn of that sharp-tongued reformer Beatrice Webb when she met them in 1898.[2] The fact was that in Sydney as in most Australian cities prominent men sought the office of Lord Mayor either to protect and advance their own business interests or in hope of a knighthood or minor honour.

Nemesis came in 1900 when Sydney and Brisbane were visited by plague. The slum streets of Sydney's Rocks were devastated. In the city as a whole there were 112 deaths.[3] Respectable citizens were horrified by the outbreak of a disease which most associated with mediaeval filth and which could not be guaranteed to stay obligingly in the poorest parts of the city. William Morris Hughes, the incisive young member for West Sydney, took great pleasure in escorting the premier, Sir William Lyne, around the filthy hovels in his electorate:

> I led him to the parapet on the edge of Darling Harbour, where, jutting out over the water, were two foul-smelling sentry-box structures smeared with ordure—the only sanitary convenience for the sixty or seventy people that lived in the street! One glance was enough to turn the strongest stomach. Sir William's face was

mottled; he tugged at his whiskers savagely. 'This is awful!' he said in a broken voice . . . We boarded the launch, and from a distance of twenty feet or so saw the walls [of the parapet] thickly daubed with excreta, and thousands of rats poking their heads out of holes in the wall . . . As we sped swiftly on our way, I said to Sir William, 'Yes, you're right it's terrible—but do you know that some, if not all, of those filthy dens are owned by Aldermen of the City Council?'[4]

It would have been carrying social justice too far to take legal action against these landlords, but as a result of the plague many of the worst tenements were vacated and subsequently razed. Action was spurred by a second outbreak of plague in 1902 which lingered sporadically until 1909. Control of the port was placed under a unified Sydney Harbour Trust and the Rocks Resumption Board was set up to advise on the rehabilitation of the area. Many of the old rookeries were swept away, among them some of the narrowest alleys and the flat-chested terrace houses which they served. Sydney may have lost a little in picturesqueness, but it certainly gained in salubrity.

The plague scare ushered in a decade of reform in Sydney. In 1902 the Public Health Act was upgraded and legislation was passed for the abatement of air pollution through industrial smoke. In the same year Neil Nielsen, one of those persistent champions of one idea who sometimes find their way into politics, rode his hobbyhorse to victory by persuading Parliament to allow him to chair a royal commission to clean up Sydney's slaughterhouses. The inquiry revealed a sorry tale of cattle driven through the dust and noise of narrow working-class streets, of offal dumped in the Harbour, of staff whose job was only rendered tolerable by liquor.[5] The royal commission recommended transfer to a modern killing centre at Homebush. Even then 11 610 gullibles were found to sign a petition protesting against the move and urging that the cattle-droving nuisance could be solved by a branch railway. It was not until 1916 that the Glebe abattoir ended its noisome career. Not that Sydney was outstandingly backward. In Perth in the early 1920s cattle were still being driven to slaughter along the main street, St George's Terrace, with cars veering to one side to give way.

Behind the Edwardian elegance of Australia's major cities lurked a number of earthy survivals of nineteenth-century improvisation. Garbage disposal remained faulty. As late as 1920 only five of Sydney's municipalities boasted incinerators. According to a report of that year:

The garbage of Redfern is deposited on a racecourse near South Sydney Hospital, that of Paddington near the Hampton Oval, and that of Woollahra on Bellevue Hill, 'The Dress Circle of Sydney' according to some house and land agents.[6]

The concept of sporting ground as rubbish dump had not advanced far in the forty years since nightsoil contractors dumped their cargoes outside the Sydney cricket ground. In most cities rubbish tips were located in the poorest suburbs. 'Perth's Collingwood' was East Perth, and that was where the rubbish tip went:

> Filled with water, overflowing with rubbish, and surrounded by mud and decay, it was "a standing disgrace", as a contemporary put it. If children were late out in the evening or late home for lunch, the young working class mothers of the area would rush around to the tip fearing the worst for their children. Not until 1904 was the tip covered with sand.[7]

It was the same with environmental hazards always. If they could be kept out of sight of the prosperous and influential remedial action was slow in coming.

Nevertheless in Sydney the reform movement gathered force. In 1909 a royal commission was set up under the chairmanship of Thomas Hughes, an unusually progressive lord mayor of Sydney who had already served on Nielsen's commission. Stimulated by a dizzying forecast that the city's population might reach as high as a million by 1930 (it turned out to be a million and a quarter), the Hughes commission made a searching investigation into many of Sydney's environmental problems. Much of their attention went to the problems of traffic flow. In a city where bullock teams still hauled drays to the wool stores at Circular Quay the first motor vehicles were now adding their noise and fume to the trams, carriages, wagons, cabs and pedestrians which thronged the streets. The commission found that unified planning was needed to cope with the problems of road maintenace and improvement, and this led them to the concept of a Greater Sydney Council with responsibility for town planning.

The need was compelling. Noting that crowding in the inner suburbs reached between 112 and 192 inhabitants to the hectare, the commission urged that municipalities should be given the power of veto on substandard structures. No buildings should be permitted with less than about 28 cubic metres of air space in the living rooms. Workers should be given every facility to move out of the inner slums into the suburbs, except for a few groups such as the waterside workers whose occupation required them to live close to the job. In the suburbs there should be wide streets, tree planting and better parks and municipal playgrounds.[8] So in the name of reform the Hughes commission reinforced the tendency to see the inner-city districts as irreversibly doomed to decay. Other Australian cities would follow their model of the inner city as confined to commerce and business, a 'dead heart' which was the target of suburban comings and goings. With the best intentions in the world the reformers fostered the suburban sprawl.

After government intervention in slum clearance the logical next step was positive action to enable the less affluent to obtain their own homes. In the same way as government-funded banks were set up to help the small farmer establish himself on the land, the state governments now provided backing for the worker who wanted to buy a home. Between 1908 and 1912, beginning with Queensland, each of the states passed legislation either enabling its bank to provide long-term loans at low interest to approved home-buyers or else, as in Queensland and Western Australia, setting up a statutory board for the same purpose.

The New South Wales government went further, and in 1912 planned the model garden suburb of Daceyville where good quality housing would be available to workers for rent.[9] It was a hopeful scheme, envisaging a playground to every twenty houses and tenants who would find the government less grasping than the profit-making landlord; but rents went up because of bureaucratic inexperience, and Daceyville came under fire as a piece of utopian socialism. Its plan was never brought to completion.

By this time Sulman's ideas were seeping through to private enterprise. In the years immediately before the First World War his influence was evident in the development of the Sydney suburbs of Haberfield and Matraville. In Perth at the same time Mount Lawley and Dalkeith were subdivided in conformity with his principles, though both were destined to be settled by residents in the middle-to-upper-income brackets, so that the goal of social betterment was ill served. Perth was also fortunate in possessing a resolute and influential town clerk, W.E. Bold, who in 1914 was sent on a tour of the Northern Hemisphere to study recent developments in town planning. As a result a partial green belt was reserved in the western suburbs and the districts of Floreat Park and City Beach were planned as garden suburbs, although again it turned out to be the affluent who lived in them.

Adelaide, with its established reputation for enlightened planning, went even further. In 1914 C.C. Reade, secretary of the International Garden Cities and Town Planning Association, toured New Zealand and the Australian states at Sulman's instigation to preach the gospel of town planning. Most of the state capitals responded by forming town planning associations, but the South Australian parliament went further and in 1916 passed the first Planning and Housing Act in Australia. Reade was invited back to serve as government town planner. In his first year of office (1917) he hosted a national conference at which much was said about the redevelopment of slums—for optimism still reigned that the end of the First World War would see the making of a better society. As a sequel J.D. Fitzgerald in 1918 persuaded the New South Wales legislature to pass town-planning legislation enabling councils to proclaim residential districts which must be kept free of commerce and industry. But there initiative petered out. Although South Australia set up a planning authority in 1920 it could only act on the government's request, it was constantly rapped over the knuckles by developers and local authorities, and in 1929 much of its power was whittled down.

It need not have been thus. The newly created State housing commissions and boards had the potential for imaginative planning, learning from the mistakes of Daceyville. After the 1914–18 war the Commonwealth government entered housing with the provision of War Service Homes. By 1939 this source of funding pumped £29.7 million into the building of 21 334 houses, the purchase of 12 987 others, and the mortgaging of 2967 more. Combined with private enterprise this gave a renewed push to suburban growth in the 1920s, and to a lesser extent the 1930s. The pity of it was that all this activity took place largely untouched by the new insights of town planning.

From being a concept intended to enhance the quality of life for all citizens, town planning was diverted into an élitist enthusiasm which for the time being left its mark only on the layout of a few corners of the newest and least developed of the prestige suburbs. Elsewhere the layout of new suburbs continued depressingly in the old pattern. Much of the suburban growth between 1910 and 1940 took place within subdivisions planned many years earlier, where it was easier to continue along old plans than to scrap them and start afresh.

At the state government level the tradition continued of grudging money for urban expenditure. After a period of comparatively strong urban influence most state parliaments lapsed under the dominance of rural interests after 1910, partly through the continued veto power of Legislative Councils and partly through the rise of the Country party, or in the smaller states of Labor parties with a strong rural component.

Nor was much progress made on the amalgamation of municipalities in the interests of better town planning. Administrative inertia was fostered by the division of responsibility between state governments and petty municipal authorities. Both, especially the latter, were open to the lobbying of landlords and real estate agents who saw little merit in government intervention, particularly if it placed limits on their own profits. Vested interests in the small inner suburbs successfully fought four schemes for municipal amalgamation in Sydney between 1915 and 1931, and two town planning bills were shelved. In Melbourne the existence of the Melbourne and Metropolitan Board of Works was held to meet every likely need for co-operation. The 'Greater Perth' movement met with partial success between 1914 and 1917, and in 1925 the Queensland government forced through the merger of all the suburban municipalities into a greater Brisbane City Council. Its usefulness was hindered by party politics, but few ratepayers demanded the restoration of the old fragmentation.

Yet before dwindling into futility the town planning movement of the early twentieth century scored one notable triumph: the creation of Australia's capital city. When federation came in 1901 the traditional rivalry between Sydney and Melbourne made it impossible that either should serve as the Commonwealth's capital, and a compromise was worked out following precedents in the United States and Canada. Melbourne would serve temporarily as the capital, but an entirely new city would be created at a site in New South Wales at least 160 kilometres from Sydney. After intensive lobbying Canberra was selected. Once again largely through Sulman's influence the

Canberra 1920s
Reproduced with permission from the Public Transport Commission of NSW

Commonwealth government was persuaded to hold a worldwide competition for its design. The winner was a young member of the Chicago school of architects, Walter Burley Griffin:

> Griffin created a highly imaginative blend of formality and informality that was outstanding. Using three natural features as apexes of a triangle and the hubs of three interlocked, spider-web series of wide roads, and using the valley between them as a meandering lake, he achieved a remarkably successful marriage between the land and a controlled geometry of radial streets. It was a complete break with traditional Australian town planning.[11]

And because it was such a radical break with the past, Canberra failed to wield the influence on urban design which it deserved. Partly this was due to its unexpectedly slow growth. The First World War directed national priorities elsewhere. Obstructive public servants quarrelled with Griffin until in 1920 he was driven from his job. It was 1927 before Parliament House was opened (in temporary quarters which have lasted over half a century) and the first reluctant public servants took up residence.

Then came the depression and the Second World War. Burley

A living room furnished in 'Queen Anne' period
From *The Home* 1 August 1930 p. 48

Griffin's vision remained largely unrealised, and his creation evoked sneers such as 'a good sheep paddock spoiled'. State parochialisms bristled at Canberra as the source of federal interference and as a white elephant gorging taxpayers' money which might have been spent on superphosphate subsidies. There was little hope that Canberra would be seen as a model to imitate. Burley Griffin subsequently attempted the challenge of expressing his ideas in an Australian setting. Castlecrag in Sydney and Eaglemont in Melbourne both stand out from the ruck as desirable places to live in; but they were judged too costly for their style of planning to be wasted on working-class housing estates, and their emphasis on preserving native trees and flowering bushes was not copied. Not that Burley Griffin planned only for the rich. One of his last and most innovative designs formed the basis for a public waste disposal unit at Leichhardt.[12]

The creators of the suburban environment in the 1920s and 1930s included few like Burley Griffin. Improved housing standards took second place to the ruling passion for ownership of a house detached from its neighbours and preferably standing in a quarter-acre (0.1 hectare) block. In 1925 the president of the Master Builders Association of New South Wales, perhaps not quite the least prejudiced of commentators, remarked that building, health and other regulations made it impossible to erect houses at a figure that had any possible relation to the average worker's resources.[13] All the same between 1921 and 1933 the number of occupied houses in Australia rose from 1 211 924 to 1 547 376, of which 51 per cent were owner occupied—and 1933 was a depression year in which the proportion of home owners had fallen.

From this growth arose a continuing demand for public expenditure on basic necessities such as sanitation, water supply, electricity, gas, footpaths, schools and police stations. Since few suburbs admitted to being adequately furnished with all these amenities there was little cash or energy left for improving the communal environment. Because back yards and front gardens provided open space for recreation Australians were not under the same pressure as European city dwellers to develop their streets for any use other than traffic or their open spaces for any purpose except competitive sport. Even where community attitudes accepted the need for amenities such as parks and open spaces, performance lagged.

Newer suburbs were often less well off than those planned in the nineteenth century. Perhaps this was a concession to morality. Open spaces were often seen as venues for illicit sex, to be policed during daylight and locked up at night. J.H. Maiden, Director of Botanical

Gardens for New South Wales, told the Hughes royal commission
that Centennial Park had a wicked reputation.[14]

Most suburban Australians took their public environment for
granted as something beyond their influence or concern. The basic
infrastructure of new suburbs remained almost unchanged, and still
showed traces of country-town organisation. There would be a row of
individually owned shops clustered near the local railway station or
strung out along the main tramline or bus route. Corner shops were
dotted every few hundred metres to meet the everyday needs of
housewives who still undertook most of their local journeys on foot,
unless a major shopping expedition called for a train or tram ride
to the central city. The straight streets were planted with modest
shrubs and trees of a size unlikely to interfere with the overhead wires
or to irritate householders by overshadowing their front lawns and
blocking their roof gutters. The domain of the private front garden
was separated from the street by a picket fence or a low hedge; ti-tree,
plumbago and privet were all popular. High walls were expensive and
unneighbourly, but the Californian practice of doing without a front
fence altogether, although tried in Canberra, was slow to gain ground.
Most householders preferred to protect their gardens against marauding dogs and children.

The front garden was the conventional but deeply important
means of self-expression for most Australian suburban dwellers.
This was the private environment in which many dedicated their
weekends to the care and maintenance of lawns and flower beds which
still followed English canons of taste. Around neatly manicured
patches of grass Iceland poppies, delphiniums and, above all, roses
were cherished and lavishly watered. Such gardens were only possible
through access to piped water, and their cultivation was yet one
more sign of that preoccupation with water which marked the inhabitants of an arid environment.

Consequently native flora were held in scant respect. Certain tropical
exotics such as the bougainvillea and the hibiscus were tolerated, but
the idea of encouraging Australian natives was almost unheard of.
It was a mark of courageous eccentricity when in 1927 a Gosford
nurseryman began to deal in Australian natives. Until after the
Second World War only one or two others in the Dandenongs behind
Melbourne followed suit. A far more common reaction was the surely
autobiographical episode described by George Johnston in *My
Brother Jack*, when the hero's decision to plant a sugar gum in his
Melbourne suburban front garden was met with derision from his
wife and neighbours alike.[15]

Piped water was indirectly responsible for a major change in Australian domestic architecture. As water supplies improved and the need lessened for a corrugated iron roof as rainwater catchment, those who could afford it showed a preference for tiles as a roofing material because they did not rust. From the late 1880s tiles were imported from France, then manufactured locally after the First World War. They were a feature of the so-called Queen Anne style of house design which dominated middle-class suburbs between 1900 and 1920; a spacious and effective hybrid which has been held to match 'the view that the period of Federation was concerned with the present rather than the past'[17] But its roomy lines were incompatible with cheap building. After the First World War public taste took against the sensible and versatile veranda, and many homes contented themselves with a modest front porch, relying on curtains or venetian blinds to keep the sunlight at bay.

Inside their houses probably only a minority of Australians enjoyed a private environment in the sense of having a room of their own. Bedrooms were shared, at first with sisters or brothers, then with a spouse. This meant that most people seldom had the opportunity of asking: 'What sort of environment would I create for myself if I were planning for myself alone?' and thus never had the incentive for developing personal taste about their living space. Creative self-expression was channelled into crafts and hobbies such as woodwork, music, knitting and crocheting.

The rich who could afford to plan spaciously were usually content to take their models from Britain, or increasingly the United States. Probably they were still few enough in number not to develop an indigenous tradition of design which might have filtered down to the mass market. Professor Leslie Wilkinson pointed to another factor when he complained in 1921 that at least 70 per cent of Australian houses were erected without reference to the architectural profession: 'Until this state of affairs is altered and until the public appreciate the difference between the beautiful, the good, and the horrid, admirable work will continue to be a raity.'[18] He did not exaggerate, but nor did he indicate how the process of education should begin.

In most houses the focus of communal living was the kitchen. The kitchen table served not only for meals but also for homework, the construction of models and other hobbies, the repair of household appliances, and as the accounts section where mothers allocated the pay packet on Friday nights. A secondary focus was the sitting room, usually furnished with a three-piece lounge suite and often with a piano. Increasingly after 1920 this was replaced by a player piano or a large cabinet radio.

There would usually be coloured prints on the wall, the semi-religious themes of the turn of the century giving way by the 1920s to a solitary Arab with his camel gazing over endless Sahara sands, or a handsome couple in evening dress conversing in a Mediterranean garden. A popular pair were 'The Sea Hath its Pearls' and 'The Earth Hath its Charms'. In such households portraits, whether of the royal family, the parental wedding or the uncle who never came home from the war, were apt to be relegated to the bedroom, but other families kept these icons in the sitting room. Differing tastes may have reflected differing social values; city as against country perhaps, or Protestant against Catholic. The walls of Catholic bedrooms were usually monopolised by a crucifix and Pellegrini prints of the Madonna or the Sacred Heart.

The spread of labour-saving devices for housewives, such as gas heaters and vacuum cleaners, was disappointingly slow. The bathroom heater and the laundry copper were still usually wood fuelled—one remembers the half million tons of firewood consumed annually in Sydney and Melbourne in the 1920s—but this marked an advance on the day in 1909 when Archdeacon Boyce found it necessary to make a point of telling the Hughes commission: 'I do not see why workmen's dwellings should not contain bathrooms.'[19]

In summer food was usually preserved in an ice chest, replacing the Coolgardie safe of an earlier generation. The iceman with his horse-drawn refrigerated cart joined the milkman, the baker and the green-grocer (and often the butcher and the grocer) among the regular callers whose visits mitigated any sense of suburban isolation felt by the full-time housewives of that era.

Until the 1920s and in many cases until the 1940s the arrival of these tradesmen was heralded by a slow clatter of hooves, because motor transport was thought less economical and convenient than the horse ('you can't train a van to amble from house to house while the goods are being delivered.') Nevertheless from the earliest years of the century motor transport gradually came to dominate the city and suburban streets. At first cars were seen as something of a nuisance. J.H. Maiden in his evidence to the Hughes commission of 1909 complained that they were worse than brick carts for damaging roads: 'They suck up the very stones'. At that time tarmac roads were still rare in Sydney. The finest were in Centennial Park, said Maiden; they were clean, smooth and quiet, but a dismal colour, and they reflected heat.

As cars increased in number they hastened the sealing of suburban

streets with bitumen, thus reducing the problem of dust. Traffic
congestion was not yet seen as an ungovernable problem. In most
cities, even at rush hours, the flow could be satisfactorily controlled
by a policeman on point duty. Traffic lights were not known until
shortly before the Second World War, and in Perth and Hobart such
exotic innovations were not deemed necessary until the 1950s.

Although the number of private cars in Australia quadrupled during
the 1920s, to reach 466930 in 1929–30, car ownership remained largely
outside the grasp of many working-class or lower middle-class families.
Even in car-owning families women often did not drive and remained
dependent during weekdays on public transport. In Sydney trams
reached their maximum patronage of all time in 1926, as did ferries
in 1927; but in both Sydney and Melbourne the subsequent decline
was due not only to cars, but also to the electrification of suburban
railways and the rapid growth of motor-bus services during the 1920s.
These tended to operate in the new outer suburbs beyond the reach of
tramlines. They were faster, and bus services could be routed more
adaptably than either trams or railways. Contrary to earlier policy,
most state governments were prepared to leave them in the hands of
private enterprise.

By bringing the beaches and the hills within easier access these
transport services extended the range of leisure activities. Until the
first decade of the century the beaches were underdeveloped, but
between 1900 and 1910 most of the by-laws against daytime bathing

Transport to Tambourine Mt, c. 1922

were repealed. The formation of the first surf clubs was followed within a few years by social acceptance of mixed bathing. For many Australians, particlarly among the younger women, the availability of sport and outdoor leisure became possible only with good public transport. The resulting social changes have yet to be fully explored. It seems certain that access to the beaches and the hills enabled many suburban families to visualise alternative environments to those in which they lived at present. This encouraged such families to dream of moving to a home in those pleasanter surroundings. The nourishing of those dreams would give a powerful impulse to the outward spread of Australia's big cities when prosperity came after the Second World War.

But the social sciences were still in their infancy, and nobody in authority thought about consulting the dreams of suburban Australia. It had always been a weakness of the town planning movement that it was seen as a question of educating the men in authority, so that politicians and bureaucrats would be persuaded to enforce enlightened standards of urban design on a receptive public. Thus it became inevitable that the town planning movement after generating such a promising start in the years before 1914 should wither away when other priorities gripped the attention of Australia's decision makers.

It could hardly be expected that much would be done to improve the quality of the Australian suburban public environment when those who lived there lacked opportunities to formulate their own tastes, let alone to mobilise themselves into effective pressure groups whose opinions required hearing. Without expectations of controlling their public environment the suburban Australians, like so many latter-day Candides, contented themselves with cultivating their own gardens.

12   Rural Australia, 1900–1945

Although most Australians lived in the suburbs many writers insisted on regarding suburban life as inherently inferior to farming. The happy ending came for C.J. Dennis's Sentimental Bloke not when he married his Doreen but when the two of them fell heirs to a small mixed farm and quit the inner suburbs for a productive and healthy life on the land: state governments saw it as their prime responsibility to encourage such settlers. Between 1890 and 1930 the area under agriculture quadrupled from 2 198 740 to 8 878 430 hectares, though during the same period the number of people engaged in primary production rose only from a little less than half a million to about 650 000.[1] The typical rural Australian was no longer the squatter or the stockman but the farmer. Although wool remained the biggest source of Australia's export income it was 1925 before Australia's sheep numbers recovered to the 100 million mark reached in 1890, and even after that two bad years of drought such as 1944–45 could pull the figure back below that level. Cattle numbers held up better— from 10.3 million in 1890 to 8.6 million in the drought-affected year 1900 and 14 million in 1934—but largely as a result of dairying.

In the pastoral industry technology changed slowly, and so did the working environment. In response to the deterioration of pastures on the frontages of natural watercourses pastoralists in most parts of Australia began to open up their back country by making dams. Following advocacy by H.C. Russell in 1879 pastoralists in Queensland and New South Wales sank artesian bores, and by 1901, 158 bores, some of them over a thousand metres deep, yielded 3.5 million millilitres daily. The development of these new pastures was not accompanied by much significant change in grazing practices. Sheep and cattle continued to trample and nibble vegetation adapted to the light grazing of migratory marsupials who changed their foraging with the seasons. Improved water often stimulated a population explosion among kangaroos and wallabies. Before long only the more hardy and drought-resistant vegetation survived. It was usually the least palatable.

In the more prosperous and well-watered parts of south-eastern
Australia, pasture improvement made considerable advances, such
as the spread of subterranean clover in the 1920s. In these regions the
pastoral landscape, already accepted as an authentic image of Australia, came to present an agreeable image of stability and continuity.
It was, for instance, not the least of Canberra's assets that it was
surrounded by grazing country of long standing where the elements of
the scenery were influenced but not overwhelmed by evidence of
cultivation and improvement—though there was also a good deal
of gullying and erosion. But probably most of Canberra's early
inhabitants merely saw their pastoral surroundings as an unwelcome
source of flies in summer.

Farming intensified and took many forms. 'Cow cockies' proliferated
in the medium- to high-rainfall country of Gippsland and the Western
District of Victoria, the Illawarra in New South Wales, Queensland's
Atherton Tableland, and the jarrah and karri country of Western
Australia. In Tasmania the entrepreneurial activities of Henry Jones,
the founder of IXL, gave a great boost to fruit growing. The Queensland cane sugar industry, having abandoned the plantation system
after the slump of the 1880s, was secured for smallfarming by the new
Commonwealth government's racial and tariff policies. But the major
crop was wheat. The first wave of settlement came between 1890 and
1914. Under the influence of superphosphate and the propagation of
new varieties of dry wheat, land was brought under the plough in the
250–500 mm rainfall areas of New South Wales, Western Australia,
the Eyre Peninsula and the Mallee. After the First World War expansion continued to find farms for returned servicemen and migrants.
But after the first decade little was done to improve the scientific
basis of wheat growing, except in the areas of disease resistance and
protein quality. Looking for payable crops many farmers subjected
their land to frequent cultivation interspersed by bare fallowing.
As a result the soil structure was often destroyed and fertility de-
creased.[2]

Not that the farmers lacked scientific advice. In the dozen years
before 1900 every government in Australia set up a Department of
Agriculture which included among its functions the spread of information about sound farming practices. By that time, starting with South
Australia's Roseworthy in 1882, agricultural colleges were established
in four of the six Australian colonies. Although the staff of these
colleges confronted the scepticism of the practical farmer for the
mere scientist, their findings were often given widespread publicity
through respected and influential journals such as the *Leader, Register,*

Queenslander and *Western Mail*; but their total influence is hard to guess. Later the application of science to primary production was given a great boost by the establishment of the Council for Scientific and Industrial Research in 1926.

Irrigation was the most widely appreciated gift bestowed on the farmer by technology. The first stirrings of official interest came in 1886 in Victoria when the young Alfred Deakin made his political name by legislation providing for the funding of irrigation projects and the reservation of access to watercourses for public use. With his encouragement the Chaffey brothers came from California to initiate Australia's first dried fruits industry by irrigation from the Murray at Mildura. Deakin's legislation led to the proliferation of many small irrigation authorities, and these were replaced in 1905 by the State Rivers and Water Supply Trust. The Victorian experience strengthened Australians in their faith in water conservation. One of the first initiatives of the new Commonwealth government in 1902 was to meet the appropriate state premiers at Corowa to discuss the allocation of Murray waters—ironically, since it was a year of parching drought when there was hardly any Murray. It was 1915 before agreement was finally reached, to be followed by the construction of the Hume reservoir and Lake Victoria.

Meanwhile the New South Wales government in 1912–15 built the Burrinjuck dam on the Murrumbidgee with the dual purpose of generating hydroelectricity and nurturing irrigation settlements for fruit growing at Leeton and Griffith. This was an achievement which for about a year in 1916–17 had no less a publicist than Henry Lawson, sent to Leeton as a last resort to dry out and earn a little money. Lawson's letter to a young Anzac serving overseas in the First World War gives an eloquent illustration of what irrigation meant to many Australians of that generation:

> . . . It is a spread of green, all chequered off, with little homes, and trees, and clear, green-fringed canals and channels—just like English brooks—you've seen them—set in the midst of a bare, scorching, dusty, red, and parched yellow Dead Land that's a lot older than Egypt. You've seen Egypt—Desert, Nile, and oasis? Well!

'The nights here are like the Breath of Paradise and look like it', he added, ' . . . the way the fruit trees and vines grow and bear is a miracle out of the Bible.'[3] It was a good theme for Australia's foremost writer, since in a dry continent the need for water conservation was one of the most essential lessons in environmental management for the Australian people to learn. Rural Australia learned the lesson well. It was only among metropolitan users of water that waste would eventually present the prospect of serious problems.

If farmers remained sceptical about scientific advice on improvements in their own farming methods, they were prepared to applaud scientific achievements in the area of pest control. The paradigm case was prickly pear. By 1925 nearly 25 million hectares of Queensland and northern New South Wales were pear infested, and there seemed no good reason why its spread should not continue indefinitely. If all the cattle in Australia were fed on prickly pear, calculated one scientist, they would only be able to keep down the natural increase without making inroads on existing infestation.[4] But Queensland and Commonwealth scientists were on the lookout for an insect predator which would check its spread. In 1914 the American cacto-blastis was tried experimentally, without marked success. But in 1925 a second attempt was made, and this time the results were dramatic. Within five years nearly all the infested country was cleared, and despite minor recurrences since, the pest has remained permanently under control. Encouraged, the Queensland authorities then moved on in the 1930s to introduce South American toads as similarly efficient predators on insect pests in the sugar cane industry. This was less successful, and the toads themselves became regarded as an unlovely nuisance and a menace to small fauna.

Agricultural scientists tended to be damned when they brought bad news and praised only when they brought good. In Western Australia experts were derided when in 1929 their use of scientific soil analysis showed that poor crop results in some marginal wheatbelt districts were due to excess salinity. A few years later some of the same men met general acclaim for their discovery that the poor performance of long-settled districts near the south coast was caused by deficiencies in trace elements such as cobalt and copper, which might be made good. Salinity on the other hand was an expensive and complex problem which would continue to grow during the following half century; it was understandable that farmers and politicians did not want to hear about it. Such attitudes were one of the strongest impediments to environmental reform. They were well to the fore in the story of soil erosion.

Like their fathers before them the pioneers of the new farming districts cleared the land with indiscriminate zeal, spurred by the urge to render every acre productive and to leave no sanctuary for vermin such as wallabies and rabbits. Soil erosion and salt creep were the consequences. Both took some decades to be recognised as calling for action. Sand drift was noted in the Victorian Mallee as early as

1878, and in 1892 a correspondent in the *Victorian Naturalist* wrote of districts where bare dunes overwhelmed pasture formerly covered with she-oaks and blackwoods.[5] In 1917 the Victorian ministry for public works set up a committee to prepare a report on the effects of erosion, but nothing followed. Meanwhile the Mallee was being taken up by wheat farmers who were slow to recognise that the practices which had served them well in the Wimmera were not suited to the new environment. 'The rotational system of burn, fallow, crop, and burn again'[6] exhausted the humus in the soil, and pressure of debt led the farmers to resort to over-frequent cropping. The resulting sand drifts flowed over the roads and railway lines and blocked irrigation channels.

Yet when Victoria's premier was taken on a tour of the Mallee in 1935 to investigate the damage he asserted unblushingly: 'I saw no erosion there'. This was no ignorant city dweller but a shrewd farmer of lifelong experience, Albert Dunstan. The Melbourne press dubbed him 'Albert the Ostrich' since they said the only way he could miss seeing the sand was by burying his head in it. But there was some evidence which even an ostrich could not swallow. In Gippsland the

Sand drift, Broken Hill 1930
Reproduced with permission from the Public Transport Commission of NSW

rivers were becoming gorged with sediment because of the lack of clearing control in their catchment areas. The Water Commission of Victoria spent over £100 000 in 1933 clearing sand from watercourses and irrigation channels. That was a substantial piece of taxpayers' money. Dunstan was obliged to consent to the appointment of a government commission of inquiry in 1937–38.

This inquiry spelt out a serious problem. Its findings were reinforced by an important symposium of surveyors, engineers and agricultural scientists in 1939. Even then it took strenuous pressure, notably from Harold Henslow, the Country party nominee on the Water Commission, before Dunstan yielded and in 1940 brought down legislation to set up a Soil Conservation Board. Yet Dunstan was as resilient as Mr Toad of Toad Hall. In the summer of early 1945 when wind erosion once again became bad in the Mallee and it rained red dust on Mount Hotham, he was still making light of the problem. 'The Mallee is Paradise' he told a newspaper reporter.[7] He was by no means the only farmer-politician whose faith blinded him to the unpleasant realities of the human impact on the Australian environment.

Other states tackled the problem more energetically. In the late 1920s and 1930s complaints grew rife in Sydney about the heavy dust storms thrown up by the summer westerlies. The public at large came to realise that much of the New South Wales wheatbelt's topsoil was being steadily blown out across the Tasman.[8] In 1933 a government committee was set up to monitor the problem, and in 1938 a soil conservation service was created to survey its extent. More than half the State's area was surveyed by 1942. Of that area nearly half was to some extent affected by erosion, but it was claimed that only 480 700 hectares (about 1 per cent of the surveyed area) was ruined beyond redemption.[9] In South Australia an act of parliament was passed as early as 1923 and some valuable work was done in the 1930s by Francis Ratcliffe, whose *Flying Fox and Drifting Sand*[10] first alerted the wider reading public to the impact of soil erosion, and achieved the status of a minor classic.

The responsibility for salt creep was harder to assign. In Western Australia the increasing salinity of rivers in the fertile South-West was noted in the early years of the century. By 1924 this tendency was linked with the clearing of native vegetation in the wheatgrowing districts at their headwaters. Yet wholesale clearing continued unchecked, and this led in time not only to deterioration in most of the region's few freshwater rivers, but also to the spread of salt creep. On the other hand the spread of the problem in the Yass district of New South Wales was associated with heavy rain rather than clearing.

Clearing on steep slopes creates the hazard of erosion
From C.J. Lloyd, *The National Estate: Australia's Heritage*, Cassell, Stanmore, 1977

Where experts disagreed it was hard to persuade governments and farmers to embark on remedial action.[11]

The clearing of land for farms also intensified competition between people and the original fauna of the habitat. In some regions this hastened the process of extinction. The tammar and toolache wallabies of South Australia, still common at the turn of the century, were no longer to be found in 1930 after thirty years of closer settlement. But the larger species of kangaroo survived, bred and competed for pasture. In the wheat districts of South and Western Australia emus appeared in plague proportions every few years, as in 1927–29 and 1932. They flattened fences and spoiled crops so that in 1932 farmers in the eastern wheatbelt of Western Australia went to the lengths of demanding a detachment of army machine-gunners to slaughter the invaders. The emu regiment withdrew without many casualties.[12]

Closer settlement may also have affected the balance of nature so as to stimulate smaller predators. Grasshoppers and locusts were bad in several seasons around 1890 in New South Wales and Victoria. 'The locusts have arrived' wrote the Welsh swagman William Evans at Maldon in December 1890;

> The train was unable to run through the swarm. They were so thick as to cover the rails and become greasy.[13]

On several occasions—1906, 1916–17, 1930, 1947—South Australia and western Victoria were afflicted with plagues of mice. In four months in 1917, 32 million mice weighing 553 tonnes were destroyed in South Australia.[14] But the most persistent pests continued to be introduced exotics such as the rabbit and the fox, which both extended their habitats during the first quarter of the twentieth century to cover practically the whole of subtropical Australia.

The impact of early twentieth century farming on the Australian environment is hard to assess. C.R. Twidale and his colleagues in South Australia have shown how the clearing of mallee scrub at Kappakoola Swamp in 1916 started the formation of bare dunes which have steadily encroached on the surroundings.[15] But they also point out that the north-western Eyre Peninsula, until 1910 a prickly-grassed stony scrubby 'desert', improved beyond recognition with the coming of settlers and a railway. The railway tanks attracted run-off from the granite rocks and formed the basis for a system of reticulation, and after the Second World War the introduction of pasture legumes such as medicagos made a lasting improvement in fertility. They concluded that 'for the success of transformation of the landscape it is not sufficient for a technology merely to be available, there must be sufficient incentive for it to be applied.[16] Specifically, a government-provided infrastructure was required for optimum agricultural development.

The new rural communities seldom shared common origins like the German Lutherans of the Barossa Valley or the Irish settlements in the Darling Downs or the Western District of Victoria. Often in districts such as the Mallee, the Murrumbidgee Irrigation Area or the Western Australian wheatbelt the government allocated blocks of land in order of application and settlers became neighbours by the luck of the draw. Sense of community grew up around the small country towns which came into being along the railway lines at distances of 25 to 30 kilometres—horse-and-buggy radius. Each of these settlements was equipped by the government with a post office, a police station and a primary school. In lobbying for these amenities the first generation of settlers developed a corporate sense of identity. Football fields, golf links and tennis courts followed as symbols of co-operative effort.

The main street, with its wide footpaths and post-supported verandas, was the main forum for business and the exchange of news and gossip. Farming families would come in from outside the town with fairly precise knowledge of when and where they might expect to meet other individuals going about their business down the street. In the late 1930s a pioneer sociologist spent an afternoon on market day in a Victorian country town noting the activities of the people in the main street. Only eleven out of ninety were alone. Sixteen were walking in groups and the other sixty-three were standing and talking. Of twenty-three cars parked in the street, twelve were empty, ten were occupied by more than one person conversing, and only one had a solitary occupant.[17] This showed the extent to which the street provided a useful public environment for country dwellers. It was one of the marks of a city's growth when the streets became too crowded for sociable loitering.

Country towns were for use rather than ornament, and their appearance showed it. Most shires planted suitably hardy trees such as sugar gums or pepper trees for shade in their main streets, but except in regions of relatively high rainfall their improvements could not go much further. The sale yards, the sporting oval, the showground and the rifle range were the limits of initiative expected of local authorities. Farmer ratepayers were quick to question the motives of shire councils who spent too much on the amenities of country towns. Little would be spent on ornament apart from the universal war memorial: usually an Anzac at attention to honour the fallen, but sometimes a cenotaph or clock tower. It was not until after the Second World War that hospitals, swimming pools or libraries came to be seen as acceptable war memorials.

A few country towns had more. Some such as Camperdown in the Western District of Victoria had the fortune to be endowed with a pleasant park through the munificence of neighbouring pastoralists. Others, such as Grafton, made a special feature of jacarandas, or some similarly ornamental tree or shrub. A few, such as Katanning in Western Australia, erected a statue in the main street in memory of a local lion. These variations on the basic theme were not imitated by the ruck of country towns. For them progress was measured understandably in the accumulation of amenities.

From around 1910 many country towns boasted electricity locally generated by a wood- or coal-burning plant and sometimes combined with an iceworks. Diesel fuel was brought in during the 1930s, but these schemes were seldom extended far among neighbouring farms. Scheme water was connected to about 300 Australian country towns by 1930, and visitors to a community enjoying this blessing seldom escaped the ritual of a visit to admire the local dam. Most country towns in the 1920s had better access to a local newspaper and a local medical practitioner than they had known in 1890 or than they would enjoy in 1980.

These improvements shed some reflection on the quality of life for farming families, but generally their conditions were slower to improve. A.J. Rose has estimated that:

> Through the inland and margins of the wheat belt of eastern Australia in 1911 any locality was likely to have from a tenth to a quarter of all its habitations walled with cloth. In some areas corrugated iron was used in a similar role and in the South Australian Mallee at that time a fifth of all houses used iron for walling.[18]

Later, if the farmer prospered, these makeshifts would be replaced by a timber house with a corrugated iron roof. Often the materials and instructions were sent out from the city by one of the major timber retailing companies, and the farmer or a local tradesman would do the rest. This meant that rural architecture was largely standardised, with little possibility of regional variations.

Another index of improving living standards could be seen in the fact that from 1920 the number of horses employed in the country districts began to fall. This reflected the shift as more and more farmers bought tractors. Others ventured on the ownership of model T Fords or utilities, rather to the detriment of the unsealed roads. The introduction of better suspension and balloon tires during the 1920s tended to cause corrugations. Very few country roads were bitumened before the Second World War; when the Americans quickly constructed a bitumen highway from Darwin to Alice Springs under the pressures of 1942, it was regarded as an unprecedented feat of highway engineering.

Given the dominant urge among many farmers to pass on their properties to their sons, it might have been thought that an Australian rural environment of some stability and permanence was coming into being. But then came the depression of the 1930s. Rural Australia was plunged into a decade of crisis from which it emerged only to be confronted by the shortages of the Second World War. The depression exposed the basic fallacy on which much rural development was based. Most politicians counted the success of agriculture in terms of the number of families wresting a full-time living from the soil. But it had never been decided whether the aim of rural policy was to get families out of the cities and settled on the land, or whether the object was the increase of productivity to secure maximum export income.

The question was seldom put this way because many politicians believed that maximum productivity would come from putting the maximum number of farmers on the land. But this was a fallacy. Even around the turn of the century when farming was comparatively labour intensive, agricultural planners tended to underestimate the amount of land required for a successful farm unit. With the gradual growth of mechanisation the smallholding steadily declined in comparative efficiency. 'Closer settlement' too often resulted in families trying to make a living on areas too small for profitable farming. Short of capital, anxious to break even, they were pushed into exploiting the land recklessly, leaving a legacy of long-term environmental damage.

Between 1930 and 1945 the depression and the war meant that improvement stood still in many regions of rural Australia. In the long run this may have led to greater efficiency. Marginal wheat farmers walked off the land; successful dairy farmers absorbed the cattle and property of their weaker neighbours. To the extent that larger and better capitalised farmers might in time be able to practise farming methods which made for sounder conservation, it could even be argued that the depression was a harsh medicine forcing Australian farming to upgrade its techinques. But such benefits were long term and uncertain. In the short term, leaving aside the considerable record of human misery, the depression and the war meant that for at least fifteen years it was virtually impossible to find the means for stopping the unwise exploitation of the Australian soil. On the contrary, the need to stay solvent forced many to flog the country and spend as little as possible on improvements.

As for most country towns, the depression stunted their growth at a point where they had not reached the capacity to attain economic take-off or to develop any role except that of service centre to local farmers. They were not market towns in the classic European sense of the word, places where traders exchanged local produce. Nor, apart from one or two exceptional instances such as the Fletcher Jones trouser manufactory in Warrnambool, had they generated specialist industries. And from 1930 their future as local service centres was shadowed first by the shortages of the depression and the war, then by the certainty that long-distance motor transport would render many of them obsolete. The stage was being set for an acceleration of the drift to the cities, and for the draining of much of the vigour of Australia's rural environment.

13 Affluent Society

Since 1945 Australia's cities have undergone a major period of crisis and transformation, and Australia's rural areas have been affected as never before by the consequences of urban growth. In common with most of the western democracies Australia emerged from the Second World War with some sense of official commitment to building a better society in which some of the more glaring inequalities of the prewar depression would be reformed. Few saw the care of the environment as an urgent priority, and many thought conservation stood in the way of progress. Old buildings were often regarded as outworn relics of a colonial past which in no way shared the elegance of the 'real' past enshrined in the stately homes of England. Thus a Sydney report of the mid-1940s saw no case for retaining Greenway's Hyde Park barracks and their survival was due largely to good luck. As for the natural environment the attitude of the twenty years after 1945 has been summed up by Clem Lloyd:

> The residue of the past was swept away by a tide of modern enterprise, conditioned by beliefs that Australia's natural environment was infinite, and that as a young country its man-made fabric was not worth preserving.[1]

The more urgent need was seen by reformers as the provision of decent housing in a reasonable urban environment. Because of the depression and the war new building was restricted between 1930 and 1945, though the later 1930s saw a revival in the building of blocks of flats, especially in Sydney. The building industry nevertheless lacked opportunities to train enough newcomers in the skills of its trades, so that by 1945 there was a serious shortage of qualified labour. Much older housing had been allowed to deteriorate. The return of the ex-servicemen and the resulting boom in marriages and young families could be expected to create heavy demand. Between 1945 and 1970 Australia also made a net gain of 2 million migrants. Although official policy encouraged migrants to live in rural areas, and in the case of the 'displaced persons' of the late 1940s actively coerced them, most found their way to the cities where they sought as assiduously as any native Australian to acquire their own homes.

Such an upsurge of demand called for a major rethinking of public policy. Either credit facilities for wouldbe homebuyers would need to be liberalised and made more flexible than in the past, or else a massive intervention would be required on the part of state governments and other public authorities to provide low-cost housing. It has been argued that the latter policy would have resulted in dramatically lower costs for householders by sparing them cumulative interest charges, insurance costs, and profits taken by real estate vendors and finance companies.[2] But the value of owning one's own home was a belief entrenched in far too many Australians to be overthrown by economic theorising.

In a society which viewed property as an extension of personality, home ownership gave at least an appearance of choice about the environment with which people surrounded themselves and their families. A highly competitive real estate business offered Australian families a choice of suburban addresses, and merchandisers vied to offer them possessions to furnish their houses. If their taste was mainly derivative and conformist this in no way sullied their pride of possession. Home ownership was commonly regarded as a safeguard against economic insecurity in old age, and if the payment of a twenty-year mortgage was the means of attaining that goal few Australians begrudged the banks and building societies their profits from the process. Given the widespread prevalence of these attitudes, it was surprising that government in the 1940s ventured as far as they did in the business of providing houses.

The initiative came, a little surprisingly, from South Australia, Here a Liberal Country League government, enjoying that special stability which comes of a really efficient gerrymander, held office continually from 1933 to 1965. Its leaders, (Sir) Richard Butler and (Sir) Thomas Playford, although no great social reformers, were not inhibited by traditional conservative misgivings about increased government intervention. When in 1936 the South Australian government set up a State Housing Trust to provide subsidised low-rental housing for its workers, its motive was not simply concern for the underdog but a wish to attract investment in secondary industry.[3] By providing cheap housing and thus keeping down living costs, South Australia not unreasonably hoped to lure industrial investors from its older established rivals in New South Wales and Victoria. The State Housing Trust barely got into its stride when the outbreak of the Second World War brought its operations to a virtual standstill. The South Australian example was nevertheless a model for others. In New South Wales, where a 'house famine' had been forecast as far back as the 1920s, the McKell government formed a Housing Commission in 1941, though here too the war ruled out further progress.

The Commonwealth government under Curtin and Chifley (1941–49) strongly favoured a national housing policy. During the war, and for as long afterwards as the courts permitted, rent control was imposed as a price-fixing measure. In August 1944 a report for the Department of Postwar Reconstruction recommended that about half the new housing required after the war should be government built. Perhaps helped by the unusual circumstance that all the state governments except South Australia were Labor, the Commonwealth government in 1945 introduced legislation to ratify a federal-state agreement on housing. Although unable to fund directly any home-building projects, the Commonwealth offered the states financial assistance to build houses either for cheap rental or for purchase.

Non-Labor spokesmen stated a preference for making cheap loans available through banks and other existing financial institutions, thus encouraging Australians to buy their own homes. This stung Dedman into asserting that it was not intended to make Australians 'little capitalists'.[4] His candour was unwise, and pointed to a defect which was to dog the reputation of state housing in Australia. If State Housing Commission dwellings were not meant for 'little capitalists', most Australians concluded they were not meant for them.

This impression was reinforced because most land zoned for State Housing Commission purposes tended to be situated in the less attractive suburbs on Crown land not previously found presentable enough for alternative use. Following the South Australian example most housing authorities preferred to situate workers' houses fairly close to their places of employment, and this usually meant lower-income areas not far from the industrial suburbs. Those who occupied State Housing Commission houses were often the less affluent members of society: blue-collar workers without the ability to save, itinerants, deserted mothers, recent migrants, in later years sometimes urban Aborigines. They were groups for the most part inexperienced in asserting their rights, lacking political strength, and without first-hand experience of good quality housing.

State housing authorities compromised uneasily between architects who wanted to adopt new planning ideas and Treasury officials intent on protecting public money. State Housing Commission estates were sometimes among the first to lay down street plans with cul-de-sacs and guided traffic flow; but the design of houses was often mediocre and unimaginative, and did little to avert the growth of serious social problems in some estates.

Postwar shortages of building materials fostered a rather stark and monotonous architectural style, without porches, verandas or spacious extras. The pressure mounted to build houses of any kind; in May 1947, for instance, the New South Wales government committed itself to building 90 000 houses in three years. Nor was there much to commend in most of the private housing erected between 1948 and 1951. The shortage of skilled tradesmen and materials, the consequent 'do-it-yourself' movement, the pressure of demand in an inflationary era, the absence of new ideas from a war-torn Europe, all made for mediocrity.

From this unfortunate start the pattern of urban growth in postwar Australia never really recovered. In the thirty years after 1945 each of Australia's state capitals was to double in population. While the city centres remained more or less identical with those of earlier times, their carrying capacity increased greatly because of high-rise building. Banks, insurance companies and other financial and industrial organisations sought to capitalise on the rising costs of urban property by tearing down their headquarters and replacing them with office blocks thirty or forty storeys high. It was curious that in an era depending on telecommunications city firms had to concentrate in the same few streets as they had in the days when office boys ran messages from one business to another and their seniors met in the street for a yarn and a stroll; but even government departments refused to take initiatives in decentralisation. The central blocks of Australia's major cities became noisy canyons dominated by the impersonal strength of the tower blocks in which the country's finance and industry were planned.

Industry deserted the city centres. Zoning policies favoured the concentration of factories and industrial developments in specific localities: thus in Sydney the southern suburbs around Kingsford Smith airport and Botany Bay took the heaviest industrial use. South Australia pioneered the notion of concentrating industry and worker housing in a specifically designed satellite city, and so Elizabeth, 17 kilometres to the north of Adelaide, was established in 1954. At about the same time Western Australia decided to site heavy industry at Kwinana on Cockburn Sound, believing that access to port facilities offset the inconvenience of locating a major source of industrial pollutants in the path of the summer south-westerly which cooled

Perth's afternoons. Victoria authorised a similar development at Westernport. Such industrial complexes usually employed a large migrant workforce, who lived either in State Housing Commission suburbs erected nearby—and hence far from the city centre—or else at a distance which required the worker of the household to monopolise the family car, leaving the rest of the family to the uncertainties of public transport.

And public transport deteriorated. In every major Australian city except Melbourne the trams and trolley buses were taken out of commission between 1950 and 1970, and bus services ran less frequently. Workers lived increasingly at a distance from their place of employment. A survey of the early 1970s suggested an average journey to work of 9.4 kilometres in Sydney and 12 kilometres in Melbourne —the need was felt for every family to own its own car. By 1970 the streets of Australian cities carried five times the number of cars there were in 1945. This not only placed the authorities with the problems of organising and building new road systems, often involving freeways which ripped the heart out of long-established inner-suburban precincts; it also, in J.M. Freeland's words, 'caused mutations to existing types of building as well as the rise of entirely new types'.[5] Service stations proliferated along every major road. Multistorey buildings were provided near the city centres exclusively for the parking of vehicles. The corner store and the corner pub gave place to the supermarket and the drive-in hotels, each surrounded by an arid acreage of bitumen. Tradesmen ceased to deliver to private homes, and the character of shopping expeditions changed. Women drove, if they were lucky enough to have access to a car, or walked (accompanied often by preschool children) to a large impersonal arena where they fetched their own purchases from the shelves and propelled them in shopping trolleys past check-out girls too busy for conversation. As the pattern of supermarkets and shopping complexes standardised, every new suburban centre began to look like every other. Even the advertisement hoardings were the same.

Thus, having been checked during the 1930s depression and the war, the suburban sprawl resumed and accelerated. These pressures forced politicians and the public belatedly to pay greater attention to town planning and environmental control. The 1940s were the first time that more government expenditure was channelled into urban than into rural areas, a trend which has since continued. But decisions on urban growth were taken in a piecemeal fashion, responding to the stimulus of immediate emergencies. The consequences were seldom without environmental fault.

An exception was Canberra, the federal capital. Here the population increased tenfold after 1945; but because this change simply spanned an increase from 20 000 to 200 000, and because growth took place under the supervision of a single planning authority enjoying adequate funding, the outcome was on the whole beneficial. From justly meriting the jibe 'six suburbs in search of a city', Canberra improved to provide a comely environment for dwellers in the national capital. Critics complained of its dominance by the car, forgetting that it was the only Australian city planned with the car in mind; they bemoaned its lack of industry or of ethnic character. A neighbouring grazier commented in 1970: 'I think Canberra is satisfactory in that it fulfills what most Australians want and I think it is as dull as bloody hell'.[6]

New South Wales provided the greatest disappointment. In 1947 the State government took Sydney's local authorities by the scruff of the neck and coerced them into accepting the creation of the Cumberland County Council. It was intended that the new body would co-ordinate planning throughout the metropolitan area, curbing the suburban sprawl, ensuring a balance of industrial and residential development, and preserving rural enclaves within easy access of the built-up districts. Its achievements were miserably disappointing. Developers and local authorities failed to co-operate. The state government lost interest, its withdrawal of support being symbolised in 1953 when it overruled the Cumberland County Council's decision on the siting of an oil refinery. Although the Council survived until its replacement by a State Planning Authority in 1963 its effectiveness had gone years earlier.

The result was that the western suburbs of Sydney exploded in a limitless sprawl, edging out towards the Blue Mountains, obliterating market gardens and open spaces, and encompassing old-established centres such as Parramatta. Decisions about the location and features of new subdivisions were left in the hands of the developers. Since the major offices, business houses, and academic institutions stayed close to the old heart of the city within a few kilometres of Sydney Cove, this meant that the metropolitan area grew increasingly lopsided, with the majority of inhabitants lacking convenient access to these central amenities.[7]

Some responded by moving back close to the centre. The run-down inner suburbs, for long stigmatised as slums, were discovered by young couples of slender means but middle-class tastes. Thus Paddington's reputation changed over twenty years. In 1948 the Cumberland Planning Scheme described the area as 'wholly substandard, requiring replacement'. In 1958 a City of Sydney Planning Scheme called for its major redevelopment. The plan called for the pulling down of rows of rather cramped and near derelict terrace houses and replacing them with very much more cramped blocks of flats, with no increase in street widths, or green space, or playgrounds, or school facilities. A cosy, human old slum was being replaced by a cruel new one. Yet in 1968 Paddington was described as a 'special area of architectural and historic interest', with a lively Paddington Society devoted to its preservation as an urban amenity. Paddington was becoming too expensive for the young and upward-mobile, They were being compelled to look at less fashionable run-down areas such as Balmain and Glebe.

Other cities followed the Sydney pattern. In Melbourne the East Melbourne Society, founded in 1954, took the lead in lobbying for the rehabilitation of an inner city area, though in the case of East Melbourne they had a district which had contrived to retain vestiges of nineteenth-century elegance more successfully than any of its Sydney equivalents. By the mid-1960s the former slums of Fitzroy and South Melbourne were attracting middle-class buyers. Meanwhile city retailers, afraid of losing customers to the suburbs, embarked on the establishment of shopping malls such as Chadstone.

The suburbs spread like squeezed toothpaste. The local authorities abandoned any pretence of providing bitumen roads before subdivision. Instead, home builders in the new suburbs had to wait several years before the coming of made roads and guttering, and then these were provided at the expense of the householders. Sewerage also lagged far behind the suburban spread. Most householders installed septic tanks, but nightcarts were still operating in the suburbs in the 1960s. In Brisbane, by contrast, although suburban growth was also extensive, the Brisbane City Council set itself the target during the 1960s of providing main sewerage to nearly all households, and by 1970 could boast a success rate of 95 per cent. No other Australian city could claim nearly as much.

The smaller Australian major cities girdled their middle-aged spread with slightly greater success. In Perth the commissioning of the Stephenson-Hepburn plan in 1955 committed the city to a policy of growth along a corridor plan, stringing development out along freeways and other major highways and access routes, and leaving substantial areas zoned for agriculture and recreational use. Adelaide also endeavoured to develop plans for future growth, spurred by the realisation that water supply might become a problem for a community with the lowest rainfall of any major Australian city. It was not until after 1965 that a succession of reform-minded governments commissioned the State Planning Authority to undertake a major transport study, restricted the spread of high-rise building, and set a target for Adelaide of a maximum population of 1.3 million. In an era when the average Australian city dweller consumed over 400 litres of water daily, such prudence was commendable, but it was confined to Adelaide. No other Australian city set any restriction on its size. Most politicians considered that the difficulty of telling people where they should live outweighed any amount of social problems caused by excessive city growth.

Yet the drift from the country continued inexorably. The depression of the 1930s and the Second World War drove many families off the land and condemned most of the others to fifteen years of stagnation without the capacity for improving their properties. With the wool boom of 1948–51 and the coming of prosperity the alternatives confronting many primary producers were 'to get big or to get out'. Because of mechanisation and the increasing sophistication of technology, farms and pastoral properties required heavier investment, consolidation into larger units, and less manpower. The farming districts were no longer the potential home of a bold yeomanry but an increasingly efficient workshop of large-scale rural capitalism.

Better education and the experience of the Second World War converted many of the younger generation of farm owners into keen advocates of mechanisation; it was through his enterprising use of new technology that Joh Bjelke-Petersen first distinguished himself among the farmers of Kingaroy.[8] In an era of relatively cheap petrol farmers invested in heavier and more complex farm machinery, abandoning the horse and the crops of oats that fed it. They adapted the four-wheel drive vehicles of jungle warfare for cross-country rural travel. Some used light aircraft and motor cycles for mustering; others welcomed the use of aviation and pesticides in crop dusting, though the lavish use of such innovations as DDT took heavy toll of native birds, as well as having unpredictable side effects on the human ecology.

Pastures were enriched by the use of subterranean clover, which although advocated as early as 1907 and spread during the 1920s, came into its own only after the Second World War. The discovery in the 1930s of the role of trace elements such as cobalt and copper enabled new farming districts to open up in the marginal lands of South and Western Australia. Pastoralists benefited further in the early 1950s when, after a chapter of delays and misadventures, myxomatosis at last provided a lethal agent of biological warfare

Wheat harvesting mid twentieth century
Reproduced with permission of the Public Transport Commission of NSW

against the rabbit. Perhaps eighty per cent of Australia's rabbit population went to an unpleasant extermination, and although surviving colonies developed considerable immunity they were never such persistent competitors for grazing.

Because of improved transport and technology the commercial slaughter of unprotected fauna went on with improved efficiency. In the seas whaling fleets hunted the humpback whale until in 1977, after years of international protest and despite the angry determination of the Western Australian government to uphold the whaling industry, the last whaling station ceased its operations because the kill no longer warranted the cost and the unpopularity. In inland Australia a continuing demand by the manufacturers of pet food for suburban dogs and cats stimulated hunters to kill thousands of kangaroos, as well as performing a more useful eradication of feral donkeys and goats. These activities eventually attracted the attention of a committee of the Commonwealth Senate in 1971–72, as a result of which recommendations were drawn up to regulate the killing of native fauna.[10] Of course the need to protect threatened species such as the koala and the platypus was by now widely recognised, but commoner species such as the grey and red kangaroo were still a subject of controversy. Graziers still saw them as a pest; conservationists (especially Americans) sometimes demanded their total protection. Between these two extremes the Senate committee's recommendations seemed to steer a sensible compromise.

Motor transport was the great agent of transformation in the rural environment. To compete with the railways producers increasingly used trucks for marketing. Country roads were sealed and upgraded, and car-owning families could cover a greatly extended range of travel. They were no longer dependent on the nearest township, but increasingly took their business to the city or to the largest of the neighbouring country towns. Many country townships accordingly stood still or decayed. Those that prospered tended to grow increasingly standardised in their appearance—their stores, their service stations, their places of recreation assimilating to the suburban model. When mining companies took the responsibility for housing their employees in the tropical parts of Queensland and the North-West their company towns made various concessions to the heat, but essentially they followed the same suburban model. Even the new homesteads of farmers and graziers often abandoned the traditional verandas for a replica of the brick-and-tile bungalows of the metropolis.

After twenty years postwar economic growth Australians gradually became aware of voices calling for concern for the quality of their environment. To some extent this concern, like so much Australian thinking in the 1960s, was derived from an American model. Works such as Rachel Carson's *The Silent Spring* and reports indicating the appalling pollution of waterways such as Lake Erie roused Americans to question the benefits of technological change and led in time to the formation of environmentalist lobbies, pressure groups and organisations such as the Friends of the Earth. In Australia public reactions were slower to surface. Australians lacked the tradition of political activism which drew many middle-class Americans into protest movements, and the myth of limitless resources still seduced many.

When an environmental movement began to surface in Australia its concerns took three forms. Some of its partisans, building on the established tradition of nature conservation, looked for stronger action to preserve Australia's remaining wilderness areas and the habitats of native fauna. Others began to see a value in the buildings left by earlier generations, and to throw their weight behind the State branches of the National Trust established during the 1950s. To these respectable and essentially conservative movements a third was added: the environmentalists who sought to arrest and diminish the spread of industrial and urban pollution, even where such measures would conflict with the claims of economic development. These developments were to give a controversial bite to the environmental movement during the 1970s.

14 Rescue Operations

The Australian Conservation Foundation was set up in October 1965. Among its virtues the Foundation established the credibility of the environmental movement as a cause who members were not all trendy radicals and subversives. Its foundation president was Sir Garfield Barwick, chief justice of the Australian Commonwealth and formerly a Liberal attorney general, but also a long-term trustee of the Kosciusko national park and a public sceptic about the virtues of unlimited economic growth. He was later succeeded by the Duke of Edinburgh.

Standing outside partisan politics, the Australian Conservation Foundation commanded wide support as a lobbying organisation capable of mobilising public opinion. From 1968 it enjoyed federal funding and embarked upon the publication of a journal, *Ecos*, and other occasional papers. Perhaps encouraged by this example, and in any case responding to rising public interest, South Australia, Victoria and Western Australia each set up an Environmental Planning Authority between 1969 and 1971 and Tasmania appointed a Director of Environmental Control. The Commonwealth government created a junior ministry in 1971. New South Wales got its Planning and Environment Commission in 1974. Queensland made do with an Environmental Control Council consisting of representatives from nineteen departments; its powers were confined to initiating investigations and attempting to co-ordinate the work of state and local authorities. The Western Australian authority showed the potential of such bodies by successfully recommending against the establishment of an alumina refinery in the vineyard country of the Swan valley in 1971, but it remained debatable how far state governments would consider themselves bound by the advice of their statutory watchdogs.

Because of its status as an independent foundation the Australian Conservation Foundation could go further in campaigning against specific threats to areas of environmental value. From 1969 it began to throw its weight into various environmental controversies, sometimes to the annoyance of state politicians. In that year the government of Victoria proposed to throw open the Little Desert region in the far west of that state for subdivision into fifty farms. As the area had been recommended by the Wimmera Regional Committee for reservation as a pristine habitat and was in any case of very marginal economic potential, the scheme had little to commend it, but the Victorian government defended its decision with great obstinacy.

The Australian Conservation Foundation spoke out in opposition. The Melbourne *Age*, then under the editorship of a great crusading journalist, Graham Perkin, took up the cudgels. Day after day the *Age* featured the threat to the Little Desert, drawing the anger of the Victorian minister for lands by revealing that two of his close relatives stood to benefit from the proposal. Grudgingly the Victorian government first modified the plan and then dropped it. At the next election the minister for lands was one of the very few members of his party to lose his seat; but the premier, Sir Henry Bolte, heeded the lesson, campaigned on a 'quality of life' platform, and later introduced an environmental protection act.[1]

Between 1969 and 1975 the Australian Conservation Foundation played watchdog on many controversial schemes for the development of natural resources, usually minerals. Its most sustained campaign sought to protect the Great Barrier Reef against the triple threat of overuse by tourists, exploitation for oil drilling and the ravages of the crown-of-thorns starfish. Other controversies arose over the preservation of wilderness areas such as Cooloola, Colong Caves, and Myall Lakes.

In 1974 the Foundation was well to the fore in opposing the mining of mineral sands on Fraser Island, off the Queensland coast near Maryborough. Against the anguished protests of the Queensland government and local developers the Commonwealth government proclaimed protection over most of Fraser Island, including all the most ecologically vulnerable portions and excluding only the sections already under exploitation. It was reported at the time that the whole island would have been placed under protection except for the protests of the minister for energy, Rex Connor, who threatened to resign over the issue: an interesting stand by one who has gone down in folklore as the arch-enemy of the mining companies. It was also notable that the Fraser government upheld the Whitlam ministry's decision after it came to power.

Not all environmental issues could be seen as pitting a public concerned for its amenities against a profit-motivated developer.

Sand mining Myall Lakes
From C.J. Lloyd, *The National Estate: Australia's Heritage*, Cassell, Stanmore, 1977

Towards the end of 1970 the Clutha Development Corporation, owners of the Illawarra district's largest coal mines, planned to build a private railway leading to a dump and loader and then along a pier from which the coal could be shipped to Japan. This proposal aroused opposition from conservation groups who feared for the deterioration of local beaches, the scarring of the Illawarra cliffs and the creation of a dust problem at the dump. It was predictable that the protesters should find support from conservationists in Sydney, and that the New South Wales government of the day would support Clutha's scheme. It was noticeable, however, that many local trade unionists supported the scheme because it would safeguard jobs, regardless of the Labour Party's opposition on environmental grounds. On the other hand some Liberals were antagonised when Clutha proposed to extend its mining operations into the Blue Mountains. The firm was seen as insensitive to local pride in popular beauty spots. Others disliked Clutha's American ownership. Eventually in February 1972 the scheme was abandoned, ostensibly because of rising costs and uncertain markets, but probably also because of the unexpectedly widespread public reaction.[2]

Environmentalists now knew that they could hope to score some success when they confronted state governments or even private developers, but there were limits to their effectiveness. Against a powerfully entrenched statutory corporation there was no redress. This emerged over the Lake Pedder controversy in Tasmania. In a state as deprived of alternative sources of energy as Tasmania, hydro-electricity held an obvious appeal as a cheap and clean use of resources, and for many years over 90 per cent of Tasmania's electricity was generated by this means. Since 1930s, control of the system was vested in a Hydro-Electricity Commission, which as a body of engineer-administrators outside party politics commanded great public prestige and a reputation for sound judgement which defied challenge by any but the expert. The Commission's advice was thus accepted faithfully by both political parties in Tasmania when in 1967 it recommended that another dam would be needed to meet the state's growing energy needs and nominated Lake Pedder as the most desirable site.

This raised opposition, first from Tasmania's foresters, then from conservationists. Lake Pedder, fringed by a beach of pinkish-white sand, was the centre of a mountain region of remarkable natural beauty. Besides, south-west Tasmania contained what was probably Australia's largest and least developed area of high-rainfall natural bush, and conservationists feared damage from the proposed development.[3] Neither the Labor government in Tasmania nor the coalition which temporarily ousted it between 1969 and 1972 took the slightest notice of protest. The word of the Hydro-Electric Commission ruled all.

It had to be admitted that the scenic qualities of the Lake Pedder region would be appreciated probably by only a minority, as most of it was wilderness country fit only for serious and dedicated bush-walkers. There was no question of massive recreational development to attract large numbers of tourists. Perhaps this told against the campaign to save Lake Pedder, as at a time when élitism was something of a dirty word it would not have been easy to sell the merits of main-taining a wilderness enjoyable only by the discerning and energetic few.

Although the Australian Conservation Foundation backed the saving of Lake Pedder it was in vain. Even when the Whitlam government early in 1973 appointed a commission of inquiry into the matter the Tasmanian government refused to co-operate. The federal commission urged a moratorium on developing Lake Pedder, even persuading the Commonwealth government to offer to meet the costs of such delay, but Tasmania remained stubborn. Against the advice of the federal committee, against a concerted chorus of protest, the

Hydro-Electricity Commission went ahead and drowned Lake Pedder.[4] So little was the Commission moved by the episode that in 1979 it reached out to repeat the process at another piece of wilderness this time on the Franklin River.

So far most of the Australian Conservation Foundation's interventions fell into the category of nature conservation. Many were prepared to applaud its role as guardian of unique natural features, whose scenic appeal could be valued as distinctive aspects of the Australian landscape. But what if the ACF started to intervene in urban Australia, the environment in which four-fifths of the Australian people spent their everyday lives, and where the rights of property were perhaps more entrenched and powerful? Would support fall away from the work of the ACF if it moved to raise Australian concern about the urban setting, and perhaps ceased to be seen as politically neutral? Or would it be strengthened by taking on new challenges, paying due regard to the inadvisability of running into too many different political fights at once? There was a limit to the extent that any Commonwealth government of either political side could be expected to apply muscle on reluctant state governments on environmental issues. Nor was the Commonwealth government always on the side of the angels. When it was proposed to erect a massive telecommunications tower on Black Mountain, overlooking Canberra, academics and naturalists campaigned vigorously against unsightliness; but Liberal and Labor ministries alike turned a deaf ear.[5]

As for the state governments, their responsiveness to pressure appeared to depend largely on accidents of personality. A Hamer or a Dunstan would show greater sensitivity than a Bjelke-Petersen or a Reece. If state governments were sometimes more amenable to organised public opinion (as over the Little Desert episode) they were also very anxious about attracting investment capital. In the outer states such as Queensland and Western Australia, where economic progress was largely seen as depending on mineral resources, there was a tendency to see the environmental movement as the creature of New South Wales and Victoria which, having achieved their own industrialisation, were now able to indulge in conscience about others.

Behind these questions lay a deeper uncertainty in the early 1970s about the direction in which the environmental movement should go. From its origins among a handful of rural and urban observers it owed its growth and success largely to support among the urban middle class. The environmental lobbies were largely made up of Australia's better-off citizens with leisure and education to enjoy the aesthetics of scenery. If the country could afford the luxury of heeding the conservationists, this was only because the early 1970s came at the end of a twenty five-year period of economic buoyancy. If recession came and jobs were at stake most governments and their voters could be expected to prefer policies which raised production rather than policies which preserved the environment.

Many Labor voters, particularly from trade unions involved in the extractive industries or from a rural background, showed little concern for environmental values. As much as their employers they were preoccupied with the creation and preservation of jobs. To capitalists, on the other hand, the middle-class environmental movement (which attracted many Liberals) was tolerable precisely because it confined its attention to the preservation of natural scenery and wildlife. Against the pressures of real estate developers and municipal racketeering the environmental movement was safely ineffectual.

One way out of this dilemma was personified by the trade union leader Jack Mundey and the 'green bans' movements which sought to bring together the middle-class environmentalists and the radical edge of the trade unions. Born in 1931, Mundey grew up in the Atherton Tableland district of North Queensland, a distinctive landscape of a European scale and greenness, comprising mixed rainforest, dairy pastures and lakes of volcanic origin. When he came to work as a builder's labourer in Sydney he was struck by the contrasting urban pollution, and soon realised that the needs of the poor and under-privileged were not sufficiently protected in town planning. Out of this environmental concern came his conviction that an alliance must be cemented between middle-class environmentalists and the militant labour movement.

From 1962 Mundey held a series of offices with the New South Wales branch of the Builders' Labourers' Federation, eventually becoming state President. As Mundey was a Communist who made no secret of his wish to secure greater acceptability for his party and who saw himself as making a fresh contribution to Communist theory, this mixture of tactics and idealism seemed hard to sell. Fellow Communists disliked compromise with the bourgeoisie, and the middle class feared the Reds. But the alliance came into being in 1970.

In that year A.V. Jennings planned to erect a complex of houses at Kellys Bush, a five-hectare tract which until that time was one of the few remaining portions of open bush in the wealthy suburb of Hunters Hill. The residents of Hunters Hill objected strenuously to this pro-posal. When the bulldozers arrived a number of housewives took up a stand in front of them and defied them to commence their work. As a last resort they took their troubles to the Builders' Labourers' Federation. Instead of merely passing a resolution of support, Mundey ensured that the Federation went out to join the women of Hunters Hill in their protest, withdrawing their labour from the project. This brought the bulldozers to a standstill, and eventually Kellys Bush was left unmolested. This was the first green ban.

This triumph encouraged action at the other end of the social scale. At Eastlakes a development company proposed to build a series of high-rise apartments on one of the few open spaces in that working-class suburb. After resisting protest the company changed its mind only after Mundey's union threatened to stop work on all its other projects if the Eastlakes proposal went through. Centennial Park, not only arguably Sydney's most valuable open space for public recreation but also the backdrop to the residences of eminent citizens ranging from Patrick White to Harry M. Miller, came under threat from the boosters. Politicians and aldermen coveted it as the ideal site for concrete palaces to house the 1988 Olympic Games. The residents came to Mundey who promised another green ban. After an adverse report from the respected architect Walter Bunning the project was abandoned.

Quickly the green ban movement spread to cover historic buildings under threat of demolition: the 1841 Congregational Church in Pitt Street, an even older colonial house at Glebe threatened by an expressway, the Royal Australian College of Physicians in Macquarie Street, a late Victorian bank in Martin Place, notable cinemas and theatres ... In the case of the Theatre Royal the developer (Lend Lease) compromised by offering to build an improved new theatre into their seventy-million-dollar complex. This offered a hopeful sign that developers and environmentalists could reach satisfactory agreements based neither on total destruction nor on a total freezing of activity and change.

The bitterest confrontation arose over the proposed redevelopment of the Woolloomooloo-Victoria Street district lying between Kings Cross and the centre of Sydney. This was a run-down medium-to-high-density working-class area, originally the home of waterside workers and allied trades but later grown more derelict. By the early 1970s it was beginning to attract a mixture of working-class, professional and artistic residents who liked its proximity to the city centre. It was open to the authorities either to foster this tendency or to leave the law of the marketplace to operate, but the state government and the Sydney City Council preferred a third option. This was to rezone the area for high-rise offices and apartments, wiping out the existing terraces and cottages, and eliminating any possibility of converting or adapting the existing old properties into a new pattern of inner-urban living. It was argued that the government's plan would eventually do more to revive the heart of the city because it would bring more people into the area than development based on single-family dwellings. It was taken for granted that a collection of late twentieth-century high-rise tower blocks would enhance the character of the neighbourhood better than a mixture of renovated old and new.

Unfortunately the local residents were not in agreement. A Woolloomooloo Residents Action Group managed to secure the abandonment of part of the scheme in July 1973, though the upshot was that many houses were left unoccupied for several years. In Victoria Street resentment grew at the conduct of a company which bought up a considerable section of its terraced houses for demolition and a thirty-million-dollar redevelopment. For three years, from January 1971 to January 1974, the residents, while paying their rent, resisted eviction and demolition. The Builders' Labourers' Federation imposed a green ban, and gave the cause widespread propaganda. Landlord and tenants set up a labyrinthine succession of lawsuits. The conflict turned vicious: there were reports of standover tactics, harassment by excessive noise at night, organised vandalism. The state government sided with the landlord company, possibly, as the *Nation Review* suggested, because its failure would have left its financial backers five million dollars in debt. At last on the night of 3 January 1974 the police were sent in to evict the few remaining residents. The houses then stood empty and derelict for several years.

The Victoria Street affair may have begun the process of polarising and radicalising the environmental movement in Sydney by revealing the tensions and viciousness which could be generated by conflicts over environmental use. It created a heightened consciousness of environmental issues outside New South Wales. More immediately the controversy made Mundey a national figure. Although his attempt to run as a Senate candidate in 1974 met with no success he was invited to participate in seminars and government committees. The green ban movement was almost becoming respectable.

Many still loathed it. The *Sydney Morning Herald* was disdainful:

> There is something highly comical in the spectacle of builders' labourers, whose ideas on industrial relations do not rise above strikes, violence, intimidation, and the destruction of property, setting themselves up as arbiters of taste and protectors of our national heritage.[8]

Such snobbery was not unique. 'What's now coming is a new type of personal property in which you have some "rights" just living in a place,' commented Alderman David Griffin, Lord Mayor of Sydney. Precisely; the fight was between those who held the traditional view that owners of private property were entitled to use it for their own economic benefit without regard for others (and the more valuable the property, the greater the loss from any form of outside restraint), and those who were demanding that property owners should be accountable to others affected by their activities. Sydney's planning laws were more than usually complicated by overlapping bureaucracies, and Sydney in the early 1970s was in the midst of a building boom. This created a high-employment situation in which the building workers could wield power by refusing to work. In some ways they inherited the traditions of those older itinerant workers, the shearers and the cane cutters. 'Mundey's one-man band', in the words of a town planner, Daryl Conybeare, achieved more than the conventional organisations of middle-class society. Yet if jobs became scarce the union's power might dwindle rapidly. 'When they're looking for work for their members, I bet their cries will fade away' forecast a senior official of Hooker Projects with gloomy relish.[9]

It was even so. With the gathering downturn in the economy after 1974, Mundey came under increasing pressure from fellow officials who thought that the 'green ban' campaign distracted attention from the major tasks of battling for improved wages and conditions and advancing the solidarity of the working class. During 1975–76 Mundey went through a troubled patch when he lost his power base in the building unions to rivals with a more conventional view of union tactics. In 1978 under ACF auspices he launched an organisation in Sydney and Melbourne, 'Environmentalists for Full Employment', designed to push the argument that capital currently earmarked for environmentally harmful or resource-wasteful projects could provide more social benefit and more jobs if the investment was redirected into alternative environmentally sound activities. Mundey's stated aim was to involve the ACF more than previously in the problems of urbanisation and suburbanisation, particularly in the massive Sydney and Melbourne metropolitan complexes.[10] But to a large extent he and the 'green ban' movement had dropped out of the public eye.

The Woolloomooloo district, saved from high-rise development by the 'green bans', was developed on a smaller scale residential basis by the New South Wales Housing Commission following Commonwealth, State and City Council agreement in 1975. Most of the old working-class residents had already dispersed to the outer suburbs.

In Victoria Street, King's Cross, where the battle had been savage, the developers retained control and the restrictions on their activities resulted in a mixture of high-rise buildings and restored terrace houses—neither within the means of the old working-class residents.

These developments highlighted the critical question for the environmental movement. It could protect the interests of the minority with taste and the means to indulge it. It could look after that other minority who were sensitive to the need for Australia to preserve areas of natural wilderness. But could it provide a lasting improvement in the daily environment of Australia's majority? And, as the economy ran into troubled waters during the 1970s, could the claims of the environment be upheld against the pressures for economic development and the preservation of jobs?

> Sydney? It's a building site now, says Kevin waiting to shovel.
>   Ambition has gobbled up the city in towers for companies
>   wanting to build more towers.
> Half of them are empty. Lights burn in them to kid America.
> My father says it's farm boys proving their point again:
> Look Mum we can fight! Look Mum we can build a metropolis!
> He and his friends keep preserving old buildings and scrub.
> against each other. No one likes what they would build now.
> Uncle Clarrie reckoned when he first knew Sydney, it was a
>   lazy dangerous town five stories high with razors up lanes,
>   trams crushing skinned corn, hawkers spitting,
> straw hats on the ferry, shopgirls indignant about everything—
> It was never a village. But now it'd hold even more people who
>   never in their lives have to know the score.[11]

15   Backlash and Forecast

In 1975 one of Australia's finest scholars, Hugh Stretton, analysed the future potential of the environmental movement as it might be shaped in three different political scenarios for the future.[1] He saw most hope in a society where material inequalities were eliminated, so that social arrangements could be negotiated between political equals. Without that sense of equality, he wrote, the underprivileged majority would always enjoy fewer of the benefits of a decent environment than the fortunate élite. The alternatives were an authoritarian society in which social costs were met by the masses, or else a continuation of the free market economy, under which the privileged would increase their relative margin of advantage over the weaker members of society.

In such a free market society—and in the 1970s and the 1980s Australia most closely approached this model—the more prosperous citizens would be able to afford to create a favourable environment in their own homes and suburbs, and would ensure that comely rural environments remained for their enjoyment. The suburbs, the housing and the places of recreation for the less well-to-do would continue to be subject to pollution, traffic problems, substandard materials and noise. The natural resources which were not protected by minority interests would be exploited relentlessly in the quest for export income.

By 1980 Stretton's diagnosis still carried some conviction. In the troubled economy of the late 1970s Australian state governments, particularly in the development-hungry frontier states of Queensland and Western Australia, grasped at every opportunity to develop natural resources on a large scale, brushing aside the objections of environmental lobbies. Only Victoria and New South Wales, the two states with the liveliest awareness of the problems of pollution and waste disposal, possessed legislation providing for the effective assessment of the environmental impact of proposed investment programmes. Meanwhile areas of rare ecological status came under threat. The mining industry, aided by modern technology, was often cast as

Woodchip pile at Eden, piped to tankers for Japanese market
Reproduced with permission from Forestry Commission of NSW

Forestry Commission nursery at Eden where seedlings of various eucalypts are raised for planting on former log dumps
Reproduced with permission from Forestry Commission of NSW

the major villain, but in fact had a better record than many others in attempting to clean up after its damage. This record dated back to the 1920s when BHP took the lead in tree planting at Broken Hill in order to diminish the dust problem. In the 1970s bauxite developers at Weipa in Queensland and in the Darling Range area of Western Australia invested in substantial programs of reafforestation, though in the latter case criticism was levelled at the choice of Tasmanian and Victorian blue gums as replacements, rather than the indigenous jarrah.

Greater controversy was caused by the growth during the 1970s of the woodchip industry, introducing techniques of clear-felling which left a trail of devastation unparalleled by any earlier timber getting. In the Eden district of New South Wales, in Tasmania and in the south-west of Western Australia debate raged, especially in regions where it was proposed to replace the cleared timber with pines, a plan favoured in order to overcome Australia's dependence on imported softwoods. Naturalists denounced the destruction of habitats of native fauna and flora, and forecast the increasing salination of watercourses in cleared country; developers and forestry officials countered with the view that timber, like any other growing crop, had to be farmed to secure the maximum economic benefit and effective policies of regrowth and conservation. The officials entrusted with environmental protection sat unhappily between these extremes as they strove to influence official policy without alienating the strong men who were the decision makers in their state.

The Commonwealth government under both Whitlam and Fraser legislated constructively. In 1975 the National Parks and Wildlife Conservation Act and the Great Barrier Reef Marine Park Act gave backing to the policy of conservation through reserves. The passing of the Aboriginal Land Rights Act for the Northern Territory in 1976 increased the scope of this policy, though South Australia alone among the states saw fit to follow suit. Nor did the Fraser government pull down the Whitlam government's plans for setting up a National Estate with a register of sites worthy of preservation because of their historical or ecological value, though the funding of this body fell short of original expectations. Yet as the states increased their pressure for control of their own economic destinies, Canberra's power to take environmental responsibility grew questionable. As oil prices rose the temptation increased to raise the moratorium on drilling in national parks, such as the Great Barrier Reef; and as the quest for export income became keener the case has been pressed more strongly for extractive mining to be encouraged without the deterrent of

environmental restraints. To some observers indeed it seemed that
the politicians remained at least slightly sensitive to environmental
lobbying, and that the real danger lay with the bureaucrat-admin-
istrator:

> What is in fact emerging as the greatest threat to the heritage is the
> power of the bureaucracy and the secrecy of its processes. The best
> remedy is exposure—more openness before decisions are taken, and
> a greater insistence on justification for whatever is being decided.[2]

Certainly some of the major ecological reverses of recent years were
due to bureaucratic insistence: the destruction of Lake Pedder, the
erection of Canberra's Black Mountain tower, the failure in 1975 of
the New South Wales government to continue supporting plans for
a complex and potentially valuable multidisciplinary study of the
Botany Bay region. This study, originating within the Australian
National University, would have pioneered the concept of creating
a master plan to permit the regeneration and future development of
a heavily industrial and considerably degraded environment; but it
fell foul of civil service jealousies, and its fate appeared to discourage
similar projects elsewhere.[3]

Nor was it evident that politicians or bureaucrats saw even partial
solutions for the problems of the urban environment in which the vast
majority of Australians lived. The problems of traffic and suburban
sprawl were not likely to be solved by rising petrol prices, because
public transport systems had been allowed to run down and because
the planning and organisation of most suburbs was based on the
assumption that most households would have access to a car—often
to two cars. During the 1970s some tentative attempts were made to
reverse this process by the provision of pedestrian shopping malls
and the alteration of zoning laws to encourage private flat-dwelling
in and among city office blocks. There was little to suggest that the
movement away from the city centres had gone into reverse on any
large scale by 1980.

This was not surprising. Australia had been settled by Europeans
for less than two hundred years. The first comers were blinkered by
preconceptions which left them unable to respond to the Australian
setting. Their children and grandchildren had shown touches of
imagination and adaptability, but the native experience was too often
overridden by the influence of overseas models, at first British, later
increasingly American. In developing Australia, stress had always
been placed on fostering economic growth and the efficient exploitation of resources. Conservation was either ignored or at best seen as
husbanding resources for future use.

It also followed that a low priority was given to the development of agreeable or efficient public environments in the cities, since such measures demanded investment without obvious immediate returns. Few citizens felt themselves to be in a position where their ideas or opinions could influence the character of their neighbourhood Decisions were therefore left to officials who from the nature of their situations, whether as elected politicians or as career civil servants, could not be expected to welcome challenge or calls for change. Where an effective concern for the environment was expressed, as in the 1880s and the late 1960s, it was very often at the end of a period of sustained prosperity when for a brief time nonmaterial considerations could be aired. Even then conservation was often seen as the protection of 'nature' or rural habitats, although the environment was often an artifact, most characteristically the city and its suburbs.

For most Australians living today the public environment will grow steadily worse. It will grow worse because decentralisation is impossible without a degree of regulation which would prove politically intolerable, and because those members of the younger generation who have moved back to the land and expressed an interest in 'organic' agriculture are seen as an uninfluential minority. No acceptable way is known of planning Australia's cities to cope with increasing numbers. Traffic congestion will increase. For most people living in the city and suburbs it will become increasingly difficult to travel to to any other environment within Australia except for holiday resorts which are in effect pieces of transplanted suburbia.

The economic difficulties of the 1980s and 1990s will embolden governments to encroach upon wilderness areas previously left intact for their scenic value; there will be more Lake Pedders and the Great Barrier Reef will be exploited. The number of people able to own their own homes will gradually decrease, and while a fortunate minority will be able to express taste and individuality in their surroundings, the majority will have no such option. Unable to influence their environment except within the privacy of their own homes, they will respond to their lack of power with apathy, leaving the developers in control.

This forecast may turn out to be too gloomy. The Commonwealth government at the June 1980 World Wilderness Conference in Cairns promised to seek the conservation of the Great Barrier Reef as part of the international heritage of the world. The Tasmanian Hydro-Electric Commission's plans for further flooding in the wilderness areas of the south-west evoked the strongest political protest movement seen in that state within living memory. The hope still survived that articulate and well-informed citizens could influence governments to make careful provision for the quality of urban and rural environments. It was even possible that the renewed concern for Aboriginal land rights might lead to a subtler appreciation of Aboriginal principles of conservation and renewal and the Aboriginal concept of a religious respect for the land with which Australians identified themselves. For if Australians were learning to abandon the old idea of their country as a hostile force to be tamed they had yet to attain that state of mind present in the wisdom of so many older cultures: the habit of viewing the Australian earth as their mother.

Notes

Chapter 1   A Timeless Land

1. C.M.H. Clark, *A History of Australia: I*, Melbourne 1962, p. 1; H.H. Finlayson, *The Red Centre*, Sydney 1935, p. 15; G.W. Rusden, *A History of Australia*, London 1883, vol. 1, p. 3.
2. C. Sturt, *Two Expeditions into the Interior of Southern Australia . . .*, London 1833, vol. 1, p. 59.
3. T.L. Mitchell, *Three Expeditions into the Interior of Eastern Australia . . .*, London 1838, vol. 2, p. 170.
4. Lt. Col. Henry Dumaresq, quoted in *Journal Royal Geographical Society*, vol. 1, 1832, p. 2.
5. C. Sturt, *op. cit.* vol. 2, p. 228.
6. J. Whitehurst, *An Inquiry into the original State and Formation of the Earth . . .*, London 1778.
7. W. Dampier, *A New Voyage Round the World* (ed. Sir A. Gray, Hakluyt Society), London 1927, p. 312; Walter Scott to Mrs James Winter Scott, 29 May 1872, quoted in G.C. Bolton 'The Valley of Lagoons: a study in exile', *Business Archives and History*, vol. 4, 1964, p. 107.
8. G. C. Bolton, *A Thousand Miles Away*, Brisbane 1963, p. 96; W.K. Hancock, *Discovering Monaro*, Cambridge 1972, p. 112; C. Turnbull, *Black War*, Melbourne 1966.
9. On this point see J. Allen, J. Golson and R. Jones (eds.), *Sunda and Sahul: Prehistoric Studies in Southeast Asia, Melanesia and Australia* 1977; S.J. Hallam 'The relevance of Old World archaeology to the first entrance of man into New Worlds: colonisation seen from the Antipodes', *Quaternary Research*, vol. 8, 1978, pp. 128–48.
10. C. Gardner, 'The fire factor in relation to the vegetation in Western Australia', *W.A. Naturalist*, vol. 5, 1957, p. 166.
11. T.L. Mitchell, *A Journal of an Expedition into Tropical Australia*, London 1848, p. 100.
12. S.J. Hallam, 'The First Comers' in C.T. Stannage, *A New History of Western Australia*, Nedlands 1981, p. 64.
13. D. Merrilees, 'Man the Destroyer', *Journal of the Royal Society of Western Australia*, vol. 51, 1958, p. 1; R.A. Gould, 'Uses and effects of fire among the Western District Aborigines of Australia', *Mankind*, vol. 8, 1971, pp. 14–24.

Chapter 2   The British Impact

1. Genesis 1:23. See also Lynn White Jr, *Machine ex Deo* Cambridge Mass.,

1968; Judith Wright, 'Education and the environmental crisis', in *Because I was Invited*, Melbourne 1975, pp. 219-23.
2. J. Swift, *Gulliver's Travels*, book II ch. 7, (ed. H. Dan's), Oxford 1959, pp. 135-6.
3. A. Pope, *Moral Essays*, IV, lines 181-90.
4. On this subject see D. Hay, 'Poaching and the Game Laws on Channock chase', in D. Hay, P. Linebaugh, E.P. Thompson, *Albion's Fatal Tree*, London 1975, pp. 189-253; C. Kirby, 'The English Game Law System', *American Historical Review*, vol. 38 1933, pp. 240-62.
5. J.P. Cooper, 'In search of agrarian capitalism', *Past and Present 80*, 1978, p. 65.
6. H. Pelling, 'Trade unions, workers, and the law' in *Popular Politics and Society in Late Victorian Britain*, London 1968, pp. 61-81.
7. For Krichauff see ch. 4; for Parkes ch. 9.
8. This argument is developed ably in J.M. Powell, *Environmental Management in Australia*, Melbourne 1976.

Chapter 3   The Weather

1. King to Camden, 7 April 1806, *H.R.A.* vol. V, p. 697.
2. W. Tench, *Sydney's First Four Years* (ed. L.F. Fitzhardinge), Sydney 1961, p. 266; Phillip to Sydney, 12 Febuary 1790, *H.R.A.* I, i, p. 144; *The Past* Enniscorthy, Co. Wexford, vol. 6, 1950, p. 83.
3. *Tasmanian Journal of Natural Science*, vol. 1, 1841, p. 11.
4. Hunter to King, 20 June 1797, *H.R.A.* I, 3, p. 26.
5. R.D. Collinson Black and R. Kinekamp, *Papers and Correspondence of William Stanley Jevons*, London 1972, vol. 1, p. 135; for Jevons see J.A. La Nauze, *Political Economy in Australia*, Melbourne 1949, ch. 2.
6. E. Smith, *The Beckoning West*, Sydney 1966, p. 167.
7. T.M. Perry, *Australia's First Frontier*, Melbourne 1963, p. 33.
8. P.M. Cunningham, *Hints for Australian Emigrants*, London 1841, p. 70.
9. *Transactions of the Philosophical Society of Victoria*, vol. 1, 18, p. 174.
10. W.S. Jevons, 'Some data concerning the climate of Australia and New Zealand', *Waugh's Australian Almanac for 1859*, Sydney 1859, pp. 47-98.
11. G. Buxton, *The Riverina 1861-1891*, Melbourne 1967, p. 151.
12. For this paragraph I draw heavily on D.W. Meinig, *On the Margins of the Good Earth*, London 1963.
13. F.H. Bauer, 'Significant features in the white settlement of Australia', *Australian Geographical Studies*, vol. 1, 1962, p. 45.
14. Judith Wright, 'South of My Days' in *Collected Poems 1942-1970*, Sydney 1971, p. 20.
15. But see G. Blainey, 'The great drought', *National Times*, 31 October-5 November 1977.
16. G.P. Marsh, *Man and Nature*, Cambridge Mass. 1965 (reprint of 1864 edition).
17. F. von Mueller, *Australian vegetation indigenous or introduced considered especially in its bearings on the occupation of the territory, and with a view of unfolding its resources*, Melbourne, 1868.

Chapter 4   They Hated Trees

1. W.K. Hancock, *Australia*, London 1930, p. 33.

2. Harris to——, 20 March 1791 (Mitchell Library CY A1597). I am indebted to Dr Alan Atkinson for this quotation.
3. *H.R.A.*, I, v, p. 67.
4. J. Atkinson, *An Account of the State of Agriculture and Grazing in New South Wales*, London 1826, p. 8.
5. T.F. Brine, *Letters from Victorian Pioneers*, Melbourne 1898, reprinted 1969, p. 56.
6. *South Australian Register*, 24 December 1845.
7. L.T. Daley, *Men and a River*, Melbourne 1967, p. 133 (and ch. 9 throughout for the Richmond River timber trade); quoting New South Wales *Legislative Council: Votes and Proceedings* 1847, vol. 2, p. 542.
8. *West Australian*, 14 January 1892.
9. W. Howitt, *Land and Labour and Gold*, London 1855, vol. I, p. 231.
10. J. Bosisto, 'Is the eucalyptus a fever-destroying tree?' *Proceedings, Royal Society of Victoria*, vol. xiii 1876, pp. 10–23; J.R. Poynter, *Russell Grimwade*, Melbourne 1967, pp. 16–18.
11. Jevons to Lucy Jevons, 9 March 1856; Collison Black and Kinekamp, *op. cit.*, vol. 1, p. 213.
12. J. Vincent (ed.), *Diaries of Edward Stanley, 15th Earl of Derby*, London 1978, pp. 346–7. I owe this reference to Dr Ged Martin.
13. J. Atkinson, *op. cit.*, pp. 83–6.
14. J.R.M. Cameron, 'Coming to terms: the development of agriculture in preconvict Western Australia', *Geowest* No. 11, 1977, pp. 30 and 60.
15. *Perth Gazette*, 2 September 1847; quoted by T. Foster, *Bushfire*, Hong Kong 1976, p. 97; also J.R.M. Cameron, *op. cit.*
16. But this has been disputed. See W.K. Hancock, *Discovering Monaro*, Cambridge 1972, pp. 26–7, quoting N.A. Wakefield, 'Bushfire frequency and vegetational change in south-eastern Australian forests', *Victorian Naturalist*, 1, 27, 1970, pp. 152–7.
17. Garroyowen (E. Finn), *Chronicles of Early Melbourne*, Melbourne 1888, p. 100.
18. W.E. Abbott, 'On ringbarking and its effect', *Proceedings, Royal Society of New South Wales*, vol. xiv, 1880, pp. 93–102.
19. New South Wales *Parliamentary Debates* 1880–81, pp. 1204–15; 1881, pp. 438–1456 (at intervals); quotations from McElhone, 1880, pp. 1204–10; Brodribb, p. 1211; Farnell, 1881, p. 455; Abbott, pp. 458–9; King, p. 1345.
20. Quoted by A.G. Hamilton, 'On the effect which settlement in Australia has produced upon indigenous vegetation', *Proceedings, Royal Society of New South Wales*, vol. xxvi, 1892, pp. 198–9.
21. *Ibid.*, p. 180.
22. Western Australia, *Legislative Assembly: Votes and Proceedings*, 1901–02, vol. 4, paper A37; minutes of evidence, question 444; also *Parliamentary Debates*, new series, vol. 23, 1902, pp. 2835–44.
23. *Commonwealth Year Book*, vol. 19, 1925, p. 701.
24. A.R. Penfold and J.L. Willis, *The Eucalyptus*, London 1961, for much of the material in this paragraph; also J. Zacharin, *Emigrant Eucalypts: Gum Trees as Exotics*, Melbourne 1978.
25. M.H. Walker, *Come Wind, Come Weather: A Biography of Alfred Howitt*, Melbourne 1971, p. 181.
26. J.B. Kirkpatrick, 'Eucalypt invasion in Southern California', *Australian Geographer*, vol. 13, 1977, pp. 387–93; K. Thompson, 'The Australian fever tree in California: eucalypts and malarial prophylaxis', *Annuals of the Association of American Geographers*, vol. 60, 1970, pp. 230–44.

27. South Australia *Parliamentary Papers* 1870–71, no. 147; 1873, vol. 2, no. 26.

Chapter 5   The First Generation

 1. A.J. Marshall, *The Great Extermination: a Guide to Anglo-Australian Cupidity Wickedness and Waste*, London 1966.
 2. Melville to Enderby, 22 November 1791; quoted by W.J. Dakin, *Whalemen Adventurers*, Sydney 1934, from the George Chalmers MSS, Mitchell Library, Sydney.
 3. Sir Joseph Banks's chief clerk, 4 June 1806; quoted by T. Dunbabin, *Australian Encyclopaedia*, 2nd edn., vol. 8, p. 56. See also M. Steven, 'Exports other than wool', in G.J. Abbott and N.B. Nairn, *Economic Growth of Australia*, 1788–1821, Melbourne 1969, pp. 285–305.
 4. King to Cooke, 1 November 1805; *H.R.A.* I, 5, p. 612.
 5. *Journal of the Geographical Society*, vol. 2, 1833, p. 133.
 6. M. Nicholls (ed.), *The Diary of the Reverend Robert Knopwood 1803–1838*, Launceston 1977, p. 55.
 7. W.J. Dakin, *op. cit.*, p. 47; M. Colwell, *Whaling Around Australia*, Adelaide 1969, p. 31.
 8. T. Dunbabin, *op. cit.*, vol. 9, p. 275.
 9. Quotations from A.J. Marshall, *op. cit.*, ch. 2.
10. G. Krefft, 'On the vertebrated animals of the lower Murray and Darling, their habits, economy, and geographical distribution, *Trans. Phil. Soc. N.S.W.* 1862–65, pp. 1–33.
11. T.F. Brine, *op. cit.*, pp. 191–2.
12. *Hobart Town Courier*, 15 July 1846. I owe this and several other references in this chapter to the kindness of Dr Stephen Murray-Smith.
13. Stokes to Sir Francis Beaufort, 31 January 1849 (Hydography Office, Taunton, England; reference from Dr Murray-Smith).
14. P. MacPherson, 'Some causes of the decay of Australian forests' *Journal Royal Society of New South Wales*, vol. 29, 1885, pp. 85–96.
15. J.T. Bigge, *Report on the Agriculture and Trade of New South Wales* (Australiana Facsimiles Editions no. 70, Adelaide 1966).
16. J. Atkinson, *op. cit.*, p. 29.
17. T.M. Perry, *Australia's First Frontier*, Melbourne 1963.
18. S.H. Roberts, *The Squatting Age in Australia 1835–1947*, Melbourne 1935, p. 347.
19. W. Howitt, *op. cit.*, vol. 1, p. 129.
20. G.F. Moore, *Diary of Ten Years Eventful Life of an Early Settler in Western Australia*, London 1884, pp. 32–3.

Chapter 6   Urban Beginnings

1. Phillip to Sydney, 9 July 1788 (*H.R.A.* I, i, p. 48).
2. Foveaux to Macquarie, 8 March 1810; Macquarie's memorandum of 27 July 1822 (*H.R.A.* I, vii, p. 233; x, p. 683).
3. Quoted by R.J. Solomon, *Urbanization: the Evolution of an Australian Capital*, Sydney 1976, p. 29.
4. Bourke to Stanley, 8 July 1834; Aberdeen to Bourke, 13 February 1835 (*H.R.A.* I, xvii, pp. 474 and 656).
5. G. Dutton, *Founder of a City*, Melbourne 1962, p. 215.

6. J.C. Hawker, *Early Experiences in South Australia*, Adelaide 1899 (Library Board reprint 1975), p. 69.
7. John Brown to Edward Gibbon Wakefield, 13 February 1837, quoted by G. Dutton, *op. cit.*, p. 217.
8. M.H. Walker, *op. cit.*, p. 37.
9. P.L. Brown (ed), *The Narrative of George Russell of Golf Hill*, London 1933, p. 133.
10. J. Slater, *The Gold Finder in Australia*, London 1853, p. 333.
11. Quoted in A.J. Marshall, *Darwin and Huxley in Australia*, Sydney 1970, p. 13. A similar account of Melbourne is given by William Howitt, *Land, Labour and Gold*, London 1855, p. 310; quoted by J.M. Powell and M. Williams, *Australian Space, Australian Time*, Melbourne 1975, p. 44.
12. Phillip to Grenville, 4 March 1791 (*H.R.A.* I, i, pp. 247–8).
13. G.T. Lloyd, *Thirtythree Years in Tasmania and Victoria*, quoted by R.J. Solomon, *op. cit.*, p. 41.
14. Bourke to Glenelg, 30 July 1837 (*H.R.A.* I, xix, pp. 55–6).
15. P. Cox and J. Freeland, *Rude Timber Buildings in Australia*, London 1969, p. 38.
16. D. Urlich Cloher, 'A perspective on Australian urbanization', in J.M. Powell and M. Williams, *Australian Space, Australian Time*, Melbourne 1975, pp. 104–49; K.W. Robinson, 'The geographical context of political individualism 1860–1914', *ibid*, 226–49.
17. R. Robinson, 'Site and Form in the valley centres of the New South Wales coast north of the Hunter', *Australian Geographer*, X, 1966, pp. 1–16; D.N. Jeans, 'Territorial divisions and the location of towns in New South Wales, 1826–1842', *ibid*, pp. 242–55.
18. *Jamestown Review*, 26 September 1878, quoted by D.W. Meinig, *op. cit.*, p. 182.
19. W.S. Jevons, *op. cit.*, p. 142.
20. A.W. Howitt to Barton Wright, 20 April 1853, quoted by M.H. Walker, *op. cit.*, Melbourne 1971, p. 52.

Chapter 7   After Gold

1. J. Slater, *op. cit.*, p. 200.
2. W. Bate, *Lucky City: the First Generation in Ballarat, 1851–1901*, Melbourne 1978, pp. 98–9.
3. J. Brown and B. Mullins, *Country Life in Pioneer South Australia*, Adelaide 1977, p. 183.
4. B. Kennedy, *Silver, Sin, and Sixpenny Ale*, Melbourne 1978.
5. M. Kelly, 'Picturesque and pestilential: the Sydney slum observed', in M. Kelly (ed.), *Nineteenth Century Sydney*, Sydney 1978, pp. 66–80.
6. D.L. Saunders, 'Terrace housing in Melbourne', (M.A. thesis, Melbourne 1959).
7. *Collingwood Observer*, 11 March 1865, quoted in B. Barrett, *The Inner Suburbs*, Melbourne 1971, pp. 29–30.
8. *Sydney Morning Herald*, 7 December 1929.
9. D. Clark, 'Worse than physic: Sydney's water supply, 1788–1888' in M. Kelly, *op. cit.*
10. B. Barrett, *op. cit.*, p. 135.
11. *Sydney Morning Herald*, 7 March 1851, quoted in D. Clark, *op. cit.*, p. 57.

12. Quoted in N.G. Butlin, *Sydney's Environmental Amenity*, Canberra 1976, p. 9.
13. *Sydney Morning Herald*, 30 November and 7 December 1929.
14. *Mansfield Courier*, 19 July 1890, quoted by J. Gillison, *A Colonial Doctor and his Town*, Melbourne 1974, p. 45.
15. C.C. Reade, 'Planning and development of towns and cities in South Australia', SAPP 63/1919, quoted in D.W. Meinig, *op. cit.,* p. 188.
16. A.J. Rose, 'Australia as a cultural landscape' in A. Rapoport, *Australia as Human Setting*, Sydney 1972, p. 67.
17. W. Evans, *Diary of a Welsh Swagman, 1869–1894*, Melbourne, 1976, p. 23; also pp. 68 and 201.
18. C.R. Twidale, G.J. Forrest and J.A. Shepherd, 'The imprint of the plough: "Lands" in the Mount Lofty region, South Australia', *Australian Geographer*, xi, 1971, p. 492.
19. SAPP 77/1875; quoted in D.W. Meinig, *op. cit.*, p. 118; see also pp. 102–8.
20. W.S. Jevons, *op. cit.*, p. 138.
21. *Ibid.*, p. 139.
22. P. Cox and J. Freeland, *op. cit.*, pp. 43–59.

Chapter 8　　The Pastoral Impact

1. O.B. Williams, 'The Riverina and its pastoral industry 1860–9' in A. Barnard (ed.), *The Simple Fleece*, Melbourne 1962, p. 415.
2. N.G. Butlin, 'The growth of rural capital, 1860–90' in A. Barnard (ed.), *op. cit.*, p. 333.
3. A. Allingham, *Taming the Wilderness*, Townsville 1977, pp. 102–3.
4. W.W. Froggatt, 'A century of civilisation from a zoologist's point of view', *Proc. Linn. Soc. NSW*, xxxviii 1913, p. 22.
5. Royal Commission appointed to inquire into the Condition of Crown Tenants in the Western Division of New South Wales; Report and Minutes of Evidence (VPLANSW 1901, 4, qn. 8482); quoted N. Cain, 'Companies and squatting in the Western Division of New South Wales, 1896–1905', in A. Barnard (ed.), *op. cit.*, p. 437.
6. R.M. Moore, 'Ecological observations on plant communities grazed by sheep in Australia', *Monagr. biol.* VIII 1959, pp. 500–513; also, G. Price, 'The moving frontiers and changing landscapes of flora and fauna in Australia', in J. Andrews, (ed.), *Frontiers and Men*, Melbourne 1966, pp. 155–73.
7. SAPP 72/1871: 'Report of the Select Committee of the Legislative Assembly on the Thistle Bill, 1871'; also SAPP 205/1862: 'Report of the Select Committee of the Legislative Council on the Thistle and Burr Bill, 1862'.
8. R.M. Moore, 'Man and vegetation in temperate Australia', D. Ag. Sci. thesis, Sydney, 1963.
9. E.C. Rolls, *op. cit.*, pp. 335–6.
10. *Colonial Times*, 11 May 1827.
11. E.C. Rolls, *op. cit.*, chs 1–9; M. Kiddle, *Men of Yesterday*, Melbourne 1961, pp. 320–22; F. Fenner and F.N. Ratcliffe, *Myomatosis*, Cambridge 1965.
12. H.A. Strong, 'Notes on the rabbit, historical and geographical', *Zoologist*, 3rd series vol. xviii (1894), p. 404.
13. (W. Evans), *Diary of a Welsh Swagman, 1869–1894*, London 1977, p. 100.

14. Queensland, *Legislative Council Debates*, vol. xxxi, p. 64.
15. C.G.N. Lockhart, 'Rabbits in Australia', *Blackwoods Magazine*, vol. 142 (1887), pp. 818–33.
16. G. Buxton, *The Riverina 1861–1891*, Melbourne 1967, p. 248.
17. *Zoologist*, 3rd series, vol. xiii (1889), p. 143.
18. Anon., 'The rabbit pest at the Antipodes: the remedy proposed by M. Pasteur', *Zoologist*, 3rd series, vol. xii (1888), p. 321–8.
19. H.A. Strong, *op. cit.*, p. 405; M. Christy, 'On the extermination of the rabbit in Australasia', *Zoologist*, 3rd series, vol. xvi (1892), pp. 377–88. The novel is R. Braddon, *The Year of the Angry Rabbit*, London 1964.
20. *Age*, 22 May 1907; *Bulletin*, 30 May 1907; L. Paszowski, 'Dr Jan Danysz and the rabbits of Australia', *Aust. Zoologist*, xv (1969), pp. 109–20.
21. K.T. Cameron, 'Queensland's struggle against rabbits, 1880–1930', *Journal of the Historical Society of Queensland*, vol. 4 (1956), pp. 1201–6.
22. E. Smith, *op. cit.*, pp. 81–2 and 101.

Chapter 9 Towards Conservation

1. Acclimatization Society of New South Wales, *Annual Report* 1863, p. 18.
2. E. Wilson, 'On the introduction of the British song bird', *Trans. Phil. Soc. Vic.* vol. II (1857), pp. 77–8.
3. E.C. Rolls, *op. cit.*, pp. 236–42.
4. *Victorian Hansard* 1861–62, vol. 8, p. 231.
5. *Sydney Morning Herald*, 10 June 1865.
6. K.I. Johnson, 'The history of the Sydney Mechanics' School of Arts from its foundation in 1833 to 1880', M.A. thesis, A.N.U. 1967, p. 270.
7. J.H. Calaby, 'The current state of Australian macropodidae', *Aust. Zoologist*, vol. 16 (1971), p. 17.
8. Western Australia, *Parliamentary Debates* (new series), vol. II, p. 85.
9. A.J. Campbell, *Nests and Eggs of Australian Birds*, Melbourne 1883, p. v.
10. A. Hasluck (ed.), *Audrey Tennyson's Vice-Regal Letters*, Canberra 1978, pp. 312–13.
11. Sir J. Barrett, *Save Australia!*, Melbourne 1925, p. 4.
12. E. Troughton, *Forest Animals of Australia*, Sydney 1951.
13. J.G. Mosley, 'History of conservation' in A. Rapoport, *op. cit.*, pp. 147–8.
14. V. Hughes, 'History of Kings Park' Hons. thesis, Murdoch University, 1978.
15. Quoted in Lane Poole to Novar, 7 July 1921 (Lane Poole MSS, National Library of Australia).
16. *Q.P.D.*, xcviii, p. 1541.
17. Australian Academy of Science and National Parks Board of Western Australia, 'National Parks and nature reserves in Western Australia', 1965.

Chapter 10 Suburban Spread

1. *Sydney Morning Herald*, 7 December 1929.
2. A.E. Dingle and D.T. Merritt, 'Urban landlords in late nineteenth century Melbourne', *Monash Papers in Economic History*, No. 1, Melbourne 1975.
3. Quoted by J. Campbell, 'The settlement of Melbourne, 1851–1893; selected aspects of urban growth', M.A. thesis, Melbourne 1970.

4. J.M. Freeland, 'People in Cities' in A. Rapoport, *op. cit.*, p. 110; also R.H. Johnston, 'An outline of the development of Melbourne's street pattern', *Australian Geographer*, VI, 1968, pp. 453–65.
5. *Q.P.D.*, xlv, pp. 160–61, xlvii, pp. 848–53.
6. C.T. Stannage, *The People of Perth*, Perth 1979, p. 270.
7. G. Blainey, *A History of Camberwell*, Melbourne 1964, pp. 78–81.
8. B. S. Marsden, 'A century of building materials in Queensland and Brisbane 1861–1961', *Aust. Geographer*, x (1966), pp. 115–131.
9. K. Lynch, 'Some aspects of domestic architecture in Queensland', *J.H.S.Q.*, 3, 1955, pp. 1076–86.
10. D. Whitelock, *Adelaide 1836–1976*, Brisbane 1977, pp. 178–80.
11. M. Gilmore, *Old Days Old Ways*, Sydney 1934, p. 73.
12. 'Smith, Sir Edwin' in *A.D.B.*, vol. 6, p. 142.
13. A.W. Hodgart, 'Melbourne's early growth—economic geography or aesthetic?'
14. M.G.A. Wilson, 'Town gas manufacturing in Australia', *Australian Geographer*, V, 1967, pp. 97–111.
15. Quoted from *Town and Country Journal* 1882 in Eric Irvin, *Sydney as it might have been*, Sydney 1974, p. 42.
16. A.J. Campbell, *Nests and Eggs of Australian Birds*, Melbourne 1883, p. iv.
17. C. French, 'A ramble through the heath ground from Oakleigh to Sandringham', *Victorian Naturalist*, vol. VII, 1890, pp. 41–72.

Chapter 11   Planners and Improvers

1. J. Sulman, 'The architecture of towns', *Australasian Association for the Advancement of Science*, Christchurch 1891, pp. 424–33; J.M. Powell, *op. cit.*, pp. 159–62.
2. A.G. Austin (ed.), *The Webbs' Australian Diary*, Melbourne 1965, pp. 23–4 and 29–31.
3. M. Kelly, *A Certain Sydney*, Sydney 1978.
4. W.M. Hughes, *Policies and Potentates*, Sydney 1950, p. 41.
5. NSW Legislative Assembly, *Votes and Proceedings* 1903, vol. 3, pp. 665–832; Report from the Select Committee on the Abattoir, Glebe Island.
6. P. Spearritt, *Sydney since the Twenties*, Sydney 1978, p. 18.
7. C.T. Stannage, *The People of Perth*, Perth 1979, p. 253.
8. NSW Legislative Assembly, *Votes and Proceedings* 1909, vol. 5, pp. 379–704; Report of the Royal Commission for the Improvement of Sydney and its Suburbs (hereafter abbreviated as *R.C.* 1909).
9. L. Sandercock, *Cities for Sale*, Melbourne 1975, pp. 16–18 and 65.
10. A. Rapoport, *op. cit.* p. 118.
11. J. Birrell, *Walter Burley Griffin*, Brisbane 1964; D.L. Johnson, *The Architecture of Walter Burley Griffin*, Melbourne 1979.
12. *Sydney Morning Herald*, 26 August 1925; quoted P. Spearritt, *op. cit.*, p. 23.
13. J. Barrett, *op. cit.*, p. 20.
14. *R.C.* 1909, qn. 3683.
15. G. Johnston, *My Brother Jack*, London 1964, ch. 13.
16. J.M. Freeland, *Architecture in Australia*,
17. Quoted by P. Spearritt, *op. cit.*, pp. 29–30.
18. *R.C.* 1909, qns. 2430–31.

Chapter 12   Rural Australia, 1900–1945

1. C.J. Dennis, 'Uncle Jim', in *Songs of a Sentimental Bloke*, Sydney 1916, pp. 93–8.
2. J. Macdonald Holmes, *Soil Erosion in Australia and New Zealand*, Sydney 1946.
3. Henry Lawson, *Letters* (ed. C. Roderick), Sydney 1970, p. 242.
4. K. Paterson, 'The formation of policy for the control of vermin and noxious weeds in New South Wales and Victoria, 1880–1930 (Ph.D., A.N.U. 1979), p. 355. Dr Paterson's useful and illuminating thesis came into my hands too late for consultation in preparing this book.
5. *Victorian Naturalist*, vol. ix (1892), p. 37.
6. D. Johnson, *The Alps at the Crossroads*, Melbourne 1974, p. 83.
7. *Ibid.*, pp. 83–7; *Argus*, 30 July 1946.
8. *Sydney Morning Herald*,
9. New South Wales Soil Conservation Service, *Annual Report* 1942.
10. F. Ratcliffe, *Flying Fox and Drifting Sand*, Sydney 1947; also A.E.V. Richardson, 'Shifting sands: the growth of the menace in Australia', *Proc. Royal Geog. Soc. Aust.* (SA branch), xxxvi (1934–35), p. 43.
11. E. Cope, *Catchment Salting in Victoria*, Melbourne 1958; D.C. van Dijk, 'Relict salt, a major cause of recent land damage in the Yass valley, Southern Tablelands, NSW' *Aust. Geographer*, xi (1971), pp. 13–21; E.P. Hodgkin, C.C. Sanders, N.F. Stanley, 'Lakes, rivers, and estuaries' in B.J. O'Brien (ed.), *Environment and Science*, Perth 1979, pp. 102–6.
12. G.C. Bolton, *A Fine Country to Starve In*, Perth 1972, p. 225.
13. W. Evans, *op. cit.*, p. 186. See also K.H.L. Kay Australian grasshoppers and Locusts in A. Keast, R.L. Cowcher, C.S. Christian, *Biography and Ecology in Australia*, The Hague, pp. 193–210.
14. *Australian Encyclopaedia*, second edition, vol. 5, p. 473.
15. D.W. Smith, C.R. Twidale, J.A. Bourne, 'Kappakoota dunes—aeolian landforms induced by man', *Aust. Geographer*, xiii (1975), p.
16. C.W. Twidale and D.L. Smith, 'A "perfect desert" transformed: the agricultural development of north-western Eyre peninsula South Australia', *ibid.*, xi (1971), pp. 437–54.
17. A.J. and J.J. McIntyre, *Country Towns in Victoria*, Melbourne 1944, p. 28.
18. A.J. Rose, 'Australia as a cultural landscape' in A. Rapoport, *op. cit.*, p. 68.

Chapter 13   Affluent Society

1. C. Lloyd, *The National Estate: Australia's Heritage*, Stanmore 1977, p. 11.
2. J. Kemeny, 'The ideology of home ownership', *Arena*, 46 (1977), pp. 81–9.
3. T.J. Mitchell, 'J.W. Wainright: the industrialisation of South Australia, 1935–40', *A.J.P.H.*, vol. VIII, No. 1, 1962, pp. 27–40.
4. *Comm. Parl. Debates*, vol. 185, p. 6265.
5. J.M. Freeland, 'People in Cities' in A. Rapoport, *op. cit.*, p. 122.
6. Mr H.B.S. Gullett, in an oral history interview, 19 November 1970; TRC 121/1, National Library of Australia; reproduced by permission of the speaker.
7. M. Ravalleri, 'Urban problems, public places, and social structure', *Australian Quarterly*, vol. 46, no. 3 (September 1974), pp. 84–9.
8. H. Lunn, *Joh*, Brisbane 1978, ch. 3.

Chapter 14   Rescue Operations

1. 'Political chronicle' in *Australian Journal of Politics and History*, xv, *3* (1969), pp. 93–4, xvi, *1* (1969), pp. 82–6.
2. J. Hagen, 'Clutha: the politics of pollution' in R. Dempsey (ed.), *The Politics of Finding Out*, Melbourne 1974, pp. 29–41.
3. R.W. Davis, 'Waterpower and wilderness: political and administrative aspects of the Lake Pedder controversy', *Public Admin.*, xxvi (1972), pp. 21–39; D. Johnson, *Lake Pedder: Why a National Park must be Saved*, Adelaide 1972.
4. Burton J.R. et al., *Interim report of the committee of inquiry into the future of Lake Pedder*, Canberra 1974; *Final report . . .*, Canberra 1975.
5. W.K. Hancock, *The Battle for Black Mountain*, Canberra 1974.
6. *Sydney Morning Herald*, 14 August 1972.
7. *Bulletin*, 12 May 1973.
8. T. Reeves, 'The society that Jack built', *Pol*, September/October 1978, pp. 66–8.
9. Les Murray, 'Explaining to the fencers', *Sydney Morning Herald*, 10 June 1978.

Chapter 15   Backlash and Forecast

1. H. Stretton, *Capitalism, Socialism and the Environment*, Cambridge 1975.
2. R. Raymond, 'Only vigilance can save our native heritage', *Bulletin*, Centenary issue, 29 January 1980, pp. 44–59 (a useful summary of present trends).

Bibliography

General
Costin, A.B. and Firth, H.J. *Conservation*. Ringwood 1971.
Dempsey, R. *The Politics of Finding Out*. Melbourne 1974.
Leeper, G.W. (ed.). *The Australian Environment*. Parkville 1970.
Powell, J.M. *Environmental Management in Australia 1788–1914*. Melbourne 1976.
Rapoport, A. *Australia as Human Setting*. Sydney 1972.
Seddon, G. and Davis M. (eds). *Man and Landscape in Australia*. Canberra 1976.

Aborigines
Blainey, G. *Triumph of the Nomads*. Melbourne 1975.
Hallam, S.J. *Fire and Hearth*. Canberra 1975.
Mulvaney, D.J. *The Prehistory of Australia*. Melbourne 1969.
Mulvaney D.J. and Golson J. (eds). *Aboriginal Man and Environment in Australia*. Cambridge 1971.

British impact
Smith, B. *European Vision and the South Pacific 1768–1850*. Oxford 1960.
Williams, R. *Country and City*. London 1973.

Climate
Perry, T.M. 'Climate and settlement in Australia 1700–1930: some theoretical considerations'. In Andrews, J. (ed.). *Frontiers and Men*. Melbourne 1966, pp. 138–54.

Forests
Jacobs, M.R. 'History of the use and abuse of wooded lands in Australia'. *Australian Journal of Science*. vol. 19 (1957), pp. 189–257.
Routley, R. and V. *The Fight for the Forests*. Canberra 1973.

First generation
Denholm, D. *The Colonial Australians*. Ringwood 1979.
Lansbury, C. *Arcady in Australia*. Melbourne 1976.
Perry, T.M. *Australia's First Frontier*. Melbourne 1963.

Early architecture
Cox, P. and Freeland, J.M. *Rude Timber Buildings in Australia*. London 1969.
Freeland, J.M. *Architecture in Australia*. Melbourne 1970.
Wilson, H. *Old Colonial Architecture in New South Wales and Tasmania*. Melbourne 1970.

Rural environment in nineteenth century
Barnard, A. (ed.). *The Simple Fleece*. Parkville 1962.
Jeans, D.N. *A Historical Geography of New South Wales to 1901*. Sydney 1972.
Meinig, D.W. *On the Margins of the Good Earth: the South Australian Wheat Frontier 1869–1884*. Adelaide 1962.
Powell, J.M. and Williams, M. *Australian Space, Australian Time*. Melbourne

1975. (Includes Cloher, D.U. 'A perspective on Australian urbanization', pp. 104–49, but mainly essays on the rural environment.)

Warner, R.F. *New England Essays: Studies of the Environment in Northern New South Wales*. Armidale 1963.

Williams, M. *The Making of the South Australian Landscape*. London 1974.

Nineteenth-century towns

(a) General

McCarty, J.W. 'Australian capital cities in the nineteenth century'. *Australian Economic History Review, 10* (1970), p. 121.

(b) Specific

Barrett, B. *The Inner Suburbs*. Melbourne 1971.

Bate, W. *A History of Brighton*. Melbourne 1963.

Bate, W. *Lucky City: the First Generation in Ballarat, 1851–1901*. Melbourne 1978.

Davidson, G. *The Rise and Fall of Marvellous Melbourne*. Carlton 1978.

Nature conservation

Australian Academy of Science. *National Parks and Reserves in Australia*. Canberra 1968.

Johnson, D. *The Alps at the Crossroads*. Melbourne 1974.

Town planning *1900–1945*

Brown, A.J. and Sherrard, H.M. *Town and Country Planning*. Melbourne 1951.

Sandercock L. *Cities for Sale*. Melbourne 1975.

Spearritt, P. *Sydney Since the Twenties*. Sydney 1978.

Sulman, J. *Town Planning in Australia*. Sydney 1921.

Rural environment in the twentieth century

Hancock, W.K. *Discovering Monaro*. Cambridge 1972.

McIntyre, A.J. and J.J. *Country Towns in Victoria*. Melbourne 1944.

Ratcliffe, F.N. *Flying Fox and Drifting Sand*. Sydney 1947.

Postwar

Boyd, R. *The Australian Ugliness*. Melbourne 1960.

Neutze, G.M. *Urbanization in Australia*. Sydney 1977.

——. *Australian Urban Policy*. Sydney 1978.

Roddewig, R. *Green Bans*. Sydney 1978.

Seddon, G. *Sense of Place*. Perth 1973.

Stretton, H. *Ideas for Australian Cities*. Adelaide 1970.

——. *Capitalism Socialism and the Environment*. Cambridge 1975.

Whitelock, D. *A Dirty Story: Pollution in Australia*. Melbourne 1971.

Index

Abbott, J.P., 44
Abbott, W.E., 44
Aboriginal archaeology and sites, 5, 8; culture, lifestyle, 4–9, 22, 25, 34, 174; hunting, food gathering, 55–6; Land Rights Act (Northern Territory 1976), 171, 174; prehistory, 5; use of fire, 7, 8, 42; women, 51;
Aborigines, 3, 21, 55, 57, 95, 117; effects on the environment, 4–5, 8–9, 55–6, 84, 174; European impact upon, 4, 9, 42, 56; extinction of Tasmanian, 4; fear of, 58; genetic origins of, 5–6; Tasmanian, 4, 7; urban, 149
Acclimatization Society (1861), the, 97
Adelaide, 13, 38, 63, 67, 93, 104, 117; Botanical Gardens, 47; forestry school, 105; 'green belt' of 62, 75; grid plan of, 62; planning, 125, 153–4; public transport, 112–13; suburban growth, 114; types of housing, 116
Age, the, 93, 160
Agriculture, 29, 135, 145, 153, 173; colleges, 136; Departments of Agriculture, 136; development, 143, 145; scientists, 138, 140
Air pollution; legislation to control, 123
Albany (W.A.), 51
Albury (N.S.W.), 68, 76, 83
Alice Springs (N.T.), 145
Alligator River, 89
Alumina Industry; environmental problems, 159; See also Mining, bauxite
Angas, J.H., 47
Animal species; See Fauna
Antarctica, 50, 54
Anthropologists, 4
Anzacs, 137; war memorials, 143–4
Arbitration system, the, 33
'Archaeology of "High" culture', 5
Architecture; profession, 128, 131, 149, 165; rural, 144; style, 150; See also Colonial
Argus, the, 69, 97
Arnhem Land, 6
Atherton Tableland (Qld.), 40, 136, 164

Athlone Place (Sydney), 66
Atkinson, James, 38, 42, 56
Austin, Thomas, 90, 95
'Australia Felix', 1
Australian, the, (C19th), 28
Australian and New Zealand Association for the Advancement of Science (ANZAAS), 45, 99, 122
Australian Capital Territory (A.C.T.), See Canberra
Australian Conservation Foundation (A.C.F.) the, 159–160, 162–3, 167
Australian Financial Gazette, the, 109
Australian Labor Party, the, 33, 126, 149, 161–3; supporters, 164
Australian National University (A.N.U.), the, 172

Ballarat, 55, 69–70, 109
Balmain (Sydney), 153
Bandicoots, 7; as source of food, 15, 54, 102; 'bilby', 54, 102
Banks, 76, 109, 125, 148–50; See also Finance institutions
Banks, Joseph, 26
Barossa Valley (S.A.); German Lutherans of, 143
Barrett, Bernard, 74
Barwick, Garfield, 159
Bass, 51
Bass Strait, 7, 42, 50–1
Bathurst, 28, 56, 67
Baudin, Nicolas, 51
Bauer, F.H., 32
Beaches, 104, 119, 133–4, 162; and bathing, 133–4; deterioration of, 161; See also Surf clubs
Bega; 'first municipal gasworks', 77
Belair National Park (S.A.), 105
Bigge, Commissioner, 56
'Bilby', the; See Bandicoots
Bishop, Charles, 50
Birger, Count, 99
Bjelke-Petersen, Joh, vii, 154, 163
Black Mountain (A.C.T.); telecommunications tower on, 172

Blackwattle Swamp Creek (Sydney), 75
Blaxland, G., 28
Bligh, Governor, 27
Blue Mountains, the 28, 60, 73, 91, 152; environmental theat to, 161; platypus in 54
Bold, W.E., 125
Bolte, Henry, 160
Bosisto, Joseph, 41, 46
Boston, 67, 116
Botanical Gardens, 47, 60, 117, 129–30
Botany Bay (N.S.W.); climate of, 26; industry in, 150; region study, 172
Bourgeoisie, the, 27, 164; See also Class and classes
Bourke, Governor, 62, 66
Bourke Street (Melbourne), 110
Bowen (Qld.), 4
Boyce, F.B., 122, 132
Brazil, 46, 49
Brighton (Melbourne), 112, 117
Brisbane, 13, 28, 61, 67, 117; City Council, 153; grid plan of, 62; lack of sanitation in, 74; public transport, 113, 119; suburban growth, 114; types of housing in, 115; urban services and utilities in, 118–19
Brisbane river, 38, 62
Britain, British, passim
British Impact, Chapter 2, passim
Britannia, the (ship), 49
Brodribb, W.A., 44
Broken Hill (N.S.W.), 71, 109, 171
Broken Hill Proprietary Co. Ltd. (B.H.P.), 171
Brunswick, 115, 117
Builders Labourer's Federation (B.L.F.), 164–6
Building; companies, industry, 147, 164–7; 'high-rise', 150–1, 154, 165–8; regulations, 129; societies, 110, 148; speculators, 71, 114, 166
Bulletin, the, 120
Bunker, Ebor, 50
Bunning, Walter, 165
Burdekin river, the, 28
Burra (S.A.), 40, 70–1
Burrinjuck dam, 32, 137; See also Irrigation, Hydro electric power
Burwood, (Vic.), 120
Busby, John, 73
Bush, the, 27, 37, 66–7, 81, 88–9, 97, 104, 106–7, 119–20; walkers, 162
Bushfires, 7, 55; and 'burning off', 8, 42; 'Black Thursday', 42
Bushmen of South Africa, the, 3
Butler, Richard, 148

Cahill, Paddy, 89
Cairns (Qld.), 173

California, 30, 46, 130, 137
Camberwell, 115
Campbell family, 82
Camperdown (Vic.), 83, 144
Canada, 50, 127
Canberra (A.C.T.), 28, 105, 127–30, 136, 152, 163, 171
Cape York Peninsula (Qld.), 5
Capital investment, 18, 32; British, 57; in primary and secondary industries, 148, 154; in resources development, 163, 167, 169; lack of small farming, 56, 77
Capitalism; agrarian, 13; and capitalists, 164; C19th industrial, 22; rural, 154; See also Class, Private enterprise
Carlton (Melbourne), 71
Carson, Rachel, 156
Carter, Howard, 5
Castlecrag (Sydney), 129
Cats; domestic, 88, 155; feral, 88
Cattle, 13, 22, 29–30, 54, 84, 95, 100, 123, 135, 138, 145; and dairying, 135, 145, 164; diseases, 86, 89; impact on environment, 81, 85, 88
Caulfield (Vic.), 120
'Cedar cutters', 38, 40
Centennial Park (Sydney), 73, 105, 132, 165; 'a wicked reputation', 130
Chaffey brothers, the, 137
Charleville (Qld.), 34, 93
Charters Towers (Qld.), 45, 71, 88–9
Chicago, 116, 128
Chifley, Joseph Benedict, 149
Children, 56, 73, 130, 172; 'a fine climate for . .', 27; and infant mortality, 116
China, 5, 12, 21–2; sparrows from, 97
Chinese, 43, 50
Christian inheritance, 11
Christy, Miller, 92
Circular Quay (Sydney), 118, 124; See also Sydney
Cities, 4, 21, 27, 45, 62, 68, 71, 77, 104, 107, 110, 112, 114, 117, 121, 123–4, 127, 133–4, 145–6, 151, 153, 173; capital, 67, 150; Central Business District, 150; changing skylines of, 119, 150; 'crisis and transformation', 147–8; inner, 115, 117, 122–3, 124–5, 150, 165–8, 172; See also names of cities
City Beach (Perth), 125
Clarence river, the, 38, 84
Clark, Manning, 1
Clarke, W.B., 43
Class and classes; conditions of working, 30, 38, 60, 71, 73–4, 91–2, 104, 112, 114, 117–8, 122–4, 129, 133, 164–8; in Britain, 12–17, 19, 21; 'in the suburbs', 117–8, 125; middle, 59, 114, 133, 152–3, 156, 163–4, 167; professional, 114, 117, 165; the wealthy, 18, 42, 74, 129,

131; *See also* Pastoralists, Capitalism, Capital investment
Climate; *See* Weather
Clutha Development Corporation, 161
Cockburn Sound (W.A.), 150
Cockatoos; 'made good soup', 54
Colac (Vic.), 83, 90
Collingwood (Melbourne), 73–4, 98, 114, 124; town hall, 110
Collins, Lieutenant-Governor, 52
Collins Street (Melbourne), 63, 119
Colonial; architecture, 66, 76; 'colonisation of Australia', 12, 49; government, 19, 112; society, 121; the Colonial Office, 3, 73
Combine harvestor; *See* Farming technology
Communists, 164
Connor, Rex, 160
Conservation; and 'Progress', 147, 172; anti-conservation, 98; early attitudes towards, 15, 22, 37, chapter 9, *passim;* of flora and forests, 38, 40, 47–8, 104–7, 165; of historic buildings, 156, 165; of wilderness areas, 156, 160, 162–3, 168, 173; water, 137; wildlife (fauna), 49, 97–9, 102–4, 165; *See also* Australian Conservation Foundation, Environmentalists
Conservationists; *See* Environmentalists
Convicts, 15, 21; labour, 38; transportation of, 49–50
Conybeare, Daryl, 167
Coolgardie (W.A.), 32, 45, 93; 'safe', 132
Coolong Caves; preservation of, 160
Cooloola; preservation of, 160
Council for Scientific and Industrial Research (1926), 137
Country Party, the, 126, 140
Cradle Mountain—Lake St. Clair National Park, 106
Crowding; *See* Suburbs, inner
Cunningham, Peter, 29, 54
'Currency lads', 52
Curtin, John Joseph, 149

Daceyville, garden suburb of, 125, 126
Dalgetys, 85
Dalkeith (Perth), 125
Dandenongs, the (Vic.), 130
Danysz, Jan, 92
Dampier, William, 3
Darling, Governor, 60
Darling Range (W.A.), 171
Darling Downs, 86, 143
Darling river, the, 28, 83, 85
Darwin (N.T.), 145
Darwin, Charles, 3
Day, Edward, 29
Deakin, Alfred, 137

Dedman, 149
Dennis, C.J., 135
Derwent river, the. 52, 54
de Salis family, 82
Diet; and suburban food delivery, 132; native game as food source, 54, 89. 91; of Irish peasantry, 12; traditional English, 27
Dingoes, 7, 88–9
Diprotodons; *See* Fauna, prehistoric
Diseases; and eucalyptus oil remedies, 37, 46; animal, 92–3; early theories about, 41; epidemic, 12, 41, 46, 57, 74, 86, 122; fear of, 121–2; workingclass, 74, 122; *See also* Children
Disraeli, Benjamin, 42
Dogs; domestic, 88, 91, 155
Domain, the (Melbourne), 117
Domain, the (Sydney), 60
Don, C.J., 98
Dress; and adaptability to climate, 27
Droughts, 28–34, 43, 55, 86, 93, 100, 118, 135; the 'king drought', 31
Dunbabin, Thomas, 52
Dunstan, Albert. 139–40
Dunstan, Don, 163
Dutton, Geoffrey, 62

Eaglemont (Melbourne), 129
East Africa, 5
East India Company, 14, 50
Eastlakes (Sydney), 165
Echidnas; legislative protection of, 102
Ecology, 1, 4, 13, 19, 44, 56, 171; ecological balance, 48, 55, 95, 104, 172; ecosystem, 7, 8; human, 154; *See also* Soil erosion
ECOS, 159
Eden (N.S.W.), 170–1
Edinburgh, Duke of, 159
Ednie-Brown, 43, 48
Elizabeth (S.A.), 150
Elizabeth Farm (N.S.W.), 65
Emus, 6; eggs, 54; extinction on King and Kangaroo Islands, 51; plagues of, 142; protection of, 98
Enderbys; *See* Whaling companies
England, English, *passim*
Environment; European preconceptions and perceptions of, 1, 8, 11–12, 13–5, 19, 121, 172; Government management of, 17–9, 33–4, 47–8, 105–7, 159, *passim*
Environmental impact; of exotic animals, 81, 88–93, 95, 97–9; of exotic plants, 47–8, 84–6; of mining, 69, 160–1, 169, 171; of pastoral industry, chapter 8 *passim*, 102, 138–142, 145–6, 154, 160; of technology, 1, 169, 171; of urban and industrial growth, 151, 160–9
Environmentalists, 53, 97, 104, 107, 156–

7, 161–2, 164–5; and 'militant labour movements', 164; and protest groups, movements, 156–7, 159, 161–9, 172, 173; 'Environmentalists for Full Employment', 167; rural and urban origins, 163
Environmental pollution, 21, 69, 73–4, 107, 110, 121–3, 150, 156–7, 164, 169; See also Air pollution, Water pollution
Environmental problems, 4, 83–6, 88–93, 95, 118–9, 120, 122, 124, 129, 138–142, 145–7, 151, 154, 156, 159–169, 171–4; conservation, 15, 22, 47–8, 106–7, 121, 137, 140, 147, 156, chapter 14, passim, 171–3, government management and planning, 17–19, 105–7, 123–4, 137–8, 140, 159–160, 171; legislative measures, 86, 88, 91, 105–7, 122–4, 159–160, 171
Eucalypts; transplanted around the world, 46; varieties of, 38, 40–1, 43, 45–7, 55, 57–8, 83, 100, 139, 143, 170–1; See also Trees
Eucalyptus oil; export trade in, 41, 46; medicinal use of, 37, 41
Europeans, European society, 1, passim; See also British impact, Migrants
Evans, Arthur, 5
Evans, William, 77, 90, 142
Eyre Peninsula (S.A.), 136, 142

Fairbridge, Kingsley, 105
Farmers and farming, 22, 30, 34, 43, 45, 56, 70, 75, 77, 107, 125, chapter 12, passim, 154; capital outlay, 57, 145, 154; 'Cow Cockies', 136; inheritance of British methods, 13–14, 83; labour-intensive, 145; land clearing, 38, 40, 42, 57, 105–6, 140–2; technology, 32, 58, 77–8, 83, 135, 137, 142–5, 154; See also Agriculture, Pastoral industry, Pastoralists
Farnell, J.S., 44
Farrer, William, 32
Fencing, 42, 57, 82, 83; rabbit proof fencing, 93; wire, 58, 83; See also Pastoralists
Fauna; as food source, 15, 54; 'exotic invaders', 81, 88–93, 95, 97–8, 104–5, 138, 142, 155; extinction of species, 54–5, 100, 142–171; killing regulations, bounties, 54–5, 155; prehistoric, 6–7; protection, 98–9, 102–4, 122; sanctuaries, 99, 105; slaughter of, 49, 88, 154, 155; species of, 49–51, 54–6, 88, 89, 98, 99–103, 105, 120, 135; Tasmanian, 7; working-class attitudes to protection of, 98; See also names of fauna
Ferntree Gully, 105
Field, Barron, 3
Finance institutions, 109–10, 125, 148–50

Finlayson, H.H., 1
Firewood, 45, 132; See also Timber industry, Trees
Fitzgerald, J.D., 126
Fitzroy, 114, 117, 153; town hall, 110
Fitzroy river, 100
Flats, 71, 147, 153, 172; See also Suburban growth, Suburbs
Fletcher Jones; 'trouser manufactory', 146
Flies, 116, 136
Flinders, Matthew, 54
Flooding and floods, 28, 38, 67; Aboriginal folk memories of, 25
Flora; exotic species, 47–8, 83–7, 130, 138, 143–44, 171; legislative protection of, 106–7; reproduction of species, 7; sanctuaries, 99; species of, 38, 40, 43, 45, 47–8, 57–8, 65, 83, 85, 100, 105, 120, 130, 139, 143, 171; See also Conservation, Trees, Eucalypts
Floreat Park (Perth), 125
Flying Fox and Drifting Sand, 140
Forestry; absence of legislation, 44, 48; Commissions, 105, 170; foresters, 106, 162, 171; Indian influence on, 47; policies, 47–8, 105–6; reafforestation, 46, 48, 171; schools, 105–6
Forests, 35, 37, 40, 99; British 'deciduous hardwoods', 13–14; destruction of, 38–9, 42, 44–6, 48, 105; jarrah, karri, 40, 47, 105, 136, 171; pine, 40, 48, 171; rainforests, 106, 164
Forrest, John; government of, 32
Foveaux, 60
France, 12, 26, 46, 92, 131
Frankland river (Tas.); environmental threat to, 163
Fraser Island; protection of, 160
Fraser, Malcolm; government of, 160, 171; See also Liberal Party of Australia
Freeland, J.M., 151
Fremantle, 62
Friends of the Earth, 156
Frogatt, W.W., 85
Fry, Commissioner, 40
Fyans, Foster, 54–5

Galah; 'byword for uselessness', 54
Galvanised iron, 78–9, 82, 115; See also Houses, housing
Game laws, the, 15, 55, 98; See also Class, Convicts
Gazette, 33
Geelong (Vic.), 55, 90, 97
Geologists and geology, 3, 50
George Street (Sydney), 110
Gilmore, Mary, 116
Giddings, 93
Gippsland (Vic.), 42, 46, 95, 136, 139
Glebe (Sydney), 75, 123, 153, 165

Gold, 29–30, 43, 58, 81, 83; diggers, 29, 38; discovery of, 4, 32, 45, 68, 79; fields, 32, 38, 93; rushes, 53, 68–71, 82, 97; *See also* Mining
Goulburn (N.S.W.), 28, 56
Goulburn river, the, 69
Government intervention; in urban system, 125–6, 133, 148–54; provision of cheap housing, 148–9; rent control, 149; *See also* Environmental impact
Goyder, G.W. (Goyder's line), 30–1, 43, 47–8, 86
Grafton (N.S.W.), 144
Grasses and grasslands, 8, 57, 84; introduced species, 85–6; native species, 85, 95; spear, 84; star, 85; tussock, 40, 84; *See also* Noxious weeds, Flora
Graziers, *See* Pastoralists
Great Barrier Reef, the (Qld.), 50, 54, 171, 173; environmental protection of, 160;
Great Barrier Reef Marine Park Act (1975), 171
Great Extermination: A Guide to Anglo-Australian Cupidity Wickedness and Waste, The, 49
'Green bans' movement, the, 164–7; *See also* Mundey, B.L.F., Kelly's Bush, Victoria Street, Woolloomooloo
'Green belt'; *See* Planning
Greenway, Francis, 147
Griffin, David, 167
Griffin, Walter Burley, 128–9
Griffith (N.S.W.), 137
Gundagai (N.S.W.), 76

Haberfield (Sydney), 125
Hall, E.S., 28
Hamer, Dick, 163
Hamilton, A.G., 45
Harris, John, 37, 89
Hart, John, 38
Hawker, J.C., 63
Hawkesbury river, 38, 65, 78
Hayes, Michael; Irish exile, 26
Heidelberg school of painters, the 120
Henry Edward, the (ship), 42
Henslow, Harold, 140
History of Australia, 1
Hobart, 26, 60, 62, 65, 67, 133; urban services and utilities, 118–19; whaling in, 51–3
Homebush (N.S.W.), 123
Home owners and ownership, 64, 70–1, 109, 115, 125, 129–30, 148–9, 169, 173; myth of, 109; *See also* Private property, Suburban growth
Hooker Projects, 167
Houses, housing; building materials for, 65–6, 71, 73, 78–9, 114–15, 131, 144, 156; Commissions, 126, 148–150, 151;

company, 156; conditions, 63, 129, 150; Federal-State agreement, 149; Government provision of cheap, 147–9; interiors, 131–2; origins of single-storey, 64, 82; rental, 125, 148–9; terrace, 64, 71, 123, 153, 166, 168; types of, 72, 114–6, 131, 156, 165; typical plan, 114–5; War Service, 126
Howard, Ebenezer, 121
Howitt, Alfred, 42, 46, 63, 68
Howitt, William, 40, 46, 57
Hughes, Thomas, 124, 130, 132
Hughes, William Morris (Billy), 92, 122
Hume reservoir, 137; *See also* Water resources, reservoirs, Irrigation
Hungerford, Thomas, 42
Hunter, Governor, 27, 54
Hunter river (valley), 38, 42, 44, 86; 'sheepwalks', 56–7; towns of, 67; vineyards, 56
Hunters Hill (Sydney); residents, 164–5
Hunters and hunting, 55; for food, 54; for sport, 54, 88–90, 103; licenses, 55, 103
Hyde Park (Sydney), 60, 73; Barracks, 147
Hydro electric power, 77, 137, 162–3, 173

Illawarra (N.S.W.), 38, 43, 65, 136; coal mines, 161
Illnesses; *See* Diseases
Immigrants, 21, 29, 73, 136, 147–9, 151; British, 62, 67; European, 22; South-East Asian, 22
India, 38, 47, 64; spotted deer from, 89
Individualism, 9, 12, 110
Indonesia, 21; water buffalo from, 89
Industrial development, 121, 150–2, 163
Industrial relations, 71
Industrial wastes, 69, 74
International Garden Cities and Town Planning Association, the, 125
Ireland, 12; Irish exiles, 26; Irish settlements, 143
Ironfounding industry, 71
Irrigation, 30, 32, 83, 137; pollution of channels, 139–40; projects, 137, 143
Islamic culture, 5

Japan, 161; woodchip market, 170
Java, 5
Jennings, A.V., 164
Jenolan Caves (N.S.W.), 104
Jevons, W.S., 27, 29, 42, 73, 75, 78, 109
Johnston, George, 130
Jones, Henry; founder of IXL, 136
Jones, Inigo, 34

Kalgoorlie (W.A.), 32, 45, 71, 88, 93
Kappakoola Swamp, 142
Kangaroo Island, 51

Kangaroos, 6; as source of food, 15, 54;
    extermination of, 99, 100, 102; legisla-
    tive protection of, 102; pet food market,
    155; population explosion, 135; shoot-
    ing licenses, 55; species of, 98, 100–1,
    142, 156; trade in skins, 54–5
Katanning (W.A.), 144
Kelly's Bush (N.S.W.); first green ban,
    164–5
Kendall, Henry, 48
Kimberleys, the, 5, 85, 95, 100
King, Governor, 25, 37–8, 51
King, Philip Gidley, 44
King Island; extinction of seals on, 51
Kingaroy (Qld.), 154
King Sound Pastoral Company, 85
King's Cross (Sydney), 165, 168
Kings Park (Perth), 105
Kingsford Smith Airport, 150
Knopwood, Robert, 52, 54
Koalas, 102, 155; killing of, 104; legislative
    protection of, 103, 155; trade in skins,
    102–3
Kosciusko National Park (N.S.W.), 159
Krefft, Gerard, 54, 55
Krichauff, Heinrich, 19, 47
Kwinana (W.A.), 150

Labour and labourers, 19, 43, 67, 109,
    148–9, 151, 165; building, 114, 164, 167;
    bush workers, 33; Chinese, 43; convict,
    38, 57, 73; demand for, 51, 71, 79, 114;
    domestic, 115, 132; migrant, 151; short-
    ages, 81, 147, 150; waterside workers,
    124, 165
Lahey, Romeo, 106
Lake Eyre (S.A.), 100
Lake Pedder (Tas.); hydro-electricity
    scheme and environmental protest, 162–
    3, 172–3
Lake Victoria, 137
Lamington National Park, 106
Land; Acts, 29, 43; boomers, 112; owners
    and ownership, 13–5, 17, 21, 41–2, 44,
    102, 109–10, 113, 125–6, 166–7;
    'quarter acre' block, 114, 129; sub-
    division of, 71, 104, 110, 114, 126, 152–3,
    160; See also Private property, Aborigi-
    nal culture, Houses, housing, Farmers,
    farming, Pastoralists
Lang, John Dunmore, 64
Launceston (Tas.); hydro electric scheme
    in, 77
Lawson, Henry, 31, 137
Lawson, William, 28
Leader, 136
Leeton (N.S.W.), 137
Leichhardt (N.S.W.), 129
Leichhardt, Ludwig, 28
Lend Lease, 165

Liberal Country League, 148
Liberal Party of Australia, 161, 163;
    politicians, 159; supporters, 164; See
    also Liberal Country League
Light, William, 62
Lillie, John, 26–7
Lindsay, Norman, 103
Lithgow, 70
Little Desert (Vic.); environmental threat
    to, 160, 163
Lizards, 7
Lloyd, Clem, 147
Local Government, 19, 75–7, 89, 110, 112,
    114–9, and garbage disposal, 123–4;
    and local businessmen, 110, 164; and
    ratepayers, 110, 127, 143; and slum
    clearance, 122; and town suburban
    planning, 124, 126, 143, 152, 165–8; See
    also Private property, Public transport,
    Suburban growth, Urban amenities
Lockhart, C.G.N., 91
London, 40, 122
Lyne, William, 122

Macarthur, John, 65
Macarthur, William, 41
Mackay races, the, 27
MacPherson, Peter, 55
Macquarie, Governor Lachlan, 17, 28, 60
McCubbin, Frederick, 81
McElhone, J.E., 44
McKay, H.V., 77
McKell, William, 149
Magic Pudding, the, 103
Maiden, J.H., 129–30, 132
Makasar Indonesians, 5
Maldon (Vic.), 77, 142
Mallee country, 33, 40, 100, 136, 138–40,
    142–3
Manning river, 38
Mansfield (Vic.), 75, 97
Marsh, G.P., 34
Marshall, Jock, 49
Marsupial lion; See Fauna, prehistoric
'Mateship', 38
Matraville (Sydney), 125
Melanesia, 21
Melbourne, 4, 13, 29–30, 34, 45, 67, 83,
    89, 97, 105, 109, 129–30, 132, 167;
    Botanical Gardens, 117; City Council,
    119; early living conditions in, 63, 65,
    73–4; grid plan of, 62, 113; growth of,
    71, 73–4, 110, 112; housing types in,
    115–16; inner city rehabilitation, 153;
    pollution in, 74; public transport, 112–
    13, 133, 151; urban services and utilities,
    118–9, 127
Melville, Thomas, 49, 50
Meredith, Louise, 69
Meteorologists and meteorology, 33–4

Mildura (S.A.), 137
Miller, Harry M., 165
Mineral resources; dependence on, 163; development and exploitation, 160, 172; exploration, 23
Miners, 22, 45, 70
Mining; bauxite, 171; coal, 45, 161; companies, industry, 18, 156, 160, 169, 171; copper, 40; environmental impact of, 69, 160-1; gold, 43, 45, 69; sand, 160-1; towns, 69, 70-1, 88-9, 109, 156
Mitchell, Major Sir Thomas, 1, 8, 42
Monaro, 4, 88
Moorabbin (Vic.), 120
Moore, George Fletcher, 58
Morris, William, 121
Mosley, J.G., 104
Mosman, Archibald, 52
Moss Vale (N.S.W.), 82
Motor vehicles, transport, 64, 89, 132-3, 143-6, 151-2, and 'transformation in the rural environment', 156; car ownership, 133, 151, 156, 172
Mount Hotham (Vic.), 140
Mount Lawley (Perth), 125
Mueller, Ferdinand, von, 34, 46, 47
Mulga, 57; See also Grasses, Sheep, Pastoralists
Mundey, Jack, 164-7
Murray river (valley), 38, 54, 83, 90, 137
Murrumbidgee, 32, 137, 143; See also Irrigation
Myall Lakes; preservation of, 160
My Brother Jack, 130

National Parks and Wildlife Conservation Act (1975), 171
National Trust, the, 156, 171
Nation Review, 166
Naturalists, 49, 54-5, 99, 106, 163, 171; clubs and societies of, 99, 120; publications, 139
Nautilus, the (ship), 50
New South Wales, 3, 27-9, 32-4, 37-8, 40, 42, 44-5, 48-50, 52, 54, 56-7, 59, 67-9, 76, 78-9, 81, 83, 86, 89-90, 92, 97, 102, 125, 148, 152, 161, 163, 166; building legislation in, 66; cat protection legislation, 88; environmental problems and planning in, 142, 159, 169, 172; fauna protection legislation 1866, 98, 102; flora protection legislation 1926, 107; infestation and noxious weeds legislation, 86, 138; irrigation and fruit-growing in, 137; Land Act 1861, 29, 43; Master Builders Association, 129; Native Birds Protection Act 1893, 99; Natural History Association 1887, 99; parks and reserves in, 73, 104-6; pastoralists, 135; Public Health Act 1896,

122-3; Rabbit Destruction Act 1880, 91; railway system, 112; Royal Commissions, 124, 130, 132; Southern Tablelands of, 82; State Housing Commission, 149-50, 167; town planning legislation, 126, 152
New York, 67, 116
New Zealand, 8, 34, 50-1, 86, 100, 125
Nielsen, Neil, 123, 124
Northern Territory, 22, 89
Noxious weeds, 85-7; See also Grasses
Nullarbor, the, 93

Oakleigh (Vic.), 120
O'Connor, C.Y., 32
Ogilvie, Will, 81
Oil industry, the, 53; exploration, 160, 171; petrol prices, 154, 171-2; refineries, 152
Ormond, Francis, 18
Overlanders, 13, 89

Paddington (Sydney), 71, 152-3; Society, 153; town hall, 110
Panshangar, 16
Papuans, 5
Pardoo (W.A.), 93
Parks and reserves, 15, 47, 60, 75, 104-5, 124, 129-30, 152; national, 19, 104-5, 106, 159, 171
Parramatta (Sydney), 112, 152
Parkes, Henry, 19, 48
Parliament House (Canberra), 128
Pasteur, Louis, 92, 93
Pastoral industry, 4, 18, chapter 8, passim, 135, 154; companies, 85; government infrastructure, 143; See also Agriculture
Pastoralists, 8, 22, 28-9, 32-3, 42-4, 57, 81, 83-4, 91, 95, 100, 135, 144, 154; and dam building, 135, 144; and graziers, 28, 34, 75, 152, 156; and landscape, 136; and overstocking, 32, 57, 85, 100; and 'ringbarking', 42-4, 83, 100; impact on environment, 56, 58, chapter 8, passim, 102, 138-42, 145-6, 154
Paterson, 'Banjo', 81
Perkin, Graham, 160
Perth, 13, 27, 40, 62, 113-4, 133, 151; 'Greater Perth' movement, 127; Kings Park, 105; lack of sanitation in, 74, 124; Stephenson-Hepburn plan 1955, 153; suburban living, 117, 125; urban services and utilities, 118, 119; See also Swan River
Pest control, 116, 119, 138; of grasshoppers and locusts, 142; 'pesticides in crop dusting', 154; See also Environmental problems
Phillip, Arthur, 17, 21, 26, 49, 59, 64
Philp, Robert, 106
Piano, the, 82, 132

Pitt Street (Sydney), 117, 119, 165
Planners, chapter 11, *passim*, 167; first town, 59, 60, 62, 67
Planning; and influence of developers, landowners, 112–3, 126, 168; environmental, 17–8, 151; 'green belt' concept, 62, 75; legislation, 126–7; public transport, 112–3; rectilinear grid plan, 60, 62, 67, 121; town, 17, 59–60, 62, 107, 113–4, 121–2, 125–7, 129, 134, 151–2, 164, 173
Playford, Thomas, 148
Platypuses, 54, 74, 102, 155; extinction of species, 54; legislative protection of, 155; trade in skins, 54, 102
Poole, C.E. Lane, 105–6
Pope, Alexander, 14
Port Adelaide, 112
Port Macquarie, 38, 60
Port Stephens, 38, 62
Possums, 56; black, 103; legislative protection of, 102; trade in furs, 103
Poverty, 109
Private enterprise, 73, 91, 117, 125–26, 169; and public transport system, 112, 133; and the 'Australian ethos', 110; investors, developers, 76, 126, 148, 152, 160–2, 164–68, 171, 173; *See also* Capitalism, Class, Labour
Private property; as 'an extension of personality', 148; investment 109; rights of, 11–12, 15, 17, 21, 74, 110, 167; speculation, 71, 114; *See also* Home ownership, Class
Public; buildings, 75–6, 110, 116, 147, 165; morality, 129–30- open spaces, *See* Parks and reserves; servants, 128, 173; taste, 131; transport systems, 110, 112–3, 116–17, 119, 133, 151, 153, 172; *See also* Railways
Pubs, 68
Putland, Mrs, 27

Queanbeyan. 32, 82
Queensland, 3–4, 27–9, 32, 34, 40, 48, 67, 77, 79, 81, 88–91, 99, 102, 104, 156, 163, 169; Animals and Birds Act, 103; City Council, 127; environmental planning in, 159; environmental problems in, 160; flora protection legislation 1930, 107; home loans legislation, 125; infestation and noxious weeds legislation, 86, 138; pastoralists, 135; Public Health Act, 122; rabbit-proof fence, 93; railway system in, 67, 93, 112; State Forests and National Parks Act 1906, 106; sugar cane industry, 136, 138; types of housing, 115–6; urban planning legislation, 114
Queenslander, 137

Rabbits, 54, 81, 85, 88, 89–93, 95, 100, 138, 142, 154; as food source, 91; myxomatosis, 93, 154; Rabbit Destruction Acts, 91–2; rabbit proof fencing, 93–4; trade in skins, 91;
Railways, 22, 58, 67–8, 70, 77, 79, 83, 93, 112; construction gans, 88; country, 112, 139, 142, 143, 156; Government ownership, 112; Hobson's Bay Railway Company, 112; private company, 161; routing influenced by landowners, 113; suburban, 104, 112–3, 130, 133
Rainfall, 8, 29–32, 34, 44–5, 117, 136; capital cities, 13, 153; wilderness areas, 162
Ramel, Prosper, 46
Ratcliffe, Francis, 140
Reade, C.C., 125–6
Real estate, 73; agents, 110, 114, 126, 148, 164
Recreation; holiday resorts as 'transplanted suburbia', 173
Redfern, 74
Reece, Eric, 163
Register, 136
Reid, William, 51
Richmond river, the, 38, 40, 84
'Ringbarking'; *See* Trees
Riverina, the, 1, 29, 83, 85–6, 92, 100
Roberts, Tom, 81
Robertson brothers (Colac farmers), 90
Robertson, John (Justice of the Peace—S.A.), 47
Robertson, John (N.S.W. pastoralist), 29
Rockhampton, 67
'Rocks, the', 60, 122–3; The Rocks Resumption Board, 123
Rodier, William, 92
Roma (Qld.), 93
Rose, A.J., 76, 144
'Rotten Row', 53
Royal Australian Ornithologists Union, 99
Royal National Park, the, 104; *See also* Parks and reserves
Royal Society of New South Wales, 44
Rural economy and settlement, 22, 28, *passim; See also* Agriculture, Farmers and farming, Pastoral industry, Pastoralists
Rusden, G.W., 1, 97
Russell, George, 63
Russell, H.C., 45, 135
Rutledge family, 82

Salamanca Place (Hobart), 53
Salt lakes, 8
Saltbush, 57, 85; *See also* Grasses, Sheep, Pastoralists
Sandringham (Vic.), 120
San Francisco, 46, 59

Sanitation, 18; collection and sanitary contractors, 74–5, 123–4, 153; problems, 73–5, 110, 122–4, 129; 'unhygienic practices', 74
'Scab'; *See* Sheep diseases
Schomburgk, Robert, 47
Scotland, 12, 46, 98
Scott, Walter, 3
Sea-elephants, 51
Sealing industry, 50–1, 53; commercial use of seal oil, 50; sealskins for fashion and export, 50, 51
Seals, 50–1; and sealers, 50–1; dwindling numbers of, 51
Sentimental Bloke, 135
Shapcott, Thomas, vii
Sheep, 22, 29, 42, 44, 54, 88, 90, 92, 100, 135; diseases, 57; feeding habits of, 57, 85; impact on environment, 81, 83–5; merino, 57, 81; shearers, 167; stealing, 55
Shingles, 66, 78; *See also* Houses, housing
Shoalhaven, 38
Silent Spring, 156
Slums, 60, 107, 112, 115, 121–3, 152; clearance, 122, 124–5; redevelopment, 126, 153; *See also* Suburban growth, Suburbs, Urban decay
Smith, Edwin, 116
Smith, William Forgan, 104
Social; justice, 123; reform movement, 124
Soil; aridity, 8, 43; conservation boards and services, 140; erosion, 8, 37, 43, 84, 136, 138–9, 140–1; salinity, 138; structure, 136; *See also* Environmental pollution, Trees
South Africa, 26, 29
South America, 26, 29; introduction of toads, 138
South Australia, 29–30, 33, 38, 47–8, 57, 62, 67, 70, 75, 83, 89–90, 100, 110, 142, 150, 154; conservation and forestry policy in, 47–8; dried fruits industry in, 137; droughts in, 43; environmental planning in, 159, 171; flora protection legislation 1939, 107; noxious weeds legislation in, 86; parks and reserves in, 104–6; Planning and Housing Act 1916, 125–6; Public Health Act, 122; Rabbit Destruction Act 1875, 91; railway system, 112; Roseworthy Agricultural College, 167; State Housing Trust 1936, 148–9; State Rivers and Water Supply Trust, 137; wheatgrowing in, 30, 77, 142
South Australian Register, 40
Spate, Oskar, 25
Spencers Gulf (S.A.), 30
Squatters, 28–9, 81–2, 84, 90, 135; *See also* Pastoralists, Farmers
'Squireens', 56

Stirling, Captain, 26
St George's Terrace (Perth), 123
St Kilda (Melbourne), 112, 117
Stokes, John Lort, 55
Stretton, Hugh, 169
Strikes, 33, 104
Strong, H.A., 92
Sturt, Charles, 1, 26, 28
St Vincent's Gulf (S.A.), 30
Suburban; Australians, 130, 134; developers, 104, 114, 152; dwellers, 99, 119, 130, 134; environment, 76, 107, 119–20, 129–30, 134; gardens, 130, 134; growth, sprawl, chapter 10, *passim*, 125–6, 151–3, 172; shopping complexes, 151, 153, 172
Suburbanisation, 167
Suburbs, 32, 74, 110, 113–4, 117, 119, 124, 135, 149–53, 169, 172–3; affluent, 74, 110, 117–8, 126, 164; garden, 125; industrial, 149; inner, 71, 73, 105, 109–10, 112–4, 124–6, 135, 151–2; middle-class, 131; new, 115, 121, 126, 129–30, 153; outer, 110, 122, 133, 167; working-class, 118, 124, 129, 165; *See also* names of suburbs, Class and classes
Sulman, John, 121–2, 125, 127–8; 'The Laying Out of Towns', 122
Surf clubs, 134; surfing, 52
Surry Hills, 72
Swan River (Perth), 26, 58, 117; as a sewerage outlet, 119; coastal plain, 4; colonists, 42; industrial threat to vineyards, 159
Swans, black, 98
Swift, Jonathan, 11
Sydney, 3–4, 13, 22, 27–8, 30–3, 43, 50, 62, 64–6, 89, 92, 104, 109, 124, 127, 129, 132, 147, 150; City Council, 74, 122, 165, 167; conservationists, 161, 164–5, 167; Cumberland County Council, 152–3; early living conditions in, 73–4; environmental problems, 124, 140, 166–7; first plans for, 20, 59–60; first settlement at, 26; growth and planning of, 110, 114, 125, 152, 167; Harbour, 49, 59, 60, 74, 117, 123; housing types, 115, 116; merchants, 51, 117; parks and gardens, 60, 73, 105, 165; pollution in, 74–5, 123–4; population of, 67, 71, 124; public transport, 112–3, 133, 151; slumbs and redevelopment, 122–3, 153; social classes in, 117; urban services and utilities, 118–9; whaling in, 52, 53
Sydney Cricket Ground, the, 75, 124
Sydney Mail, the, 99
Sydney Morning Herald, the, 74, 166

Tambourine Mountain (Qld.), 106
Tamworth (N.S.W.); first electricity, 77

Tank stream, the, 60; pollution of, 73
Tasmania (Van Diemen's Land), 4, 6, 22, 32, 75, 88, 89, 136; bounties on native game, 54; environmental planning in, 159; environmental problems in, 162–3, 171; fauna protection legislation 1860, 98; forestry policy in, 48, 105, 171; fruit growing industry, 136; hunting licenses, 55; hydro electric power in, 77, 162–3, 173; Ornithological Society 1888, 99; Public Health Act, 122; Rabbit Destruction Act 1871, 91; Scenery Preservation Act 1915, 106;
Tasmanian tiger (thylacine), 6–7, 101
Tench, Watkin, 26
Tennyson, Lady, 102
Thargomindah (Qld.); first hydro electricity, 77
Thylacine tiger; See Tasmanian tiger
Timber industry, the; and suburban market, 115–6; commercial use of native timber, 38, 40, 43, 45, 69, 88, 171; companies, 79, 144; exports, 38, 40, 45; government involvement in, 38, 40, 66, 105–6; manufacture of weatherboards, 58, 79, 115; mechanisation of, 66; See also Forestry, Trees, Firewood, Woodchip industry, Conservation, Environmental problems
Toorak (Melbourne), 17
Tourism, 106, 160, 162
Town and Country Journal, the, 119
Town building and towns, 60, 64–7, company, 156; country, 68–9, 70, 75–7, 110, 112, 114, 143–4, 146, 156; dwellers, 22, 58, 63, 67, 81, 104, 121; new, 58, 59, 62, 121
Towns, Robert, 53
Townsville, 67, 89
Trade unions, 33, 164; and greenban movement, 164–7; unionists, 161; See also Strikes, Labour, Class
Traffic congestion; See Transport
Tramways, 112–3, 116, 119, 124, 130, 133, 151
Transport; air, 23, 154; and traffic congestion, 121, 124, 133, 172, 173; private, 112–3, 116, 161; public systems, 110, 112–3, 116–7, 119, 133, 172, road systems, 23, 144–5, 151, 153; studies, 154
Trees, 49, 130; clearing of, 34–5, 37–8, 40–5, 57–8, 69, 100, 105, 140–2, 171; conservation of, 38, 40, 47–8; native species, 38, 40–1, 45, 47–8, 57–8, 65, 83, 100, 105, 139, 143, 171; planting of exotics, 47–8, 171; ring-barking of, 42–5, 83, 100; See also Bushfires, Forestry, Timber industry
Trollope, Anthony, 70, 77

Trotman, H.S., 27
Twidale, C.R., 142
'Typically Australian', 58, 81
Tyson, 'Hungry' Jimmy, 86, 92

Unemployment, 104
United States of America, 8, 22, 42, 50–1, 59, 67, 104, 109, 116, 121, 127, 131, 172; conservationists, 156; construction of Darwin to Alice Springs highway, 145; introduction of cacto-blastis, 138; mining companies, 161
University of Adelaide, 105
University of Melbourne, 5
Urban; amenities and costs, 18, 45, 73–7, 110–2, 117–9, 122–4, 129, 153, 173; Australians, 99, 107; decay, 111, 124; design, 134; environment, 121, 130, 147, 172–4; expenditure, 126; growth, 22, 50, chapter 6, passim, 73, 78, 119, 147, 150–3—affecting rural areas, 147; landscapes, 58–9, 68, 119; reclamation, 121; sprawl, 60, 62
Urbanisation, 67, 99, 167

Van Diemen's Land; See Tasmania
Vaucluse (Sydney), 17
Veddahs of South Asia, the, 3
Verandah, the, 64, 66, 76, 78, 82, 114, 131, 143, 150, 156
Victoria, 1, 29, 32–3, 40–2, 45, 57, 67–9, 81, 97, 99–100, 106, 137, 143, 148, 151, 163; cat protection legislation, 88; environmental problems and management in, 139–40, 142, 159–60, 169; Field Naturalist's Club of, 99, 120; flora protection legislation 1930, 107; Forestry Act 1876, 48, 105; Game Protection Act 1860, 98, 102; noxious weeds legislation, 86; parks and reserves, 105–6; Public Health Act, 122; Rabbit Destruction Act 1880, 91; railway system, 112; Western district of, 82–3, 88, 90–1, 136, 142–4
Victorian Naturalist, 139
Victoria Street (Sydney); redevelopment and green ban, 165–6, 168
Von Mueller; See Mueller

Wagga Wagga (N.S.W.), 76, 102
Wales, 12, 46
Walker, William, 46
Wallabies; extermination of, 99, 100, 138, 142; Kawau Island colony, 100; legislative protection of, 102; population explosion, 135; species of, 100–2, 142
Walsh, W.H., 91
Warrnambool (Vic.), 146
Waste disposal, 129, 169
Water; artesian, 30, 77, 135; Commis-

sions, 140; conservation, 137; consumption, 154; pollution, 73–5, 122, 140, 156; O'Connor pipeline, 32; resources, reservoirs, 44, 73–4, 135, 137, 162–3; salinity and river systems, 140, 171; sewerage and drainage, 117, 118–9, 153; storage, 73, 79, 115; shortages, 74; supply and services, 18, 73–5, 110, 115–6, 129–31, 138, 144, 153; See also Irrigation
Waverley (Sydney), 118
Weather, 8, 50, 70, 114, 118; effect upon town planning, 63; See also Chapter 3, passim
Webb, Beatrice, 122
Weipa (Qld.), 171
Wellington Valley (N.S.W.), 3
Wentworth, William Charles, 23, 28
Western Australia, 22, 27, 32–3, 40, 45, 48, 57–8, 89, 100, 136, 144, 150, 154–6; agricultural scientists in, 138; convict colony of, 55; environmental planning in, 159; environmental problems in, 169, 171; fire control legislation in, 42; Forests Act 1918, 105; Game Act 1912, 102; home loans legislation, 125; parks and reserves, 105; Public Health Act, 122; rabbit proof fence, 93–4; water salinity and river systems in, 140, 171; wheatbelts, 142–3
Western Mail, 137
Westernport (Vic.), 151
Whales, 49–50, 52, 54; and whalers, 50; humpback, 54, 155; 'near extinction' of, 50
Whaling industry, 50–4, 155; commercial use of whale oil, 50, 53, 119; closure of last station, 155; companies, 50, 53; 'competition from American whalers', 52; decline of, 53
Wheat industry, 30, 86, 155; and erosion of topsoils, 140; and superphosphate, 136; exports, 77; growers, 77, 139, 145; varieties of wheat, 32, 136; wheatbelts, 33, 100, 138, 140
White, Patrick, 165
White, Samuel, 90, 95

Whitlam, Gough; government of, 160, 162, 171; See also Australian Labor Party
Wildflowers, 106–7
Wildlife Preservation Society, 99
Wilkinson, Leslie, 131
William and Ann, the (ship), 50
Wilson, Edward, 97, 98
Wilson, Samuel, 18
Wimmera (Vic.), 89, 139; Regional Committee for reservation, 160
Winds, 30, 63; 'brickfielder', 63; -power, 100; See also Meteorology, Weather
Wirrabeen (S.A.), 90
Wombats, 6–7; as 'acceptable food', 54; legislative protection of, 102; trade in furs, 103
Women, 73, 81, 109, 134, 151, 165; and Victorian clothing, 27; as housewives, 56, 65, 78, 107, 115, 130, 132—and bulldozers, 164; as mothers, 131; 'checkout girls', 151; dependence on public transport, 133–4; 'deserted mothers', 149; See also names of women
Woodchip industry, 170–1
Wool industry, the, 30, 52, 57, 135; boom 1948–51, 154; markets and prices, 32, 57, 95; stores, 124; See also Sheep
Woollahra (Sydney), 118
Woolloomooloo; Residents Action Group, 166; Victoria Street redevelopment, 165–7
World Wilderness Conference (1980), 173
Workers; See Labour and labourers
'Working man's paradise', 4, 30; See also Class
World War I, 126, 128, 131, 136–7
World War II, 128, 130, 133, 142, 144–5, 147, 149, 154
Wragge, Clement, 34

Yarra river, the, 74, 117
Yass (N.S.W.), 76, 140

Zoological gardens; Society (1857), 97; Royal Park, 97